The Progress City Primer
Stories, Secrets, and Silliness from the Many Worlds of Walt Disney

Michael Crawford

Progress City Press

Orlando   Chapel Hill   Los Angeles

2015

Copyright © 2015 by Michael Crawford

All Rights Reserved

Published in the United States of America
by Progress City Press, L.L.C.
www.progresscitypress.com

P.O. Box 690127
Orlando, FL 32869

Cover Design by Celeste Cronrath
theluckyorange.com

No part of this book may be reproduced or transmitted in any form without the prior permission of the publisher.

This book is an unofficial text and is not authorized, endorsed, or sponsored by The Walt Disney Company or any of its subsidiaries or affiliate businesses. All copyrighted and trademarked material, including names, places, and characters, are the sole property of their respective owners. Images, except where specified, are the sole property of The Walt Disney Company and are taken from promotional and press materials. They are reproduced in part here solely for educational and editorial purposes.

Library of Congress Control Number: 2015910584
ISBN 978-0-9862050-6-4

Dedicated to my family -

My parents, brother, aunts, uncle, and grandmother, who made all the silliness possible.

"I love the nostalgic myself. I hope we never lose some of the things of the past."

"Whenever I go on a ride, I'm always thinking of what's wrong with the thing and how it can be improved."

"It's silly to build a wall around your interests."

Walt Disney

Table of Contents

Preface ix

Walt

The Taming of the Mouse 3
The Future Fantasias of 1940 7
Walt's Elephants 23
On Location With Walt 25
Walt & Ike 35
Walt and the Winter Olympics 45
Walt Disney vs. the Air Pirates 59

The Imagineers

George McGinnis & the Underground Train of Tomorrow . . 65
The People Moving People 71
Smokey and the Figment 79
Travels with Herb 85

The Vacation Kingdom

In the Beginning, There was Project Future 91
A Model Kingdom, 1968 95
The Lake Buena Vista STOLport 105
Take the auto-train! 117

Looking Back at Tomorrow

The Tripartite Plan, 1975 123
Master Plan 5, 1977 133
Iran So Far Away 155
Ahead of the Curve 157
Your Very Own WorldKey 161

Welcoming Our New Go-Bot Overlords 165
To GYRO and GERO in the Wabe. 169
Tomorrow's Windows 179

The Wonderful Weird of Disney

Little Orange Memories 201
Experimental Prototype Callgirls of Tomorrow. 207
Greatest. Press. Release. Ever.. 209
The Ballad of Bisontennial Ben 213

A Disneyland Interlude

A Stroll Down Liberty Street 225
Pooh For President 235
Third Theme Park - It's Dot Com!. 241

Neverworlds

The Disney-MGM Studio Backlot 257
Port Disney 267
Disney's America 285

Appendix

Dining With Disney 311

Preface

It all began so innocently.

The year was 2007. I was sitting on a park bench, eating a handful of peanuts, when I gazed wistfully at the horizon and said to myself, "I feel that there should be some kind of a website enterprise built where a guy and his fellow nerds could talk about Handwiches together." And that's how Progress City started.

Or maybe not – it's kind of hazy. In actuality, Progress City emerged when I finally got off my hinder and did something I'd been putting off for years – reviving my old (*old*) Epcot history website from the internet dark ages of the mid-1990s. Static websites had since been replaced by blogs and instead of building my shrine to classic Walt Disney World all at once, I thought, I could just create it piecemeal over a period of years.

It helped that the path had been blazed by several in-depth Disney history blogs such as *Passport to Dreams Old and New* and *2719 Hyperion*; these followed in the footsteps of seminal sites like *Widen Your World*, and began to fill the void of truly obscure Disney historical research and analysis.

That was the main reason that my brother Jeff and I started *Progress City, U.S.A.* – to talk about things that few others were writing about at the time. To make silly and obscure jokes, to reference the old Disney movies and shows that we grew up on, and to really poke around the oft-forgotten back corners of the Disney experience that defined our childhoods.

Everyone has a favorite ride, or film, or book, which was not a beloved bestseller but loomed large in their life. They're the things we love most – the goofy TV special from 1989 that we taped on VHS but no one else remembers, or the obscure magazine we had as a kid and read until the binding fell apart. It's always thrilling to discover others who, too, remember these things, and it's even more fun to share them with people who missed them the first time around.

I started writing for my own amusement and never suspected that many (or any) others would be interested, but this experience has instead exposed me to an endless stream of great, hilarious, and interesting folks. People interested in Disney history comprise a fascinating community, and nearly everyone, from the loftiest "Disney Legend" to the masses of everyday fans like myself, have been incredibly kind. I'm extremely grateful for everyone who has read along and commented over the years, and thank everyone for joining in on the silliness.

A few people have asked, in the past, that I collect some of my posts in print. I will freely admit that I always worried that this seemed a bit shady, but have assuaged my guilt by expanding the following stories from their original versions and adding in some previously unpublished tales. Hopefully that brings balance to our social contract.

The stories collected within have no real overall rhyme or reason; the Disney entertainment empire is so vast that it's always fun to just pick favorite bits and bobs from here and there to discuss. As Walt would say, lots of little "things" one might find interesting. I certainly hope that you do, and I thank you again for reading.

I.
Walt

.01

The Taming of the Mouse

The Disney studio has long faced a problem regarding what, exactly, to do with its beloved mascot Mickey Mouse. The character, once irreverent and borderline anarchic, has evolved over the years into a somewhat staid corporate icon. People tend to forget that those early black and white Mickey shorts were as hilarious as they are; Mickey came off as a cross between Chaplin and Douglas Fairbanks, finding himself in a number of out-sized adventures based on the popular fiction of the day.

The company itself has addressed this issue quite openly over the years, with occasional campaigns to revitalize the character for new generations. Mickey makeovers have ranged from his pastel-suited 1980s "Don Johnson" phase to more recent attempts to return to his subversive roots in the *Epic Mickey* series of videogames and the popular 2013 animated short, *Get a Horse!*

But Mickey's descent into suburban ennui isn't something we can pin on latter-day executives. This is actually an issue that goes all the way back to Walt's day – way, way back as a matter of fact.

It seems that the issue of what Mickey would or wouldn't, or should or shouldn't, do goes all the way back to his infancy. In 1930, just two years after his theatrical debut and at the height of his popularity, a number of theaters and localities were already up in arms about the scandalous antics of the world's favorite cartoon character.

Under the headline "The Censor!", a story appeared in the November 16th, 1930 issue of the *New York Times* about just such a case. "Although there is no morality clause in the contract of Mickey Mouse," the paper reported, "that vivacious rodent of the animated screen must lead a model life on the screen to meet the approval of censorship boards all over the world."

Forbidden were drinking or smoking, and Mickey was not allowed to "cut any suggestive capers." Keen attention had to also be paid, said the *Times*, to avoid "wounding various national dignities."

This was in reference to a German censor who had rejected the 1929 Mickey short *The Barnyard Battle*, in which Mickey leads an army of mice against invading felines. German officials found the cats, which wore helmets resembling those of the nation's army at the time, "offensive to national dignity."

Even more amusing was the case of the 1930 short *The Shindig*, which found itself banned in Ohio. Not only did the cartoon take the shocking liberty of exposing Clarabelle Cow's udders (udders being a very common source of gags in early Disney/Iwerks films), but Clarabelle's introduction came as she reclined in her barn reading a copy of Elinor Glyn's *Three Weeks*.

Glyn's saucy novels had caused outrage among moral watchdogs in the early 20th century, making a reference to her works seem hilariously out-of-place in a Mickey Mouse cartoon. Amusing, yes... to everyone except Ohio censors.

Perhaps it's no surprise that Mickey drew the eye of such folks; after all, busybodies and self-appointed crusaders for virtue have plagued popular entertainment since time immemorial. But rarely have the efforts of the thought police centered so heavily on the wardrobes of animated mice or the reading habits of cows.

The November 23rd, 1930 *Los Angeles Times* published a fictitious interview with Mickey Mouse about the issue; reporter Philip Scheuer claimed to have found the actor "cowering under a desk at the trim motion-picture plant where his antics are recorded, holding Minnie Mouse with one affrighted paw and looking very, very unhappy." "I'm immoral," confessed Mickey, before detailing the list of problems his films had encountered.

He mentions the Glyn issue ("That's nothing," quipped the reporter. "Everybody except the cows has read it by now.") as well as Clarabelle's infamous udders – the cow's skimpy wardrobe had gotten her banned in Canada as well. Also drawing Canadian ire was the 1930 Silly Symphony *Frolicking Fish*, where a playful – dare I say, frolicking – fish happily slaps the rump of a ship's mermaid figurehead.

In the end, it was a newer Disney character, Donald Duck, who would become the studio's resident scamp and all-around troublemaker. He was able to get away with things that Mickey simply couldn't anymore; a victim of his own success, the Mouse was forced to become a role model.

"Mr. Disney isn't really a bad man," Mickey told the *Times*. "You know what he does when a state or somebody cuts out a scene from one of my pictures? He supplies another one to take its place!" The *Times* explains that scenes deemed problematic couldn't just be cut from films or the "synchronization goes blooey"; to keep the film matching its soundtrack, new filler scenes had to be animated and sent to the film exchange via airmail when a segment was found objectionable.

In the end, it would have probably been cheaper to confiscate Clarabelle's library card.

.02

The Future Fantasias of 1940

"Maybe we ought to open up on those things instead of playing down to our medium or our public. That's the very thing we like to have, a challenge."

— Walt Disney

This single, simple quote speaks volumes in explaining the devout admiration and never-ending fascination that many hold for the works of Walt Disney. It also helps to explain my great love of *Fantasia*, his studio's 1940 masterpiece. My interest stems not only from the film itself, but from the underlying concept of the entire project; *Fantasia* was not meant to be a film unto itself, but rather a constantly renewing experiment in animation and music that would blur the lines between art forms and between what was considered "high" and "low" art. To prepare for this, the Disney studio was planning a stream of exciting new animation to be added to the *Fantasia* repertoire.

This leads to another major reason for my fascination with the film. During the creation of this so-called "Concert Feature", there were a number of alternate numbers considered for the film and its planned follow-ups, and several other approaches to the concept were developed in the decades that followed. For someone like myself who is obsessed with "the Disney that never was", *Fantasia* is a treasure trove of unproduced material. In some ways this material is unique, as, arguably, if the desire existed it could be developed today and folded into a revival of the project. The concepts are as valid now as they ever were, and a simple raid of the animation morgue would provide material for any number of fascinating segments.

Many of those ideas for *Fantasia*'s proposed sequels were discussed in a story meeting for the "Future Concert Feature," held on May 14th, 1940. Attending the meeting were Walt and conductor Leopold Stokowski, as well as orchestrators Fred Stark and Ed Plumb, arranger Herb Perry, Bill Cox, director Ben Sharpsteen, story man Joe Grant, and Bob Carr, Director of Educational Research for the studio. Transcripts were typically kept for these sorts of meetings on the Disney lot, and they never fail to provide a captivating look at the creative process in the artists' own words.

The discussion begins as the group tries to hammer out a lineup for a full-fledged *Fantasia* sequel, and ends with an emerging plan to slowly produce new animated segments to rotate in and out of the *Fantasia* program on a periodic basis. There are enough clues here to help us imagine what a full *Fantasia* sequel would have been like, though, and as a bit of alternate-universe filmmaking it sounds astounding. At the very least, it allows fellow *Fantasia* nerds such as myself to create their own "Future Concert Feature" mixtapes.

As Sharpsteen explains, the key element in selecting pieces for the *Fantasia* followup would be their popular appeal – how well-known and liked they were. Thus, at Stokowski's suggestion, the film could have kicked off with the Overture from Mozart's *The Marriage of Figaro*, which he called "very gay – sparkling – like champagne." Other numbers Stokowski suggested for the film's overture included Dvořák's *Carnival Overture* ("Full of life, full of color and vitality"); Wolf-Ferrari's *Secret of Suzanne* ("Gay and fine"); the Overture from Rossini's *Barber of Seville* ("Gay and marvelous"); and an unnamed piece by Alexander Scriabin.

Rejected as opening numbers were Mendelssohn's *Fingal's Cave*, which he thought too "poetic and gentle for a beginning"; Mozart's *Don Juan* which was "a little too tragic"; and von Suppé's *Light Cavalry Overture*, which is rejected after Sharpsteen points out that it had been heavily "burlesqued" already in the studio's cartoons. The other serious contender to start off the film, aside from *The Marriage of Figaro*,

The Future Fantasias of 1940

A proud Walt Disney (right) and studio artist T. Hee (center right) watch as legendary choreographer George Balanchine (left) and *Rite of Spring* composer Igor Stravinsky examine character maquettes from *Fantasia*'s *Dance of the Hours*.
© Disney

was *Le carnaval romain* by Berlioz, which Stokowski brings up often and seems keen on inserting it into the lineup.

Next in the lineup for this future *Fantasia* was *Peter and the Wolf*, which would eventually be animated for inclusion in 1946's *Make Mine Music*. Stokowski speaks glowingly of the piece:

> "I think it is top-notch – wonderful music, wonderful humor, wonderful story – I'm all for it. I think it's the greatest thing Prokofiev has ever done. You can have records of it, but they don't give you an idea – the records are perfectly played, but the music of course is highly humorous, it's fantastic and grotesque."

When Walt enters the meeting, Stokowski suggests moving *Peter and the Wolf* to a point later in the program; "I was going to say in the second half," he tells Walt, "but it shouldn't go near *Till Eulenspiegel* because they have something in common." Richard Strauss's tone poem *Till Eulenspiegels lustige Streiche*, or "Till Eulenspiegel's Merry Pranks", was selected for the new *Fantasia* because of the comedic possibilities afforded by its hero, trickster folk hero Till Eulenspiegel. Said Walt, "I think we can get big laughs out of [it] because of his pranks, surprise gags."

Walt was also excited about the comedy inherent to *Peter and the Wolf*, as seen in this quote which shows how intricately he was planning this project, and how involved he was in his films at this time:

> "I see us interpreting [Peter and the Wolf] *as a highly stylized, caricatured type of thing – the characters would have a certain stylized handling, and the whole thing would be broad caricature – the wolf, all the characters would be like a comic ballet. I don't mean like a Donald Duck; I mean their movements and everything, like the Ballet Russe might do it. It would be comic, not in the sense of big laughs, but light."*

Stokowski suggests moving *Peter and the Wolf* to the end of the film's first half, and asserts that the end of the first half and the end of the film itself are "the two important things to build to." The first half of the film would have been lighter in tone, worrying Stokowski that the second half had comparatively little humor.

One of the whimsical segments mentioned for the first half of the film was John Alden Carpenter's *Adventures in a Perambulator*. This piece was developed by Disney artists, and a reconstruction of its storyboards was presented on the *Fantasia Anthology* DVD set in 2000. Also proposed was the *Polka and Fugue* from the 1926 Czech opera *Schwanda the Bagpiper*; *Schwanda* was inserted to the lineup to replace Puccini's *Madame Butterfly*, which seems to have originally wrapped up the first half of the film. Ed Plumb points out that with *Schwanda*, the artists "could go a lot further on the fantastic side than the opera does." This is opposed to *Madame Butterfly* which, says Stokowski, "has to be done quite seriously."

According to Bob Carr, one of Walt's general directives for the sequel was to feature "fewer numbers but bigger numbers." The only issue was that many of the pieces best suited for animation were on the short side. The solution, then, was to combine similar smaller pieces by the same composer; for the second half of the new film they proposed a selection of four short pieces by Debussy – three tone poems, including *Sirens* and *Sunken Cathedral*, and the third movement of *La mer*. Another short number under consideration was Weber's *Invitation to the Dance*, which would have featured the Peter Pegasus character from *Fantasia*'s *Pastoral Symphony*.

Stokowski objects to this plan, as he feels the excerpt from *La mer* was "awfully difficult to understand." Walt's response reveals a philosophy that goes a long way towards explaining why his films from this era are so highly regarded:

> Walt: *"What's difficult to understand about it? Doesn't it sound like the sea?"*
>
> Stokowski: *"It isn't clearly done. It's subjective, like you dream about the sea – it's not definite."*
>
> Walt: *"You said* The Rite of Spring *was difficult to understand, remember? Maybe we ought to open up on those things instead of playing down to our medium or our public. That's the very thing we like to have, a challenge."*

That simple quote perfectly crystallizes why Walt's early features were such masterpieces, and why the work he oversaw retains such a devout following decades after his death. It should be chiseled in granite and read aloud before every meeting at every studio. Much as he would do with theme parks later on, Walt was intent on pushing the boundaries of the animation field and was convinced his audience would follow. (And, incidentally, it's interesting to see that Stokowski had been cautious about the inclusion of *The Rite of Spring* in the original *Fantasia*.)

The next piece mentioned is Beethoven's *Minuet in G*, although Stokowski feels it doesn't belong at that place in the program. Bob Carr points out that it had been inserted as a "rest place" between Debussy and the next piece, Stravinsky's *The Firebird*, but the general consensus is that Debussy is placid enough without having to take a breather afterward. Stravinsky's piece was, of course, included as the finale of *Fantasia 2000*; that abridged version of the 1919 arrangement of the *Firebird Suite* was much shorter than the version under consideration in 1940, which Walt estimates at thirty minutes in length.

Another piece on the list for the second half of the film is Bizet's *Carmen*. Herb Perry suggests that it could be done humorously to lighten the tone of the second half, and Walt agrees, saying "If we did *Carmen* I would like to kid it. I mean have beautiful music and beautiful voices, but kid the other angle. Like *Dance of the Hours*." Stokowski disagrees again, saying that "it's such beautiful music, I think you shouldn't do it that way. I think you should leave it alone in that case." Walt seems content to leave it at that: "I don't think we can get it in the first place."

Also mentioned was Mendelssohn's *Spring Song*, which Walt says they can "kid", as well as Sibelius's *The Swan of Tuonela*. The Sibelius piece would receive a lot of attention from Disney artists in subsequent years; a number of beautiful story sketches by Danish illustrator Kay Nielsen were used to create a reconstruction of the segment for the 2000 *Fantasia* DVD.

Stokowski seems intent on including a Strauss waltz, mentioning them more than once. Walt cautions that *The Blue Danube* and *Tales of the Vienna Woods* "were done by a rival outfit, and they weren't done very well." Walt seems similarly determined to animate Rimsky-Korsakov's opera *The Golden Cockerel*, suggesting that "we could stylize the characters; instead of being too human, they would be fantastic." We can see here just how far ahead Walt was thinking with regards to future *Fantasia* sequels, and just how far he might have pushed the medium had things gone differently:

> "In the next one I would like to see us do something like The Barber of Seville or like Coq D'Or *with good voices*, but instead of having to look at the singers themselves we'll take them, take these beautiful voices, and draw to them. The Coq D'Or *gives us more latitude. But I don't want us to be doing anything with our medium that competes in any way with live action, because the field of fantasy is wide open – it hasn't been explored, and the others have tried to do it but it just falls flat. So I think we should do the fantastic things."*

With the first half of the film building to *Peter and the Wolf*, the finale of the entire film would have to be a showstopper rivaling *Fantasia's Night on Bald Mountain* and *Ave Maria*. What was planned would indeed have been spectacular, combining elements of Dvořák's *New World Symphony* with Negro spirituals. It would have been, in Stokowski's words, "a very big thing."

The well-known spiritual *Goin' Home*, written by William Arms Fisher and performed famously by Paul Robeson, is based on themes from the second movement of Dvořák's composition. For the *Fantasia* sequel it would have been arranged for a chorus, and would emerge in the film from the second movement of the symphony. Said Carr, "We'll just develop the spiritual a little further – use the same *Goin' Home* motif that is used in the [second movement], but develop it further." The choral elements would then blend back into the original Dvořák symphony for its well-known finale.

It would have been an impressive thing to see. Stokowski estimates that the segment would run about forty minutes, but "we could cut it down to twenty, not counting the spirituals." Walt cautions against this, giving more insight into how he wanted to expand the *Fantasia* concept in its sequel and what he had learned from the film's production so far:

> "You wouldn't have to cut it that much. I think in the present Concert Feature, we have cut some of the things too much. We didn't know at the time; we've never gone that long with anything like that, we were frightened – but I think, with the experience

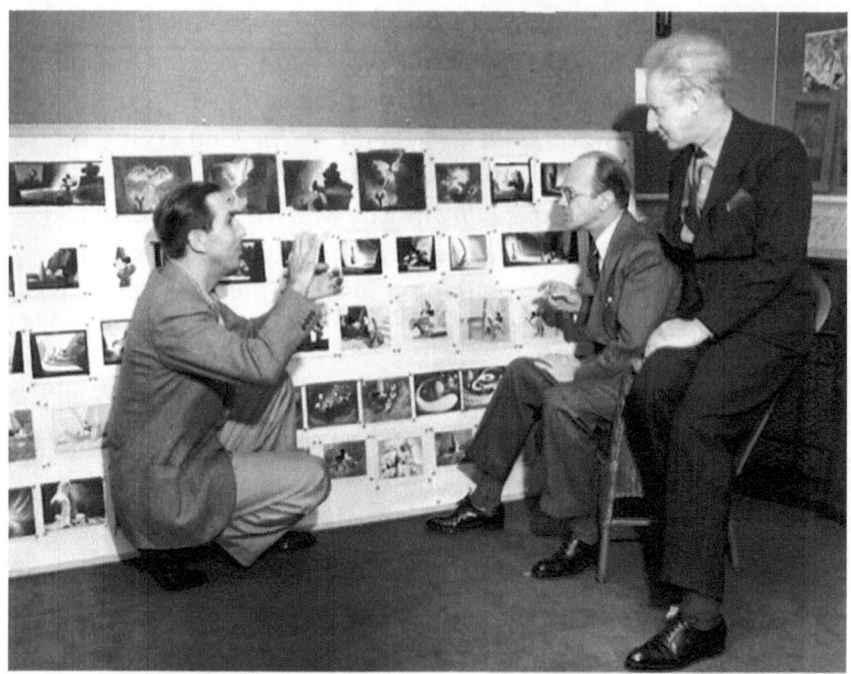

Walt acts out a scene from *The Sorcerer's Apprentice* for Stokowski and *Fantasia*'s host, musicologist Deems Taylor. © Disney

we have had, that we could take a number that would run thirty minutes without any trouble at all, if there is enough variety within the thing itself. I would want to take one of Wagner's things and try to take it, as it is, for thirty minutes."

The notion of ending a *Fantasia* sequel with an animated interpretation of Dvořák's masterpiece, possibly with a guest vocal appearance by Paul Robeson, should be staggering to animation and music lovers alike.

As *Fantasia* fans will know, the eventual (but unrealized) plan for continuing the film was to occasionally substitute individual new segments into an ongoing *Fantasia* program. The proposal for this strategy, as opposed to making a full sequel as a separate film, seems to come during this 1940 meeting. After Stokowski expresses concern about *Schwanda the Bagpiper* and *The Firebird* being included on the same program, Ed Plumb wonders similarly if *Peter and the Wolf* and *Till Eulenspiegel* should be separated in favor of including one each in other future features. This is when Walt proposes an alternate approach:

> Walt: "You know, this is just a thought, but we might just take one number at a time – say, make one or two musical numbers a year. Then we can run it with the first Concert Feature. We might run the first Concert Feature the second time, only this time we'll have, say, Till Eulenspiegel, or Clair de Lune, and we would keep adding to it and changing the program, just like the Ballet does."
>
> Stokowski: "So people would go twice in one week..."
>
> Walt: "They'd want to see their favorites again, and then we'd have one or two new numbers. It's something the Ballet has always done. And I see a number I like listed, and I go back to see it again – it never changes; the same scenery, the whole thing."

This is an interesting peek into Walt's cultural awareness, illustrating an apparent interest in the ballet. It's also a now somewhat poignant look at how he thought this film would be received, and how it would continue to live as something that people would continually revisit. I wish he had been right about that; perhaps if more theaters at the time had been able to accommodate the film's unique and expensive Fantasound format, things would have been different.

Walt mentions Debussy's *Clair de Lune* as a piece they could swap in to the *Fantasia* program, and it would in fact be animated as the first planned addition to the film after its release (in fact, at the time of this meeting Walt had already obtained the rights to its music as well as the rights to *Till Eulenspiegel* and others). When hopes to continue *Fantasia* faded away, the completed animation for *Claire de Lune* was re-edited and re-scored for the *Blue Bayou* sequence from 1946's *Make Mine Music*. A restored version of *Claire de Lune* was released as a short subject in 1996, and included on the *Fantasia* DVD in 2000. Ever the showman, Walt suggests an innovative way to use the piece:

> "I thought we wouldn't open with [Claire de Lune], but later on we'd put it in certain nights – we might even pass out the word

that if there's enough applause at the end there will be an encore, and then if there's applause they'll run that."

With a new mandate to make piecemeal additions to the "Concert Feature" in lieu of crafting a complete sequel, an idea Walt deems "a more practical approach to the thing," the team starts to propose segments to be animated. Stokowski asks to retain *Schwanda the Bagpiper*, *New World Symphony*, and *Peter and the Wolf*, as well as *The Firebird* and the Debussy medley. He continues to push for a Strauss waltz, suggesting *Die Fledermaus* as a possibility.

Walt expresses a number of considerations for which numbers should be selected, indicating that he had probably been mulling this decision for some time. One of these concerns was having material that would be appropriate to the available staff:

> "I would like to have a group of them to choose from, so that I can move them in according to the way production is moving. For instance I might have a group of men that would be ideal for *The Sea* or *Sirens* or that combination, or it might be better to start *Till Eulenspiegel*. In other words we'll have to record about four of them – that's the only way to do it – and then we can select from those four the best ones for the plant to work on"

Another consideration was the length of the pieces. Walt mentions the need for some short numbers as well as longer pieces. "One night," he explains, "we might want to replace *The Rite of Spring* with something of equal length, another night we might want to replace *Toccata and Fugue*." Cost was always an issue too; Walt suggests that *The Swan of Tuonela* would not only be "swell" but also "very inexpensive for us to do." He expounds on this later:

> "We have to think, too, of numbers that won't be too expensive to make. For the next year or so, with the market the way it is, it's probably better for us to take shorter numbers which would be less expensive to produce, and still be effective on the program. I know I could handle *Peter and the Wolf* in a simple way. I think *Till Eulenspiegel* we can handle too."

This is interesting for a number of reasons, not the least of which is that it shows that contrary to popular opinion, Walt wasn't completely oblivious to budgetary issues. Considering that this meeting was held in 1940, well before America's entry into World War II but after European markets had started to vanish, Walt's concern was somewhat prescient while still, unfortunately, over-optimistic. Disney's financial woes would last far more than a year.

A number of ideas followed for potential segments. Stokowski proposes *Rhapsody in Blue*, choosing it over Gershwin's *An American in Paris*; many decades later, it would indeed be animated for inclusion in *Fantasia 2000*. Perry brings up Mendelssohn's *A Midsummer Night's Dream*, asking if Warner Brothers' 1935 adaptation of the Shakespeare play might have taken away the possibility of adapting the piece. "No," says Walt, "because very few people saw that, after all."

Walt suggests Respighi's *Pines of Rome*, pointing out its popularity and that it would be easy to do and inexpensive. He was prescient, as the piece would also be picked for inclusion in *Fantasia 2000*. When Stokowski suggests Mussorgsky's *Pictures at an Exhibition*, Walt brainstorms wildly:

> "I think we could do something funny with all the pictures. That would be good, because people hear it so damn much and they can't quite imagine it, and we could really show the pictures that the music is supposed to represent. We could do a lot with them. There's a house on stilts, and a Mr. Goldberg and Mr. Schmoola [sic] – you could do something with that – and the eggs…"

More ideas are batted around, as Stokowski reads from a previously prepared list of possible pieces. The variety of potential segments is fascinating, and fires the imagination with regards to what could have been. The list even includes Alexander Mosolov's 1926 avant-garde Soviet futurist piece *Iron Foundry*; when Stokowski asks about it, Carr says that they played it and "it's just screeching, sort of."

Stokowski notes the inclusion of Stephen Foster's songs on the list, which he dubs "wonderful". "I would certainly do those," he says.

When Walt is concerned that they had been over-played of late, with a revival of Foster's material having played in the area recently, Stokowski says he's "never heard them well done." "I think the Negro Spiritual idea is good," says Walt, before again bringing up the enticing prospect of enlisting "good voices" like Paul Robeson. "The Hall Johnson Choir would be good," suggests Plumb.

When Stokowski asks about Wagner material they might have considered, Carr points out that they'd made "a sort of stream-lined story" out of popular segments of the composer's material. This would have certainly been an interesting project – sections of Wagner's best work pieced together to tell a narrative.

But the Disney artists had even grander ideas than new individual segments for *Fantasia*; Carr points out that they have an entirely separate list of suggestions for feature-length projects. These sound incredibly ambitious and intriguing:

> *"It was the idea of taking a big story, like the Story of Atlantis, and to the different episodes putting movements selected from different symphonies, and run it as a feature-length picture with an entirely symphonic background."*

Stokowski agrees that this would be feasible, adding that "it's a big idea." Carr continues:

> *"T. Hee made a suggestion for a feature which would be the whole story of music, the history of music, right up to the present time. We go through all countries, all times."*

This idea would later be explored in a number of projects, notably the Oscar-winning short *Toot, Whistle, Plunk and Boom* (1953) as well as 1953's *Melody*.

Another feature suggestion was similar to a concept Disney was concurrently developing about the life of storyteller Hans Christian Andersen. Disney had started work on the project, which would combine live-action footage with animated fantasy sequences, the year before, and a few months before this meeting had entered discussions with independent producer Samuel Goldwyn about co-producing the live-action segments of the film. The talks for that film trailed off over the years, although Goldwyn would eventually release the Danny Kaye-starring musical *Hans Christian Andersen* through RKO in 1952.

Back in 1940, though, the artists were apparently proposing another biographical film about Russian composer Pyotr Ilyich Tchaikovsky. Says Carr, "Bill Roberts suggested this Tchaikovsky story, a story of his life with his music – it would be some live action, about 10% live action and 90% animation."

Stokowsky points out, in an amusingly oblique fashion, a problem with this idea:

> Stokowsky: "I don't think his life would be good, but I think his music could be made into a wonderful thing. I don't think it's possible to put his life on the screen because of the central feature of his intimate life – you just can't mention it very well, though they have now this Oscar Wilde play which frankly does so."
>
> Carr: "Yes, it's a very debatable thing."

I'm amazed they would even worry about issues in Tchaikovsky's private life; after all, pretty much any biographical Hollywood picture from that era was whitewashed completely beyond recognition, if not simply fabricated outright.

One of their feature ideas might sound familiar to fans of Disney theme parks. Says Carr, "Another suggestion for a feature length picture was what we call tentatively the American Journey; we go geographically over all America, and also historically, and musically we would go all the way from cowboy songs up to Roy Harris." This general concept would be used much, much later as the basis for the beloved 1974 Disneyland attraction *America Sings*.

Then there's this intriguing prospect, tying in to earlier proposals dealing with Negro spirituals, the works of Stephen Foster, and other pieces of Americana and roots music:

Carr: "Then another shorter thing would be to take the development of Negro music from real jungle chants, beginning in Africa, through the old slave songs, into spirituals and blues, and finally William Grant Still and a Negro symphony. Do ideas like that seem labored from a musical point of view?"

Stokowski: "No, no – I think they're very interesting."

Carr: "Then there was another idea – William Grant Still is here in Los Angeles, and we could commission him to write an African Symphony to fit a scenario that we would lay out."

Stokowski: "Yes, that could be done, too, and he would do it well."

This plan not only sounds like a fascinating project, but it also presages by forty years the very similar *Heartbeat of Africa* show at Epcot Center's designed-but-unbuilt Equatorial Africa pavilion. Mass-market entertainment featuring black performers, songs, or culture were rare to begin with in 1940, and it was even more difficult to find those subjects treated with any amount of respect. It would have been interesting to see such a project produced by Disney, who would later hire James Baskett for a film that made him the first black actor to win an Academy Award.

The last suggestion brought up in the meeting sounds more traditional – "a special number on Disney hits in the past" – and it seems funny to consider a retrospective piece happening so early in the company's history. As a more "comfortable" sounding notion, it goes to point out just how bold some of these other proposals were. And that's what really impresses about *Fantasia* – it's just as bold today as it was in 1940. Walt was the only one with courage enough to do it.

Similarly impressive was the cultural awareness on display in the meeting. Walt was obviously a brilliant guy but he'd hardly had a traditional education; still, he seems well versed in not only the music itself but the stories behind the pieces. The musical selections the staff mulls cover a wide range of eras and styles ranging from traditional classical music to then-modern symphonic pieces as well as traditional and modern song. Most importantly, Walt was willing to put the efforts of his company behind bringing what was seen as "high culture" to the movie-going masses. He believed in the project, and was willing to back it up.

Few of the ideas mentioned in this meeting would ever come to anything. Some projects were developed further, some even reached the animation process, and still others were revived for *Fantasia 2000*. But deep in the animation vaults there are still slews of these proposals, just as exciting today as they were then, and hoping against hope to be discovered.

.03

Walt's Elephants

Herbert Ryman was one of Disney's greatest artists, working for the studio on and off from 1939 until his death in 1989. Trained as a fine artist, he served as a Hollywood production designer between stints at Disney; he worked for Walt first as an animation art director and, later, the third person hired to what would become Walt Disney Imagineering.

Herb was much closer to Walt Disney than the average studio artist, perhaps because both were raised in the Midwest and shared many common interests. Herb was also a rarity in that he felt free to tell Walt no when he didn't want to do something, and walked away from the studio on occasion to pursue other interests. Whether it was for that honesty, or simply because Walt recognized his immense talent, the two worked together often over the years. When Walt needed a large piece of artwork to help sell Disneyland to financiers, he called upon Herb – who didn't even work at the studio at the time – to come in over a long weekend and create that first iconic overview of the park.

Walt was such a fan of Ryman's abilities that he hired the artist to paint a portrait of his daughter Sharon. Herb had traveled to Walt's new home in Holmby Hills, near Beverly Hills, when his boss came up to him and held out his hand. "Herbie, have you ever seen anything like this?" he asked. Ryman admitted he hadn't, but guessed that the tiny brownish object was a bean of some sort.

Walt said that it was, and challenged Herb to guess what was inside the small, hollow bean. When Ryman demurred, Walt exclaimed that there were forty-nine elephants inside. He explained that the trinket had been a gift from a "very important Chinese gentleman" after the opening of *Snow White and the Seven Dwarfs*. The man had told him that the gift was appropriate since the film featured seven dwarfs – seven being a "magical" number – and that seven was also Walt's lucky number. Multiply seven by seven and you get forty-nine, which was "seven times as lucky." And so the bean contained forty-nine miniscule hand-carved ivory elephants. As long as the elephants stayed in the bean, the man said, Walt would have good luck for his entire life.

Opening the bean revealed the tiny elephants, each about the size of a grain of salt according to Herb. They were too small to see any detail, so Walt asked Sharon to bring them a magnifying glass for closer examination. They poured out the elephants and counted them out with a needle before Walt put them in Herb's hand. But as Ryman admired them through the magnifying glass, Walt unexpectedly jostled his elbow. The elephants flew through the air and down into the room's deep pile rug.

"Now, Herbie," Walt said, "see what you've done. You've brought me bad luck." "Well I didn't bring you bad luck," Herb replied. "You knocked my elbow!" Thankfully Walt's wife Lillian had seen the incident and came to Herb's defense, and agreed that Walt had instigated the elephant stampede.

Getting down on their knees, Herb and the Disneys began a search for the stray elephants. It wasn't easy, searching for the tiny elephants in the deep woolen jungle of the rug; Sharon fetched tweezers and a flashlight and the group searched for some time. They never did find them all; Herb later estimated they recovered about thirty.

Herb would continue to protest his innocence, later pointing out the success Walt continued to have with Disneyland, Walt Disney World, and all his popular films. "But still," Herb pointed out, "I sometimes think of the luck he might have had if I hadn't lost those elephants!"

.04

ON LOCATION WITH WALT

One might have thought, in the fall of 1955, that Walt Disney would have more pressing things to do than hang around on a movie set in the remote and rural backwaters of northeastern Georgia. After all, Disneyland had opened only a few short months earlier and still required a great deal of attention. So did the full slate of other productions underway at the Disney studio, including several live-action pictures as well as the constant stream of new episodes needed for the *Disneyland* television series. It would take a very special project to wrest Walt away from his new wonderland – a project like *The Great Locomotive Chase*.

Directed by Francis Lyon, *The Great Locomotive Chase* was written and produced by Lawrence Edward Watkin. Watkin was a frequent Disney screenwriter, having come to the studio in 1947. His first Disney credit had been 1950's *Treasure Island*, the studio's first completely live-action feature; his 1942 novel *Marty Markham* was later adapted into the beloved *Spin & Marty* serial for television's *Mickey Mouse Club*.

The Great Locomotive Chase had been considered for production ever since the Disney studio began to develop live-action films; according to author Michael Barrier, the story was at one point the leading contender to become Disney's very first non-animated offering. It's easy to see why the story captured Walt's imagination – it's a tale of derring-do and a "true-life" historical adventure that takes place almost entirely on speeding locomotives. Disney's love of trains was already well documented at the time, and was widely remarked on in the press when the film went into production.

The film dramatizes the Andrews Raid of 1862, following Union spies deep behind Confederate lines on a mission that could have dramatically cut short the Civil War. Fess Parker, a newly-minted star thanks to his stint as Davy Crockett, was cast as James J. Andrews - the leader of the raid.

Andrews had gained some renown in the south as a Rebel blockade runner while secretly working for the Federal government. In April of 1862, Andrews led twenty-two men into Georgia where, in full view of Confederate sentries and 4,000 troops, they stole a train while its crew and passengers were eating breakfast. Andrews planned to drive north from Big Shanty (current-day Kennesaw) to Chattanooga, destroying track and trestles as he went, making it impossible for the Rebels to send reinforcements from Atlanta into Tennessee as the Union attempted to take the state.

What Andrews didn't count on was intrepid conductor William Fuller, whose train, the *General*, Andrews had stolen in Big Shanty. Fuller chased after Andrews for eighty-seven miles, until finally he was able to commandeer the steam engine *Texas* which raced – backwards! – until it chased down Andrews near the town of Ringgold. Andrews and his men were rounded up and tried as spies, although some later managed to escape and tell their story. They were among the very first to be awarded the Congressional Medal of Honor (Andrews himself, as well as fellow civilian William Campbell, were ineligible for the award).

Disney's version of the tale is told through the eyes of William Pittenger (John Lupton), a survivor of the Raid who went on to write several books about the event. Jeff York, who as Mike Fink had proved such an able match for Fess Parker in *Davy Crockett and the River Pirates*, was cast as the belligerent William Campbell. Chasing after the Raiders as the relentless conductor Fuller was screen veteran Jeffrey Hunter. On the set, Hunter was introduced to William Fuller Jr., the elderly real-world son of his character.

The railroad along which the original events took place continues as a major rail artery to this day, and even by 1955 it had been

Walt Disney poses for a snapshot at the Clayton Cafe in Clayton, GA. Clayton was a center of activity during the filming of *The Great Locomotive Chase*.
© Georgia Department of Archives and History

straightened and modernized so as to be unusable for a period piece. Searching for a suitable substitute for the winding rails of the 19th century, Disney eventually discovered the shortline Tallulah Falls Railroad fifty miles to the east.

The Tallulah Falls Railroad, or "Old TF" in local parlance, seems itself like something out of one of Walt's rural fantasies. Formed in 1897 from elements of previous failed railroads, by 1907 the TF would stretch fifty-eight miles from Cornelia, Georgia to Franklin, North Carolina. The TF had opened up the isolated area to the outside world, allowing summertime visitors to witness the majesty of the Tallulah Falls (marketed as the "Niagara of the South", while the Tallulah Gorge was promoted as the "Grand Canyon of the East") and enabling residents of the mountains to trade and communicate freely with the outside world.

The *Texas* steams along during filming on the Tallulah Falls Railway.
© Georgia Department of Archives and History

Locals turned out en masse to be costumed as extras when filming took place in Clayton, GA. Some were even given speaking roles.
© Georgia Department of Archives and History

Eventually the boom-days of the Victorian resorts turned bust, and when Walt arrived in 1955 the TF had been in receivership since 1923. Locals had started referring to it as the "Total Failure", and even spectacular views from the train as it wound a thousand feet above the floor of the Tallulah Gorge couldn't keep passenger service from ending in 1946. The TF had hauled only freight and timber since. With only one train running daily, the sleepy little line would make a perfect playground for Walt as he brought a bit of Hollywood to remote Rabun County.

The TF was well suited to Disney's needs. As it wound through the steep Georgia and Carolina hills, the railroad used forty-two trestles in its fifty-eight mile route. All of those, save one, were wooden and of great vintage.

For his steam-driven stars, Walt personally recruited a number of vehicles from the B&O Railroad Museum in Baltimore. Starring as the *General* was the *William Mason*, a 4-4-0 American built in 1856 and still in use today (it appeared as *Wanderer* in the 1999 feature *Wild Wild West*). Also on loan from Baltimore were the *Lafayette*, a replica of an 1837 locomotive, as well as two Civil War era coaches, a baggage car, and two ammunition cars.

Another 4-4-0 American, the *Inyo*, was borrowed from Paramount Pictures to portray the *Texas*. The vehicles were all shipped by rail to Cornelia, where they were transferred into the care of the Tallulah Falls Railroad. All in all the *Inyo* and *William Mason* logged more than a thousand miles during filming – all back and forth over a single thirty-five mile stretch of track.

It wasn't easy working with the old trains; engines of that era didn't have brakes, and could only stop quickly by throwing their wheels into reverse. This made work tricky for the actors, as well as the camera car which followed for filming. Signals between the vehicles had to be precise in order to prevent potential injuries or accidents.

The TF provided engineers and conductors to run the trains during filming, but during breaks Walt took the trains out himself. Walt spent several weeks on location, where he became a fixture in the small towns along the route. He could be seen daily on the set, speaking to old railroaders and poking around the locomotives. He even raided the costume department for a vintage Confederate cap so he would fit in to the period atmosphere.

Filming began in late September 1955, and lasted about six weeks. Casting calls allowed locals to take part in the filming, and many obtained speaking roles. "Anytime anybody came to town to make a movie we all went down and tried out for it," recalled local John Kollock in a *Foxfire* interview. "Since my voice is kind of North Georgian, I got a part as one of the engineers." Kollock's scenes were filmed at a station built for the production north of the tiny town of Otto, across the state line in Macon County, North Carolina. "They built a siding and the station right out in the middle of nowhere," he later recounted.

Onlookers watched as hotels were built without second floors (movie magic filled in the rest with matte paintings), and marveled as the Disney crew wrecked boxcars "on purpose." When the script called for the trains to race into a tunnel, but no tunnels were to be found on the TF, a fake tunnel entrance was built into the side of a hill. Even the trains themselves, which so convincingly steamed and smoked like wood-burners, had been converted to run on diesel.

Disney provided a huge economic boost for the area, and especially for the men working the TF. As local Ernest Anderson recounted decades later, "You ought to have been around when Walt Disney was making that picture up there. He really paid you something. He gave you fifty dollars a week extra, just to buy your Coca-Colas with, outside of your salary; then you got your dinner and supper made."

"[Walt] hired a whole lot of people from around here to work on the film," recalled Anderson. "The women and girls in the picture dressed just the way they used to seventy or eighty years ago: long sleeves, collars way up around, the skirts a-dragging," he said. "Disney hired a lot of people for the movie – and when you signed up, your pay started when you stuck your name down. I got paid two weeks before they got up there to work."

Clayton Mayor W.S. Bearden, in costume as a railroad switchman, converses with Fess Parker during a break in filming.
© Georgia Department of Archives and History

Locals, used to days of hard labor, seemed bemused by the "hurry up and wait" nature of filmmaking. Actors and extras would gather in the morning at the Clayton train station, where the costuming and makeup departments were located, before taking a bus to the shooting location. "At that time of the year there's a deep fog up in that valley, so we would get up there and sit around by the fire and wait until the fog lifted," John Kollock told *Foxfire*. "It was nine or ten o'clock in the morning before we would even start work, and then we would work the rest of the day. I was up there for a week or so waiting around."

Kollock played the engineer of a train steaming south from Chattanooga, and acted in a scene opposite Fess Parker. "When we finally got around to shooting it," he later said, "we shot the whole thing in about an hour and then I was through." While Kollack appeared to operate the train, blowing its horn during the scene, the locomotive was actually operated by TF personnel who were contracted to work the engines. Clad in their usual work clothes, they didn't even have to dress up for filming – although they had to operate the trains lying down, with actors standing overhead.

Two locals managed to be cast in plum roles that actually earned them on-screen credits. W.S. Bearden, then mayor of Clayton, portrayed a railroad switchman whose skepticism nearly derails the Andrews plot. His scenes bickering with Fess Parker earned him accolades from the local press.

Fourteen year old Doug Bleckley was discovered while working behind the counter at the local Pic-Ric Café; he was cast as the young *Texas* fireman who assists in the pursuit of the raiders. Bleckley actually made two trips to Hollywood following production; the first was for post-production needs, while the second was for an appearance on the *Mickey Mouse Club*. He even was offered a contract at the Disney studio, should his family agree to move to California; his mother, however, turned down the opportunity.

These local celebrities alongside many others were featured on an episode of the *Disneyland* television show in May 1956. *Behind the Scenes with Fess Parker* was hosted by the star himself, and offered a look at on-set moviemaking magic while introducing viewers worldwide to the residents of Georgia and North Carolina seen in the film.

Everyone got in on the act – the porter from the hotel where the Disney crew stayed, their waitress from the local restaurant, drug store clerks, and the wife of a local grocer. There was the president of the county Chamber of Commerce, a prominent restaurateur from Atlanta, and the manager of the Pic-Ric Café. Even the pastor of the First Baptist Church, one J.E. Dillard, was cast as an on-screen preacher. At first reluctant to take the small speaking role, he insisted on reading the film's script and consulting with a fellow pastor before deciding. Eventually he agreed to take the part, only after getting signed permission from each of the deacons of his church.

Incidentally, the film's impact was not limited to the tiny hamlets along the TF between Clayton and Franklin. The film's Midwest premiere was held in yet another small town along a rail line – Marceline, Missouri. The small Uptown Theater in Walt's childhood hometown earned the honor not only of a premiere, but also a visit from Walt and Roy and their wives. The film opened to a packed house of children on July 4th, 1956, and played in continuous shows until 1:30 AM the next morning and over a subsequent four-day weekend. Walt and Roy greeted each child as they entered the theater that Fourth of July, and before the film began Walt addressed the crowd. "My best memories are the years I spent here," he told the rapt audience. "You children are lucky to live here."

The weeks that Walt spent on location had a lasting impact on the residents of Rabun and Macon Counties. To this day, local businesses showcase framed pictures of Walt on location, or dining in their establishments. A rumor even persists that he considered purchasing the TF to turn it into a scenic railway, but was dissuaded by its millions of dollars of accumulated debt and back taxes. Nevertheless, the day Disney came to town left its mark on the imaginations of these mountain communities. In the words of Ernest Anderson, "Walt Disney sure was a fellow."

.05

WALT & IKE

During his lifetime, Walt Disney crossed paths with several American presidents. It seems remarkable that a poor kid from the Midwest would find himself rubbing elbows with some of the most powerful men in the world, but Walt had fans in the White House as far back as the Roosevelt administration. It was Dwight D. Eisenhower, however, with whom Walt would become particularly close.

Walt had stumped for Ike during his 1952 campaign; Eisenhower was the first major presidential candidate to advertise heavily on television, and Disney studio personnel volunteered their free time to produce an animated ad called "We Like Ike". Two versions of the ad were created to air that October; one was twenty seconds long and the other one minute in length.

This resulting ad was extremely catchy, so much so that it remains fairly well known today. In the ad, an infectious jingle repeats the phrase "Ike for President" while a parade of cartoon Americans march by on their way to vote for Eisenhower. Ike was so grateful for the ad that Walt and his wife Lillian were invited to the inaugural festivities and subsequent ball.

Reports at the time credited the lyrics to Gil George, a "Democrat for Eisenhower"; this was actually a pseudonym for Disney studio nurse Hazel Gilman George, Walt's longtime physical therapist and confidante.

Surprisingly, "Gil George" contributed a number of memorable lyrics to Disney television and film projects over the years, writing alongside studio composer Paul Smith. Her credits included dozens of songs for the *Mickey Mouse Club* including "Talent Round Up" and

"Beauty Is As Beauty Does" as well as familiar tunes such as "From All of Us to All of You" and the theme for *Old Yeller*.

The Eisenhower ad resulted from the relentless efforts of renowned aviatrix and devout Republican Jacqueline Cochran, who herself had played an instrumental part in convincing a reluctant General Eisenhower to run for president. She secured the participation of Disney studio officials, who were organized under the auspices of Roy O. Disney. Roy was credited as the ad's producer and, according to Cochran, "was the sparkplug of the entire project and who got it under way."

Disney staffers worked on a strictly volunteer basis on the ad, although Cochrane later estimated their efforts amounted to an in-kind donation of $25,000 or more. The only cost came from the laboratory fees for printing the film reels; the ever-industrious Cochrane secured a $1,000 donation from Eisenhower backer Paul Helms to cover the expense. Cochrane also ensured that the commercial spots would get frequent airplay on national television hookups and in theaters, directly lobbying media magnate and Eisenhower supporter Jock Whitney to assist in this.

The roster of Disney talent that worked on the Eisenhower commercial is a remarkable sampling of the studio's most talented artists. Supervised by producer Bill Anderson and directed by Disney vet Hamilton Luske and assistant director Clyde Jones, the cartoon married Gil George's lyrics with music by Paul Smith. The song was performed by Jud Conlon and his Rhythmaires; Conlon served as a musical arranger for the studio, and his group was a frequent presence on Disney soundtracks, including those of *Cinderella*, *Peter Pan*, and *Alice in Wonderland*.

Animating the ad were three of Walt's famous "Nine Old Men", Eric Larson, John Lounsbery, and Wolfgang Reitherman. They were joined by George Rowley and assistant animators Fred Kopietz and Art Stevens. Story men Hal Adelquist, Milton Banta, William Berg, and Winston Hibler worked on the short, as did layout artists Ken Anderson, McLaren Stewart, Ken O'Connor, Lance Nolley, Charles

Ike and Walt in the 1960s.
© Disney

Philippi, and Bruce Bushman. Backgrounds were contributed by Claude Coats and James Trout, and artist and future Imagineer Rolly Crump served as an inbetweener. Jimmy MacDonald, sound effects legend and voice of Mickey Mouse, also participated.

The result of their efforts was well received by the Eisenhower campaign and got frequent airplay that October. In a letter to Cochrane from Bill Anderson after the election, Anderson pointed out, "We have been advised by these stations that these cartoon spots were played more than any of the other Eisenhower television films." Anderson sent Cochrane, Eisenhower, and several members of the campaign staff autographed animation cel setups from the short. Roy Disney also wrote to Cochrane, saying, "The boys and girls all enjoyed working on the project and, of course, we are all very happy at the outcome of the election."

Several years later, in 1957, Walt was selected to receive the Milestone Award from the Screen Producers Guild. Writing from the White House with congratulations, Eisenhower was effusive with praise:

> "Your genius as a creator of folklore has long been recognized by leaders in every field of human endeavor, including the most discerning body of critics, the children of this land and all lands. Now, I am glad to express what I have long felt, a deep appreciation for your skill and the ways you have applied it in many worthy causes.
>
> "As an artist, your work has helped reveal our country to the world, and the world to all of us. As a man, your sympathetic attitude toward life has helped our children develop a clean and cheerful view of humanity, with all its frailties and possibilities for good."

Walt was obviously pleased with such high praise; he replied to the president, "It is my earnest desire that we will always be able to do the things that will merit your esteem." The next year he did just that, when the *Mickey Mouse Club* aired a documentary segment entitled "Inside Report on Washington". The film was delivered to the White House, and, as Eisenhower reported to Walt, "I thought you would like to know that my older grandchildren, as well as the other members of the Eisenhower family, thoroughly enjoyed the film."

After leaving the White House, Eisenhower finally visited Disneyland with his family, remarking, "We've heard about Disneyland for years. Almost dropped in a time or two. Something always came up." His wife, Mamie, told reporters, "This is grandpa's gift to the children." Drawing a throng of reporters and park guests, the former president posed in a fire chief's helmet on the Main Street, U.S.A. fire truck and took in the sights from the Disneyland and Santa Fe Railroad, the Monorail, the Submarine Voyage, and more. "Oh, I love it," Ike proclaimed.

In their six-hour visit, the President got in on the act, taking the wheel of the "Yangtze Lotus" on the Jungle Cruise. "Oh boy, Mamie,

Ike doffs his fire chief's helmet to the assembled reporters on a visit to Disneyland, December 26, 1961. © Disney

look at that!" he exclaimed when the Mark Twain steamed into view; he admitted to the assembled media, "I suppose you might say I'm enjoying this as much as the children – no, more."

Halfway through their visit, the Eisenhowers begged off for a breather. "You kids enjoy the wilder rides," the President told his family. "Grandma and I are going to rest." After a 45-minute break in Walt's apartment above the firehouse, they took an electric car to meet the family in Frontierland where they rode through the Painted Desert on the Mine Train Through Nature's Wonderland.

While taking in the *Golden Horseshoe Revue*, one of Eisenhower's four grandchildren was called onstage to learn a balloon trick from Wally "Pecos Bill" Boag. "Now why don't you go back and show this trick to your grandfather," Boag said. "It'll make him a big man in the neighborhood." Ike roared with laughter along with the crowd. Before leaving the park he raved, "I never dreamed it was this entertaining. We enjoyed every minute of it and hope to be back soon."

Following that visit in December 1961, Eisenhower wrote to Walt to express that his family had a "splendid time" at Disneyland. Said Ike, "I congratulate you not only on the imaginative but realistic exhibits, and assure you that as much as I have heard about Disneyland, it exceeded all my expectations." He even relayed that his granddaughter Mary Jean "became so attached to one of the hostesses that she almost refused to leave."

The two men continued to correspond in subsequent years. In March 1966, Walt wrote a rather charming letter to the President; his request for an autograph provides a glimpse at the man who rose from humble origins to befriend world leaders:

> *Dear General Eisenhower –*
>
> *Back in 1918, I was with the AEF in France although too young for military service, but I did manage to join up with the American Red Cross as an ambulance driver and chauffeur. During this time I had the honor of driving General Pershing's 11-year-old son, John, to Neufchateau. Then later on, through Miss Howell, I received a copy of the General's memoirs autographed to me.*
>
> *And now, getting around to the point of this preamble and more or less complete the cycle, I would sincerely appreciate your autographing the copy of your book, Crusade in Europe, which I am forwarding to you under separate cover.*
>
> *May I also take this opportunity to thank you for your part in the Freedoms Foundation presentation. With all the awards I have received during my forty years in Hollywood, this is the only one I have received for just being an American—a heritage we all take too much for granted. It was a real honor to have you make the presentation.*
>
> *And now one more favor—would you mind inscribing the enclosed photograph taken at the Freedoms luncheon. With the added touch of your inscription to this picture, I am hoping I may be able to better impress my grandchildren one of these days.*

The luncheon to which Walt refers took place in Palm Springs in 1963, when he was given the George Washington Award by the Freedoms Foundation at Valley Forge. Walt was the fifth individual to be so honored, cited for "sustaining the ideals and principles upon which America has been founded" and his work in passing those values on to children. In presenting the award personally to Walt, Eisenhower proclaimed:

> *"Freedoms Foundation at Valley Forge honors Walt Disney, ambassador of freedom for the United States of America. For his educational wisdom and patriotic dedication in advancing the concept of freedom under God; for his unfailing professional devotion to the things which matter most; human dignity and personal responsibility; for masterful creative leadership in communicating the hopes and aspirations of our free society to the far corners of the planet."*

The George Washington Award – a medal mounted on a plaque – and a framed photograph of Walt receiving it from President Eisenhower were among the select few artifacts which Walt hanged on the wall of his own personal office. They remained there in a place of honor until the day he died.

Over the years, Eisenhower had encouraged Walt's involvement in the People to People Foundation, which the President had helped establish in 1956. When the organization was incorporated as a non-governmental entity in 1961, Walt became a trustee; in 1964, he attended group meetings in Guadalajara and Mexico City. Eisenhower found Walt's participation "a great asset," and felt his attendance at the meeting of Trustees had "a tremendous impact." Writing to hotelier Hernando Courtright, Eisenhower said, "My son reports that Walt Disney was the hit of the whole affair."

The organization formed a new executive committee in 1965, and Walt was nominated for membership. He declined, feeling that with his other obligations, he would not be able to devote the proper amount of attention to the important work underway at People to People. "I am sure my work load will lessen as the years go by," he promised,

Walt accepts the George Washington Award from former President Eisenhower in Palm Springs on February 22, 1963. © Disney

"and then I will welcome opportunities to serve a worthwhile cause like this, when I can be of some use to the organization." Although he declined the nomination, he did contribute a gift of $50,000.

In 1966, General Eisenhower had begun to raise money for the founding of Eisenhower College, a small liberal arts school bearing his name. To aid in fundraising, and to honor Dwight and Mamie Eisenhower's fiftieth wedding anniversary, Walt filmed a promotional spot that June on a soundstage where work was underway on *The Happiest Millionaire*.

Walt even managed to plug his upcoming musical by filming on the Biddle mansion set and pointing out that the movie was set in the same year, 1916, that "a young Lieutenant named Dwight D. Eisenhower married Mamie Geneva Doud." He wrapped up the pitch by adding, "Now a lot of the General's good friends feel this is the perfect opportunity for the citizens he has served so faithfully to express their deep affection and regards." Since Eisenhower College was the project closest to the General's heart, Walt said, viewers "can offer no better congratulations than sending a donation." The school went on to open in 1968.

Eisenhower returned the favor the next month, when Walt and Lillian celebrated their 41st wedding anniversary. Ike and his "bride of 11 days and 50 years" sent the couple a telegram wishing Walt and Lilly "a full measure of health and happiness."

In October 1966, Eisenhower wrote to Walt expressing his plans to resign as head of People to People and relating that many thought Disney would be his "logical successor". "I most sincerely hope that when such a suggestion is made to you," said Eisenhower, "that you will give the idea your most careful and sympathetic consideration." Walt did not pursue the position, but only two months before he passed away in December 1966 he accepted a three-year term on the group's Board of Trustees.

After Walt's death, in April 1967, Eisenhower issued this tribute:

> *"To many tens of millions, Walt Disney brought good cheer and happy hours with entertainment that lightened their hearts and refreshed their minds. To Americans of all ages and all walks of life, he was unique. Children loved his characters and his portrayal of them. Parents honored him and were obligated to him for his far-reaching aid in the sensible upbringing of families. Grandparents saluted him as a genius with films that were messages of fun and education and character building. His appeal and his influence were universal... not restricted to this land alone, for he touched a common chord in all humanity. We shall not soon see his like again. Fortunately, all he stood for will live on in the memory of those who were privileged to know him in his person or in his products. His work will endure so long as men and women and children retain a sense of wonder, a need for bright laughter, a love of the clean and decent. Consequently, Walt Disney's name and his creations will endure through generations. In honoring him, we salute an American who belongs to the world."*

.06

WALT AND THE WINTER OLYMPICS

In October of 1966, Walt Disney was declared "Showman of the World" by the National Association of Theatre Owners. His creative legacy was so diverse, spanning so many realms of entertainment and outdoor recreation, it's remarkable to think that before 1955 he was "merely" a producer of motion pictures. In the last eleven years of Walt's life, the scope of his entertainment empire expanded greatly; the one-time cartoon maker was now a fixture of theme parks and World's Fairs, of television and sporting events. At the nexus of this activity came the VIII Olympic Winter Games of 1960, where Walt and his creative team expanded the bounds of their activities while forever changing the way the Olympics were presented.

The tale of the 1960 Winter Olympics, held in Squaw Valley, California, seems itself taken from a fairy tale. Initiated as a publicity stunt by Alexander Cushing, the Harvard-educated owner and only resident of the struggling ski resort, the Squaw Valley bid shocked the world by beating out some of the great ski resorts of Europe in International Olympic Committee (IOC) voting in 1955.

The only problem was that Squaw Valley was hardly prepared to host an international sporting event. At the time, it boasted only one chairlift, two tow-ropes, and a fifty room lodge. Upon hearing about the California bid, IOC President Avery Brundage told Cushing, "The [United States Olympic Committee] has obviously taken leave of their senses." Cushing turned the resort's size into an advantage, however, presenting it as a blank slate upon which a world-class facility could be custom built to suit Olympic needs.

The newly-formed California Olympic Commission had five short years to build a fully-functional, Olympic-ready facility in the mountains near Lake Tahoe. So undeveloped was the location that at the close of the 1956 Winter Games, Squaw Valley had no local government to accept the Olympic flag from the mayor of previous host Cortina d'Ampezzo. An IOC member from California had to accept the flag on Squaw Valley's behalf.

Bringing the Winter Games to California meant harnessing the luster of Tinseltown. In 1958, Organizing Committee President Prentis Hale visited the Disney studio in Burbank and, after joining Walt for lunch, asked him to become Chairman of the Pageantry Committee for the upcoming Games. This would involve programming the opening and closing ceremonies, the victory ceremonies for each event, and the Olympic torch relay. Disney agreed, saying later, "I didn't know then what I was getting into!"

Walt was no stranger to the skiing world; Mount Disney in the Sierras was named in his honor after he helped finance the Sugar Bowl resort in 1939, and twenty years later he unveiled his own man-made mountain when the Matterhorn Bobsleds debuted at Disneyland. For Squaw Valley, he recruited from within his own organization to build a committee that would undertake a then-unprecedented level of Olympic pageantry. Ron Miller, assistant director at the studio and Walt's son-in-law, was named Pageantry Coordinator. Another assistant director, Joseph McEveety, was named Olympic Torch Relay Director, and manager Edsel Curry became Director of Special Projects. Walt Disney Productions Vice-President Card Walker was named Director of Publicity. Walt also called upon the talents of a few friends; Art Linkletter, television star and host of Disneyland's live opening special, became the Vice-President in Charge of Entertainment, and Western Air Lines president Terrell Drinkwater was named Vice-Chairman in Charge of Budget.

Filling the role of Pageantry Director was Tommy Walker, once bandleader at the University of Southern California and then Director of Customer Relations at Disneyland. Walker hit the road to line up support for the event; he conferred in Salt Lake City with the president of the Music Educators National Conference about recruiting young

Walt Disney shows off a model of the planned facilities for the 1960 Olympic Winter Games. © Disney

musicians for the festivities, and sought the help of Japan's largest fireworks manufacturer in developing the ceremony's pyrotechnics.

Supervising the musical aspects of the production were Choral Director Dr. Charles Hirt from the University of Southern California and Band Director Clarence Sawhill. After a meeting with the Music Educators National Conference in March 1959, the Committee was granted permission to work with the California and Nevada Music Educators Associations to recruit musicians and singers from public high schools in those states.

The response was overwhelming. When applications were distributed in fall 1959, more than thirty bands and seventy choral groups applied to be part of the Olympic ceremonies. After listening to hours of mailed-in auditions, Hirt and his committee selected eighteen bands and thirty-seven choruses from the two states. A musical program was chosen for the event, and in December 1959 Hirt and Sawhill gathered at UCLA to record a demo of the choral and instrumental numbers to distribute to participating schools. Groups practiced first individually, and then in one of four regional rehearsals held in Reno, San Francisco, Fresno, and Los Angeles. There was no free ride; students had to raise money back home to fund their trip to Squaw Valley. All told, 3,680 students – 1,322 band members and 2,358 choir members – participated.

Youth participation was critical to the success of the Games; acting as official flag-raisers, messengers, and crowd control during the event were 125 Explorer Scouts under the leadership of Scoutmaster William King. Walt himself was quoted as saying, "I have always said that the spirit of American youth cannot be daunted, and I think this was dramatically proven by their unselfish and wholehearted effort before and during the VIII Olympic Winter Games."

This effort extended to the all-important torch relay, which brought the Olympic flame by foot more than six hundred miles from the Los Angeles Memorial Coliseum – site of the 1932 Olympic Summer Games – to Squaw Valley. More than seven hundred high school runners from the California Interscholastic Federation took part, joined by a number of former Olympic champions. The athletes were each assigned one-mile sections of the route, where they practiced by toting eight pound shot-puts.

Meanwhile, a rush was on to create an Olympics-worthy resort out of the wilderness. It was estimated that two thousand visitors a day arrived in the summer of 1959 to tour the construction site, and Walt himself made several visits to coordinate the entertainment efforts. What he would have found in the works was an Olympics after his own heart – full of innovations and "firsts".

Previous Olympics had lodged guests and athletes in local hotels and homes, but the remote location of Squaw Valley necessitated the construction of custom-built housing for participants. Thus, the very first Olympic Village, consisting of four dormitories, was created. Artificial ice was used for the first time in Olympic history for the skating events; waste heat from the refrigeration plant was used to heat buildings, melt snow from roofs, and provide hot water. It was EPCOT on ice.

Other innovations included new timekeeping equipment capable of measuring time to the hundredth of a second; IBM supplied fifteen technicians and two RAMAC computers to tabulate results and output data in English and French. For the first time television rights were sold for the Games, with CBS buying exclusive rights for a mere $50,000. The network eventually broadcast thirty-one hours of coverage during the games, and when officials needed to consult tape of an event to determine whether a skier had missed a slalom gate it inspired the concept of instant replay.

The look of the Games was heavily influenced by Disney artist, designer, and Imagineer John Hench, who was named Decor Director. At Walt's suggestion, inspired by the ancient Greek custom of commemorating Olympic champions with marble sculptures, Hench designed thirty sixteen-foot "snow" statues for placement along the Avenue of the Athletes and in other significant locations throughout Squaw Valley. To learn about snow sculpting techniques, Hench visited the Dartmouth College Winter Carnival and Ice Festival in February of 1959 as well as a similar event in Quebec; he then designed the statues, which were in turn created by Floats Inc. of Pasadena. Nine of the statues were female: four skiers, three figure skaters, and two speed skaters. Among the twenty-one male statues were nine skiers, seven hockey players, three speed skaters, and two figure skaters.

Two larger, twenty-four-foot statues, one male and one female, were created to flank the Tower of Nations. The Tower, another Hench design, stood seventy-nine feet tall and twenty feet wide. Suspended upon the metallic grid which composed the Tower's frame were the Olympic rings as well as thirty aluminum crests, each five feet by six, denoting the participant nations. The Tower marked the staging area where the opening and closing ceremonies were held, as well as the medal ceremonies for each competition. This was another innovation for this Games, as victory ceremonies had not traditionally been held for public viewing.

Around the area occupied by the Tower of Nations were thirty aluminum flagpoles, one each for the thirty participating nations. The effort to build the Squaw Valley facilities was an expensive one, so sponsorships took on an importance previously unknown in Olympic history. To help offset the tens of millions of dollars in construction costs, corporations, cities, and individuals were approached to sponsor individual flagpoles and snow sculptures; sponsor names were engraved on the items, and they were allowed to claim them after the Games had ended. For $2,000 one could purchase one of the snow statues; Palm Springs, Pasadena, Burbank, and Inglewood were among the cities that agreed to do so. Today, some of the flagpoles can be found in locations as widespread as the Walt Disney Studios Commissary in Burbank, the Walt Disney Elementary School in Marceline, Missouri, and at the first tee of the La Quinta Country Club in La Quinta, California.

Disney also helped fund a "symphonic carillon", which rang out three times a day and could be heard throughout the valley. Installed by a Los Angeles electronic engineer, the 161-bell carillon and 61-note vibrachord harp used twenty-four speakers and was provided to the Olympic committee without cost.

One lasting Hench contribution to the Olympic legacy was the torch. While torches had been used in previous Games, Hench completely redesigned the version used in 1960. Subsequent Games have adapted their torches to local cultural traditions, but their overall forms all hearken back to Hench's design.

All did not go smoothly in the run-up to the Games. Walt had originally announced plans for the torch to be flown from Olympia, Greece by "jet airliner" to Los Angeles, but the Greek Olympic Committee did not receive a request to ignite the flame at Olympia until January 1960 and refused to do so for logistical reasons. A last minute shuffle in the plans meant a return to the ritual followed during the 1952 Winter Games in Oslo, wherein the torch was ignited at the chalet of Norwegian skiing pioneer Sondre Nordheim.

Also uncooperative were officials in Melbourne, Australia, site of a recent Olympics, to whom Disney technicians wrote for a formula that could fuel the torch throughout the Games. The Australians refused to divulge their secrets, so Disney staffers had to concoct their own fuel mixture.

Two flagpoles from the 1960 Olympic Winter Games flank the entrance to the Walt Disney Studios commissary in Burbank, California. © Progress City

Even the avian community caused trouble; Squaw Valley was the first Winter Olympics to feature a release of doves at the opening ceremony, but it was worried that doves would linger in the valley and freeze to death. Homing pigeons were recruited to play the role of "doves of peace", since they would know to leave the valley and return home after they were released. This troubled the fellow in charge of the ice rink, who was wary of releasing thousands of nervous birds over his pristine ice. The schedule of events was shuffled so that the ceremonial cannons would fire only after the pigeons had been released and were heading for home.

More complications came when it was decided to use the original Olympic Anthem that had been written for the first modern Games in

Athens in 1896. The Disney musical department attempted to obtain a score from Olympic headquarters in Switzerland to no avail. Eventually they were able to track down a copy in Japan, but it was in Japanese and they had to decipher it as best they could.

Hench's giant snow statues encountered trouble on the way from Pasadena; a tarp on one of the diesel trucks transporting them came loose, and its exhaust covered the white statues with soot. Bob Henry, executive vice president of Floats Inc., who had been tasked to build and deliver the statues, was forced to find a way to wash them as quickly as possible. After delivery, 100-mile-an-hour winds at the Olympic site blew one of the statues over; the press reported that Henry soon left for New York so as to get as far away from the statues as possible.

At last, the time for the Games neared. California's racing pigeon organizations visited to make trial runs with their "doves of peace". The day before the ceremony, the combined bands had their first group rehearsal. Four Army cannons, firing four-inch shells, were brought in and aimed at surrounding mountains to prevent avalanches, yet it was a torrential rain the week before opening that threatened to wipe out the packed-snow parking lots that had been so carefully created for visitors.

The Olympic torch, which had departed Morgedal, Norway – the "cradle" of winter sports – on January 31st, was carried above the North Pole by an S.A.S. DC-7 to Los Angeles. Passed at Los Angeles International Airport to Olympic shot-put champion Parry O'Brien, it was taken via helicopter to Los Angeles Memorial Coliseum where it began its journey to Squaw Valley by foot in the pouring rain. Over a period of nineteen days it traversed a route scouted personally by McEveety, past small towns that greeted it with celebrations and festivities along the way.

On February 18th, 1960, Walt Disney and his staff awoke and were greeted by a blizzard. With the ceremony – and coast to coast television coverage – scheduled to begin at 10 AM, the whiteout conditions presented several difficulties. Snow on the roads prevented people from making the perilous drive to Squaw Valley, and hindered the network crews and announcers from reaching their locations.

Ten inches of snow fell that morning; CBS host Walter Cronkite appeared to have been broadcasting from the Arctic wastes. Many of the high school musicians hadn't dressed properly for the conditions, and stood freezing to their instruments during dress rehearsal – not that they could see the conductor through the snow, anyway. The pigeon wranglers insisted that they couldn't release their birds in such weather. And Vice President Richard Nixon, assigned to proclaim the opening of the games, was forced to drive in from Reno as his helicopter couldn't operate under the conditions. No one knew if he was going to make it on time.

Someone had to decide what to do. The alternative to an outdoor ceremony was a much smaller indoor ceremony, which the TV crews favored. But Dr. Charles Hirt, the choral director, objected to having to leave out so many of the young musicians who had worked so hard to be a part of the festivities. Art Linkletter later reported that Walt remained unfazed throughout; Disney merely said that they would go on and it would hopefully clear up. Walt even press ganged Linkletter into service as a television host, despite the fact that he was not meant to be there as a broadcaster. But although the ceremony was postponed fifteen minutes to allow more spectators to arrive on the snowbound roads, where bumper-to-bumper traffic extended for twelve miles outside of town, they couldn't stall forever.

Finally, with everyone gathered and ready to go, the skies cleared. To everyone's astonishment, the snow ended and the sunshine began, and the opening ceremonies of the VIII Winter Olympics were underway.

The festivities began with a sustained drum roll and the raising of thirty national flags, as the United States Marine Band played "The Parade of the Olympians". The 740 athletes then entered the arena, with each national delegation heralded by a salvo of fireworks. This was advertised as the first-ever use of daytime fireworks, a Disney tradition that continues in the theme parks today.

After the athletes were seated, Prentis Hale, President of the Olympic Organizing Committee, delivered a welcome. Squaw Valley marked the first Olympics of the Space Race era, and Hale's speech acknowledged the nationalist tensions that had marked preparations for the games:

"You can return home as the world's best-equipped ambassadors of unity and peace. Before we pay so much attention to conquering outer space, we should devote ourselves to conquering inner space: the distance between nations."

Avery Brundage, President of the IOC, then introduced Vice President Nixon who declared the games open; Nixon had driven forty-six miles through the snow from Reno to deliver a fifteen-word address. The massed band and chorus joined the Marine Band in playing the newly-orchestrated Olympic Hymn, the first time the 1896 piece had been presented at a Winter Olympics. Two thousand pigeons were released, and once they were clear there was an eight-round cannon salute – one salvo for each of the previous Winter Olympic Games. A newly-composed piece, "These Things Shall Be", was then performed by the massed bands and chorus.

Once planned for delivery by helicopter, the Olympic torch made the last thirty miles of its route via cross-country skier. It arrived on-site courtesy of Olympic champion Andrea Mead Champion, who appeared with the flame atop the peak of Little Papoose and blazed down the slopes accompanied by an honor guard of eight skiers to deliver the torch to Olympic speed skater Kenneth Henry. As the massed bands played the piece "Conquest", Henry lit the ceremonial torch, officially beginning the Games.

Chimes rang throughout the hills, and as the Marine Band performed "God of Our Fathers", participants joined in the Olympic prayer, which was narrated by actor Karl Malden. This was a somewhat controversial decision at the time, as such an event had not always been included in previous Olympics. There might have been a bit of Cold War showmanship at play here; Tommy Walker was quoted as saying that the prayer was optional, but "Walt felt that

The Miracle of Squaw Valley - At long last, the sun shone down upon the Opening Ceremonies of the VIII Olympic Winter Games. © Disney

prayer represents one of the freedoms of America and that we should definitely have it."

After the prayer, American figure skater Carol Heiss recited the Olympic oath on behalf of all the athletes, the first female Olympian to ever do so, and the assembled bands performed a new orchestration of "The Star-Spangled Banner". The ceremony ended, appropriately, with a bang; as the athletes paraded out, 30,000 balloons were released and shells were fired. Exploding with bursts of flags from each nation, they drifted back to earth via parachutes.

Five minutes after the end of the ceremony, the snow began to fall once more.

While the 6,500 spectators fell short of projections due to the weather and traffic, the show delivered as promised. But even with all the rave reviews for the "Miracle of Squaw Valley", Walt still had tricks up his sleeve. The Squaw Valley Olympics were the first to be scheduled with live entertainment for the athletes in mind, and when Walt first announced his plans he proclaimed that "nothing is more important than creating lasting goodwill among our visitors, and we shall do everything we can to make their stay a happy one."

Again, he delivered. Entertainment Vice-President Art Linkletter brought in a slew of his Hollywood friends every evening, resulting in appearances by Bing Crosby, Roy Rogers, Red Skelton, and Jack Benny. Actress Marlene Dietrich posed for pictures with the German hockey team, and the media was well tended to, thanks to "official press hostess" Jayne Mansfield. The Academy of Motion Pictures Arts and Sciences delivered films for the athletes, which were presented (along with free refreshments) nightly in the enclosed Olympia Theater.

A standout favorite was actor Danny Kaye, who managed to lead a number of international delegations in a chorus of "Row, Row, Row Your Boat". Press reports from the time describe Kaye performing rollicking musical numbers in a dozen languages, working Korean, Japanese, and Russian participants into his act. Decades later, many of those in attendance remembered having been in tears over Kaye's antics.

One memorable evening, Walt brought up the entire *Golden Horseshoe Revue* from Disneyland to present to the Olympians. Wally Boag, Betty Taylor, Gene Sheldon, Henry Calvin, Don Novis, and three stuntmen all performed to a rapt audience, and the staged "saloon brawl" at the end of the evening was so raucous that a frightened security officer reportedly rushed to the phone to summon help.

Walt had one last idea for entertaining the participants, who due to their own busy schedules rarely got to see the medal ceremonies as they took place. So every evening, while emceeing that night's entertainment lineup, Linkletter would introduce the new champions who had won medals that day. They would then have a drawing, with the winner getting a free phone call home – a rather remarkable prize in those days. One evening the winner was said to be so excited that he could barely speak, and it was only when they got through to his hometown operator that he remembered his family didn't own a telephone.

After ten days, 665 athletes from thirty nations had competed in twenty-seven events, and it was time to return home. On February 28th, 20,000 spectators filled the stands of Blyth Memorial Arena to witness the closing ceremonies. Flag bearers surrounded the rostrum as the national anthems of Greece, the United States, and Austria were played. IOC president Brundage declared the games closed, and the Olympic torch was extinguished. Thousands of balloons were released to end the ceremony.

Disney's Olympics, the largest Winter Games held to that point, received rave reviews. The once-skeptical IOC chair would go on to say they were the "greatest games ever staged." Army Archerd, in *Variety*, called Disney's opening ceremony "the greatest show on Earth", and a reporter for the *Los Angeles Times* proclaimed that "It is my conviction that you'll never see anything of that kind so well done in your lifetime." Even the Russians were impressed; one of the heads of their delegation approached an Olympic security chief and asked what chemicals had been used to control the weather during the opening ceremony.

The 1960 Winter Olympics would cast a long shadow, influencing the look and feel of the Games up to this day. Many of Disney's team would contribute to future Olympics, most notably the 1984 Summer Olympics in Los Angeles. The events of Squaw Valley would also affect Walt; it marked the first time he had met the world outside of Disneyland, and began the outreach efforts he would continue in 1964 at the New York World's Fair. It also sparked a concerted effort to build his own winter sports resort at Mineral King in California, a project he would pursue for the rest of his life.

But at the time many simply wondered how Walt had managed to make things work out so perfectly. Was it divine intervention? Some sort of nationalist statement from the gods of Olympus? In Disney's own press materials they claimed that if it was a miracle, it was a well-planned miracle. But perhaps Walt said it best; according to Linkletter, after the improbably perfect opening ceremony Walt explained it thus: "It's just that if you live right, things happen the way they're supposed to."

.07

WALT DISNEY VS. THE AIR PIRATES

During the 1970s, Frank Stanek lead planning efforts at WED Enterprises and headed the development of Tokyo Disneyland, but back in 1964 he was a young cast member managing the business affairs of Disney's *it's a small world* attraction at the 1964/65 New York World's Fair. Walt Disney had visited the fair several times, but Stanek wouldn't have his first real conversation with Walt until a coincidental encounter on the tarmac at LaGuardia resulting from – of all things – a shortage of nickels.

In the early 1960s the nation was experiencing a coin shortage. Depending on region, various denominations of coinage became difficult to obtain in bulk, making things hard for operations like Disneyland that required lots of cash-on-hand on a daily basis. In California, nickels in particular became scarce. This wasn't an issue in New York, and Roy Disney had befriended the manager of a bank near the fairgrounds who made sure Stanek had everything he needed to operate the ticket booths for his attraction.

Carl Freeberg, who ran the cash control department at Disneyland, grew tired of the situation and made a call to New York. "We're having trouble getting nickels," Freeberg told Stanek. "If you can get me nickels, I talked to the company aviation department, and they will fly the nickels back to me in California."

Walt never flew himself, but he was an aviation buff and had been an early adopter of planes for corporate purposes. The studio had been operating a Beechcraft Queen Air, which Walt had used to scout sites for "Disneyland East", but before the Fair opened in 1964 Disney upgraded to a Grumman Gulfstream 1 twin-engine turboprop.

Recalls Stanek, "He set up a shuttle system, and every week or thereabouts he would fly a load of Disney executives, creative people, whatever, sometimes with their wives, and he would fly them to New York for the fair." Landing at LaGuardia Airport, Walt and his guests would be just a short drive from the fairground in Queens.

With Disney's jet shuttling back and forth almost weekly, it gave Stanek an easy way to supply Disneyland with nickels. Carl Freeberg consulted with the aviation department, who said that there was room on the airplane to carry an additional 200 pounds of weight, and Stanek became, in his words, "the logistics expert on shipping nickels to California." A bag of nickels straight from the bank is $200, and weighs forty pounds. Five bags of nickels, worth $1,000, weighs 200 pounds and was therefore equal to one passenger on the Disney aircraft.

So, Stanek put in an order for extra nickels from the bank and drove them to the airfield. The pilot said that they needed to distribute the weight throughout the craft, so, says Stanek, "we would stick them underneath the seats and spread them all throughout the aircraft." The system worked well; Disneyland got their nickels, and everyone was happy. Every now and then a call would come in from California, and another batch of nickels was sent westward.

"One day," recalls Stanek, "I get a call and Carl needs the nickels again and he says the plane's in town. It was, I don't know, Saturday morning or Sunday morning." The plane was to take off early – 7:30 or eight in the morning – so Stanek picked up the nickels at the bank the night before and, before the fair opened the next morning, took them in the company station wagon down to LaGuardia. The Disney craft was parked in the section of the airport devoted to private planes, separate from commercial aviation operations.

The pilot was there preparing for the flight, but, says Stanek, "What am I? I'm 24 years old. I say to myself, 'I'm not leaving this money – it's my money until that plane gets in the air.'" The nickels were loaded on the plane, but Stanek lingered on the tarmac waiting for it to depart.

The scene of the crime: Walt's Grumman Gulfstream 1. Not pictured: *Nickels!*
© Disney

"And the next thing I know," recalls Stanek, "Walt Disney is standing next to me."

"He's an early riser, so he got there with his wife before anybody else did. He had three or four other executives and their wives with him. I said, 'Good morning, Walt,' and he said, 'Good Morning.' He says to me, 'What model aircraft is that over there?' I said, 'Well, I don't know.' And then he says to me, 'Who owns that aircraft? Is that Frank Sinatra's aircraft?' And I said, 'I don't know.'"

Stanek was starting to get worried. "Now I'm thinking to myself, he's going to ask me another question and it's going to be three strikes and I'm out. And so I said to Walt, 'I'm sorry Walt, I don't really work here and I know nothing about aircraft – I work for you!' He said, 'Oh! You work for me!' I said, 'Yep, I'm out at *small world* and here's what I do,' you know. I introduced myself of course, and he said, 'Well what are you doing here?'"

Stanek filled Walt in on the situation with the nickels, and his unique way of keeping Disneyland stocked with coins. "Of course he knew Carl Freeberg," says Stanek, "because everybody at Disney knew everybody at that time. I said, 'I'm sending Carl some nickels.'"

Most of us, at that point, would probably not have a lot to say about the nickel situation. That's why we're not Walt Disney.

"He listens to this story," remembers Stanek, "and he called his wife over. He said, 'Lilly, come over here. This is Frank Stanek, and guess what he's doing? He just put $200,000 worth of coins on the airplane!'"

So, $2,000 had become $200,000. Just a little exaggeration, right? Hardly.

"Now we're going to fly off with this money on our airplane," said Walt. "Can you imagine if we're over Las Vegas and we get attacked by air pirates?"

Stanek laughs as he remembers Walt's excitement. "He's spinning this story right there to both of us, but he's really addressing his wife. It was the most interesting, tremendous experience – you saw how Walt was thinking all the time about some kind of a storyline, about some creative thing."

At eight in the morning, even. Inspired by a story about currency shortages.

"He had this whole plane attack," says Stanek, "and they were under attack by air pirates and he was developing this whole storyline." Eventually the rest of Walt's party arrived, everyone said their goodbyes, and the plane departed. It was, no doubt, an interesting flight. Says Stanek, "I'm sure he spent the rest of the flight back thinking about that story and telling everybody on the plane about it."

Walt Disney Versus the Air Pirates – somebody should get to work on that script.

II.
The Imagineers

.08

GEORGE McGINNIS & THE UNDERGROUND TRAIN OF TOMORROW

Odds are that if you're reading this, you've put together a school project at one point or another. Maybe it was your elementary school science fair, or maybe it was your doctoral dissertation in particle physics. Either way, you've spent some time working on one of these projects. Maybe you won a blue ribbon for your idea, or received an award or some grant funding. But did any of you get a visit from Walt Disney and a decades-long career as an Imagineer?

George McGinnis did.

This veteran Imagineer, responsible for Epcot Center's *Horizons* attraction as well as many others, got his big break in 1966 when, as a student at the Art Center College of Design in Los Angeles, he was pursuing a B.S. in Product Design. For his senior project, McGinnis drew up a proposal for a high-speed train system to serve the northeastern rail corridor of the United States. That same semester, he had also submitted the design in a contest sponsored by the Alcoa corporation.

It lost, coming in second place to an all-aluminum garden cart.

Thankfully for George, he had better things than Alcoa on the way. You might say a great big beautiful tomorrow was in store, because Walt Disney was about to build a city of the future and he was personally going to recruit McGinnis to help out.

What's always amazed me about Walt's EPCOT planning was how prescient he was in recognizing problems that still plague our cities and urban areas today. Key to the entire project was innovation in the field of transportation; his idea was to get cars off the roads, replacing them with a series of peoplemovers, monorails, and trains. As the jammed freeways that caused concern in 1966 would, unfortunately, only grow worse over the next forty years, the efforts of Disney and his Imagineers seem quite timely in retrospect.

The same could be said of McGinnis's train proposal, which directly addressed problems currently being hashed out in 21st century America. Issues like geopolitical conflict, global warming, and simple expense have forced people over the last several years to re-examine the American dependence on gas-burning automobiles. Faced with melting icecaps and $5-a-gallon gasoline, many drivers have turned to our nation's rail system.

The problem facing would-be rail riders is that, after years of neglect and underfunding, the American rail network is woefully behind the times. Aside from the vast swathes of the nation that are completely without access to rail transport, even high-traffic corridors on the coasts are operating on obsolete infrastructure that prevents an adequate level of service. Amtrak's most advanced train, the Acela line, is the only high-speed rail service in the nation, and even that is typically forced to operate, on the average, at about half of its maximum possible speed. Although it's by far the nation's fastest train, its reliance on legacy track which winds through heavily populated areas forces the Acela to operate at speeds far below typical "high-speed" specifications and far, far behind advanced rail service in Europe and Japan.

McGinnis's proposal bypassed all that, proposing a train route which, like the Acela, would run from Washington, D.C. to Boston with stops in Philadelphia and New York City. In his vision, underground tunnels would allow for straight, fast routes that did not depend on winding legacy track or grade crossings in populated areas. While this might sound like an expensive fantasy, it was based on a report by the Rand Corporation that estimated that advances in tunnel boring would reduce the expense of such a project enough that tunneling costs would intersect with those of land acquisition for an above-ground project by as early as 1970.

McGinnis's proposal solved the issue of loading and unloading passengers, which adds inconvenient delays to high-speed routes, by

George McGinnis (l) demonstrates his high-speed train model to Bill Mitchell, Vice President of Styling for General Motors. © George McGinnis

designing a train that wouldn't stop at every station that it serviced. The train would indeed stop in major cities like Boston or New York, but in smaller towns like Providence or Wilmington riders would board and disembark via a separate vehicle. Powered by linear induction, the boarding vehicle would actually match the speed of the moving train, physically dock with it, and transfer passengers and cargo via a large turntable mechanism. Thus, high-speed trains could service a number of stations along their routes without ever breaking their stride.

It was an ambitious plan, and something that certainly feels of a kindred spirit to EPCOT's ideals, but for McGinnis it was just a school project until the acting president of the Art Center brought it up in a conversation with Walt Disney. John Thompson, who had previously served as editor of the *Ford Times*, had similarly introduced Walt to another Imagineer of renown, Bob Gurr, more than a decade earlier.

This time, he later related to George, he told Walt, "McGinnis will bring his train over on his back to show you."

Wouldn't you?

McGinnis's project had already received some attention; it had been inspected at the Art Center by Bill Mitchell, Vice President of Styling for General Motors. In a funny coincidence, Mitchell and McGinnis had graduated from the same high school in Greenville, Pennsylvania (albeit eighteen years apart). They shared a love for cars, too, but even this brush with executive celebrity probably couldn't prepare McGinnis for when John Thompson told him that Walt Disney wanted to see his train.

Sure enough, Walt came to the Art Center to see George's project. With him, he brought Gurr, Dick Irvine, Roger Broggie, and John Hench – future Imagineering legends, all.

So, no pressure.

Thankfully things went perfectly – almost. McGinnis's model was a working one; equipped with micro-switches, tiny motors with friction drives would turn the semicircular transfer compartments on the train. It had always worked perfectly… until Walt pushed the shuttle and it jammed. As McGinnis would later say, "My hand never worked so fast unjamming it." Walt, perhaps deciding to take it easy on a nervous student, simply remarked, "This would have to be failsafe." "Yes, sir!" McGinnis replied, and quickly pointed out the built-in emergency braking distance on the diagram.

That glitch aside, McGinnis's demonstration must have gone well; after Walt left, George Jorgensen, head of the school's Industrial Design department, told McGinnis that Walt wanted him to come up to visit WED Enterprises and ride the test track for the then-under-development WEDWay PeopleMover. Walt's visit to the Art Center marked the first time that McGinnis had ever heard of Progress City, and now he was being asked to come help develop its transportation system. While McGinnis was, in his words, "elated", he had a vision of full-sized trains in his head. Instead, he would eventually design model vehicles for the Progress City diorama which served as

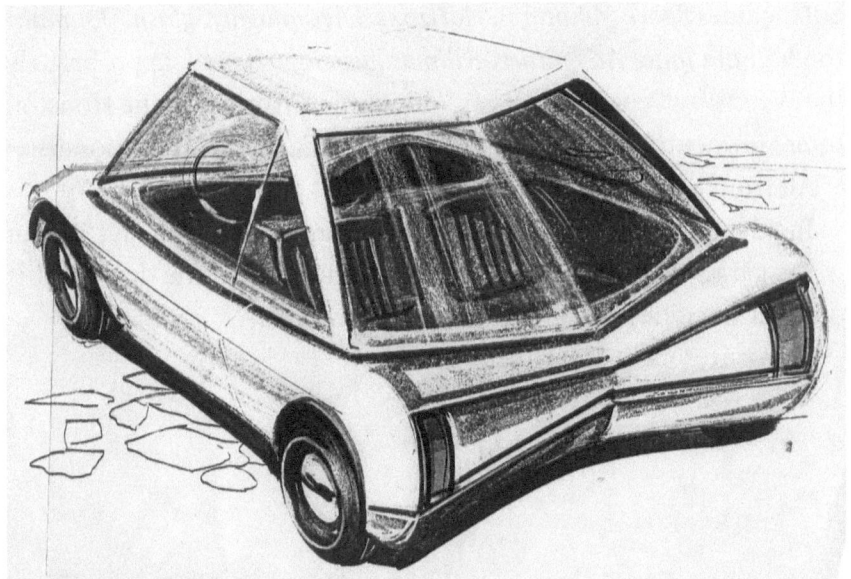

McGinnis designed this futuristic electric golf cart for the residents of Walt's Progress City - a project soon to be known as EPCOT. © Disney

the finale for Disneyland's *Carousel of Progress*. His designs included transportation systems for Progress City and later EPCOT, from peoplemovers all the way down to golf carts.

One amusing aspect of the tale is how, as always, one could say that "Walt works in mysterious ways." As Bob Gurr would later tell McGinnis, on the way back to Glendale after viewing the train proposal Walt remarked offhandedly, "We can use another industrial designer at WED." Sure enough, George got his invitation to come take a look at the PeopleMover prototype. After touring the department, Walt handed him off to Dick Irvine, who took George into his office and invited him to become an Imagineer. As Irvine would tell him during that first interview, "Nothing goes out the door without Walt's approval."

Talk about the ultimate quality assurance.

And so McGinnis became an Imagineer, taking over a cubicle surrounded by a handful of prominent art directors. Later he would get an office next to Gurr's, which he calls "one of the most important things to my career at WDI." His list of subsequent projects is long, but includes *Space Mountain, Horizons, Dreamflight, Splash Mountain,* the *Indiana Jones Adventure, Kilimanjaro Safaris,* and, appropriately, the WEDWay PeopleMovers at Walt Disney World and the Houston Intercontinental Airport, as well as the Mark V and VI monorails.

All from a "toy" train.

Incidentally, McGinnis still has his train model – he says it's out in his garage with his old 1971 Datsun 240Z, which he drove to his office at Imagineering every day for twenty years.

He assures me it still runs great.

.09

The People Moving People

The first few decades of Walt Disney Imagineering were marked by a series of escalating technical innovations. These advancements built on previous achievements, while preparing Walt Disney Productions for subsequent phases of development. Under Walt's guidance the profits and knowledge gained from each new project were funneled into the next, with every step pushing the limits of the company in new and unexpected directions. At the time of his death, Disney was preparing for the greatest challenge of his career – the creation of Walt Disney World in Florida and the design process for the "city of the future" that he called EPCOT.

The original concept for EPCOT was a massive and risky undertaking, which sought not only to entertain or inform but to completely change the way the American public thought about their cities and communities. EPCOT would be a complete, functioning city designed not only to provide services for its residents and guests but also to act as a test bed for new technologies and theories of urban design which could then be exported to the country at large. EPCOT would not be built so that one could travel to Florida and ride a monorail, it was designed so that guests might be able to one day ride a monorail in their own community. Corporations and designers would come to EPCOT to test and refine their designs, which would then become part of the urban fabric nationwide.

When Walt Disney died in 1966, the seeds of EPCOT's demise were sown. EPCOT was such an exotic and expensive project that many believed it couldn't be built, but those same words had been spoken about many projects ranging from *Snow White and the Seven Dwarfs* to Disneyland itself. Disney scholars will disagree to the end of time whether, had Walt lived, EPCOT would have been completed. Knowing Walt's track record, though, I can't help but to believe it would have happened. Without Disney himself at the helm, however, the project unfortunately had no eloquent champion or unified vision.

Yet even after Walt's death, Walt Disney Productions didn't immediately abandon the plan for EPCOT. Walt's brother Roy rededicated the company to the purpose of completing Walt Disney World in Florida by 1971, and in the process of creating the resort Imagineers developed and prototyped many technologies intended for use in EPCOT. The master planning process in Florida mirrored the guiding principles behind EPCOT, and even as the concept of EPCOT-as-city faded into history, a great number of the programs created to prepare for its eventual execution continued their work.

One of these divisions was Community Transportation Services, a branch of the company founded in 1974 "in response to numerous requests from cities, airports and shopping centers interested in applications of the company's monorail and WEDWay PeopleMover systems." Disney had debuted both the monorail and PeopleMover in his theme parks with the intention of promoting both technologies for use outside the berm. The PeopleMover, which opened at Disneyland in 1967, was created specifically in preparation for EPCOT. A refined design, which opened at Walt Disney World in 1975, would mark the first use of linear induction motors for public transportation.

The CTS division was to spin off these technologies for outside use, helping to fulfill the mandate of EPCOT even as plans for the city itself fell by the wayside. CTS would "consult in the master planning of new short-range intra-city mass transportation systems, license Disney-developed systems for these applications, and administer their construction and installation."

Disney seemed a natural fit to pioneer such applications. After all, they'd already had decades of experience as "people moving people", and had transported more than half a billion people by the time CTS was founded. As a 1975 brochure for CTS points out, "Every mode of Disney-developed transportation, for land, water, and elevated use,

"What can we do to put you in a monorail today?" © Disney

has been designed for a common goal... to move large numbers of people safely, comfortably, and in a pleasing manner." And now, just as Walt intended with EPCOT, this expertise could be transferred outside the berm to improve the lives of everyone.

There certainly seemed to be a market for this expertise at the time; Disney had long been approached by cities, airports, shopping centers, and other entities to consult on their transportation needs. CTS served as a formalized way to offer clients practical knowledge of the design, operation, construction, and maintenance of advanced transportation systems, and was intended to bring this experience to bear in the planning and development of new short-range, intra-city public transit.

A number of brochures and booklets were released over the years to promote the division, detailing the products available to potential buyers. A booklet dated June 1974, for instance, showcases a selection

A variety of PeopleMover configurations were available for potential buyers.
© Disney

A sleek vision of the future: Commuters glide in air conditioned comfort above crowded surface roadways thanks to CTS monorails. © Disney

of CTS's monorail-based systems. It appears that the main goal of the CTS designs was flexibility; the document touts their modular construction and the wide array of configurations available to customers.

All told, there were eleven basic designs of the modular cars; designs were created for standard, medium, and narrow gauge tracks. Trains were available with high or low ceilings, and wide, standard, or narrow bodies. The modularity of the design allowed for cars to be as long as desired and feature any number of seating arrangements. Trains could have cabs on one or both ends, or could even operate without drivers. This allowed CTS customers to order anything from low-profile single vehicles to wide-body 250-passenger monorail trains. Three of the CTS series vehicles were designed to run on surface tracks, while the rest used elevated tracks or rails.

A 1979 booklet promoting Walt Disney World's Mark IV monorail reads like a brochure from a car dealer's showroom. It details the history and current usage of the trains, as well as their 99.9% operational readiness ratings. Several variants of the Mark IV were available, numbered Series 900/1000/1100, with both high and low ceilings and long- and stub-nosed cabs.

CTS also touted the benefits of monorail service for cities and riders: "Operating over existing freeway medians," they said, "versions of the MARK IV Monorail can easily eliminate tens-of-thousands of would-be drivers and place them in the quiet air-conditioned comfort of a swiftly moving electric monorail train." This could reduce traffic congestion, air pollution, and avoid the rising gas prices of the era. The monorail's elevated beamway meant this capacity could be added without the need for massive new right-of-way acquisition. CTS also claimed that the per-mile maintenance costs of beamway were far less than highways or other rail systems.

By 1982, CTS had been rechristened WED Transportation Systems and had just completed the first and only installation of a WEDWay system outside of a Disney park. In August 1981, the fourth generation PeopleMover debuted at the Houston Intercontinental Airport. The Disney-designed system beat out four other transportation alternatives in competitive bidding, when it was determined to be the technically superior and most cost-effective offering.

Boasting a 99.8% operational readiness rating at Walt Disney World, the WEDWay offered high reliability with a zero-emission drive system that was environmentally friendly. The WEDWay trains featured a bare minimum of moving parts, which kept down maintenance; vehicle weight was lowered by embedding the system's electromagnetic motors in the track, which allowed the trains to continue operating even if a single engine failed. Advanced – for the time – control computers prevented the possibility of train collisions and provided a level of automation that required minimal staffing.

The Houston system differed from its Orlando cousin in that its cars were larger and enclosed. Trains came to a full stop at stations, where travelers were admitted through elevator-like boarding gates. The trains had higher capacity than the Walt Disney World variants, and traveled at twice the speed. A complete trip from one end of the train's route to the other lasted seven minutes.

Houston's WEDWay was unfortunately the last PeopleMover system to be installed; none of the Disney parks built afterward would feature the WEDWay and there have been no further outside contracts for the technology. Disney had intended to use the PeopleMover in Epcot Center, where it would carry guests from the Main Entrance into Future World, but that never came to fruition either. Still, the WEDWay continues to hold an appeal today. When you look at the transportation issues plaguing our modern cities, passages like the following sound awfully intriguing:

> *The current WALT DISNEY WORLD WEDWay operates in a closed loop with continuously moving cars. A further developed system is being designed which will permit cars to remain idle until summoned. A "destination command" panel on each vehicle will enable passengers to push the appropriate button corresponding to their desired destination. Vehicle doors will close automatically, permitting the car to be dispatched to the new location. Off-line loading will enable vehicles to bypass*

THE PEOPLE MOVING PEOPLE 77

The Houston Intercontinental Airport's installation of a fourth-generation PeopleMover marked the first outside-the-berm application of WED transportation technology. © Disney

The original control room of the Houston Intercontinental Airport PeopleMover. Operators could monitor the entire system from this console. © Disney

unwanted locations and continue without time-consuming stops. Track switching will be controlled by the destination command in the vehicle.

It's a fascinating peek into a hopeful era of Imagineering and a time when Disney was trying to forge into new frontiers. With more people than ever longing for functional mass transportation in cities worldwide, wouldn't it be nice to have a CTS-designed rail system to take you to work in the morning? Can you think of any city or community that could use a highly reliable, low-cost, zero-emission mass transportation system? Just grab a brochure on your way out...

.10

SMOKEY AND THE FIGMENT

The true payoff of being a nerd and doing research is that moment when you find a bizarre connection that you absolutely never expected and which completely blows your mind. It happens fairly often in the Disneysphere, I think, because over the years the company has employed so many creative and technical personnel who have led long and prolific careers. Or maybe it's just because life is random, like the fact that the director of *Mary Poppins* had a daughter who dated Elvis. Whatever the reason, sometimes we're fortunate enough to find fascinating connections.

So what magical connection could possibly link this…

© Disney

….to this?

© Universal Pictures

Well, I'll tell you.

One of the most notable, subtle, and even beloved aspects of the original Epcot Center was its overall aesthetic. Carefully crafted down to the minutest detail, the park's art design presented a grand and unified statement which tied the individual pavilions and attractions into a thematic whole. Fonts, logos, and signage were consistent throughout the park, giving the entire enterprise a sleek, clean, and futuristic feel. While each pavilion would have its own visual style, and its own unique logo, it would still fit into the overall color design and visual vocabulary of the entire park. This gave all of early Epcot a very comforting vibe, absent of visual contradictions and with a consistent sense of place.

This also meant that very little of Epcot Center's decor came "off the rack"; everything from large marquees and directional signs to stationary and restaurant menus had to be specifically designed to fit into the park's distinct look. Signs and printed collateral used a single set of approved fonts and styles, and everything felt "Epcot" whether it was a Japanese teppanyaki menu or a postcard for *Horizons*.

To accomplish the rather daunting task of decorating the massive new park, Imagineering's graphics department grew to an unprecedented size and handed out assignments to a slew of designers. Years of input, discussion, and revision ensued prior to the park's opening. In the end, specific artists were put in charge of individual tasks. One might be responsible for directional signage in the Germany Pavilion, for instance, or for bathroom signage, or parking lot graphics, or paper napkins and cups for each individual restaurant. Someone designed binders for attraction instruction manuals; someone designed safety procedure signs. Everything in Epcot with either words or pictures, on-stage or off, crossed some designer's desk.

Of course, while every little detail mattered to the whole, some projects were bigger than others. One notable Epcot design element was the iconic logos which represented each pavilion in Future World. In the run-up to Epcot Center's opening, responsibility for these logos was given to designer Norm Inouye, of the Imagineering graphics department. Inouye had several high-profile design projects in the

Epcot Center's pavilion logos brought a sense of consistency. © Disney

final days of Epcot's creation; he was in charge of a number of signage efforts, the marquees for the Imagination Pavilion's Magic Eye Theatre and ImageWorks, and many graphics throughout CommuniCore. He even designed the elegant and much-loved fountain which once graced the entrance to the park, seen on page 79.

So, a pretty impressive resume all around for Mr. Inouye. Now, meanwhile, about twenty years earlier...

In 1959, future Epcot sponsor General Motors produced a turbine-powered concept car, the Firebird III. The vehicle's designer, Norm James, based its hood emblem on a stylized firebird design he had seen in the Phoenix airport. About a decade later, in 1967, the first production Pontiac Firebirds rolled off the assembly line (under the auspices of none other than John DeLorean). A souped up version of the Firebird, the Trans Am, debuted in 1969; both cars featured a small emblem reminiscent of the original Firebird III. In the meantime, another General Motors concept, 1969's Banshee II, had appeared with a firebird logo designed by none other than... Mr. Norm Inouye.

Inouye worked for General Motors Graphics from 1968-1971. In 1970, designer Bill Porter approached Inouye in the company cafeteria with an idea for a new graphic to grace Trans Am hoods. "Hey, Norm,"

Maybe if Epcot Center had featured a "Screaming Chicken" pavilion I wouldn't have always preferred KITT and the General Lee. © General Motors

Porter later recalled asking, "how about doing a big huge bird for us, something like this?" Porter sketched out an idea on a napkin, which Inouye took and developed into the iconic firebird – the "screaming chicken" – which would remain a muscle car staple for years to come.

But first they had to sell it. At the time, G.M.'s vice president of design was Bill Mitchell, with whom we've visited previously in chapter eight. He was known to walk through the various design departments to keep abreast of new doings, and one day happened to stroll through the paint department. By that time, Inouye had sent his designs to 3M, who created two large prototype firebird decals for the new 1970 Trans Am show cars. Mitchell, who had something of an aversion to splashy design as well as a touchy temperament, furiously called up Porter and, claiming the decals made it look like the cars had "an Indian blanket on the hood", ordered them removed immediately.

In was only in 1973 that Porter's successor, John Schinella, was able to revisit the concept and convince Mitchell to use the firebird design. It debuted as an optional graphics package that year; for the low, low price of $53, Trans Am buyers could have their own flaming avian rampant. Of course it was the second generation 1977 Trans-Am

Special Edition which starred in *Smokey and the Bandit*, and guaranteed that the "screaming chicken" would be a fixture on toy cars throughout the era in which I grew up.

The Trans Am would continue to evolve; its third generation design starred in *Knight Rider*, a more critical staple of my childhood. And, naturally, its Pontiac brethren would grace the halls of the TransCenter in Epcot's World of Motion pavilion for years afterward. Unfortunately, the Bandit never teamed up with David Hasselhoff and Leonardo da Vinci for a Walt Disney World adventure, but I guess Epcot was already cool enough as it was.

In our next episode, how *The Cannonball Run* inspired Disney's Animal Kingdom...

.11

TRAVELS WITH HERB

Despite his humble Midwestern beginnings, Disney artist and Imagineer Herbert Ryman eventually became a world traveler, with an astounding array of experiences and encounters under his belt. Many of his early excursions were in the American Southwest, before his career took off at Metro-Goldwyn-Mayer in 1932; these road trips provided ample scenery to inspire and develop his artistic skills. It would be his later globetrotting adventures, though, that would inform his worldview and help shape some of the work that is most relevant to Disney fans – his conceptual paintings for Epcot's World Showcase in the 1970s and 80s.

Ironically, Ryman was once chagrined at his lack of worldly experience. Working on an adaptation of Pearl S. Buck's *The Good Earth* at MGM, he found himself heeding the call of the outside world. He'd worked so hard on creating exotic scenes for various films, but that was just film fakery – Herb wanted to see these things first-hand.

Things came to a head in 1936 when Ryman, fatigued by four years of nonstop work, was sketching set designs for *Mutiny on the Bounty*. A chance conversation with actor Donald Crisp led to an exhortation for young Ryman to take a break from his work and see a bit of the world while he was still young.

Mulling this advice, Herb received that same day a letter from his cousin, Halvern Norris, who was serving in the American Foreign Service as Vice Consul to Siam. Norris was wrapping up his five-year stint in Bangkok, and in his lengthy letter he encouraged Ryman to pay a visit and see the sights. Satisfied with the portent of this coincidence, Herb took leave from MGM and headed to the steamship office to book passage to Siam. He didn't have to worry about paying; in his pocket at the time were thirteen paychecks from Metro, all uncashed because the workaholic Ryman had not been able to leave his office long enough to visit the bank.

It turned out that for the price of passage across the Pacific Ocean to Siam, Herb could take the long way there and, in the process, see the world. For no extra cost he was able to circumnavigate the globe, stopping in the Caribbean, Europe, and at several other points before eventually reaching Bangkok. For someone worried about his lack of travels, Ryman was about to catch up in high style.

After circling the globe, with many stops along the way, Ryman reached Siam. While his adventures there were too innumerable to list here, it led to a number of fascinating and coincidental meetings. Prominent diplomats. Artists. Authors. The royal family. The Peking Man. It had to be pretty exciting for a young guy from Illinois. But, like so many young people in extraordinary times, Ryman wouldn't really understand the full import of his travels until later. He didn't realize, at the time, what was really happening around him as he trekked through Indochina – the first stirrings in the east that would eventually lead to a World War.

But these concerns weren't on Herb's mind. In his travels from 1936-37, he saw everything that he could possibly fit in to his itinerary. Despite the fact that the world was a much larger and stranger place in those days, even in the distant outposts of the Orient people knew about Hollywood. And, whenever locals would find out Herb worked in pictures in Hollywood, he was invariably asked about one person. Not any of the legends of MGM, where he actually worked – Garbo, Gable, or even Lassie. Everyone wanted to know one thing: Did Herb know Walt Disney?

He didn't. But, after answering truthfully a few times and seeing the resultant disappointment and instant disinterest from once-curious strangers, Ryman decided to give the people what they wanted. "Yes, I know Walt Disney!"

Don't be too hard on Herb – his harmless white lie was only a year or so distant from being 100% true.

Safari, so good - Ryman enjoys a piece of cake at his Imagineering farewell party before embarking on an adventure to Africa in 1983. © Disney

From Siam, Ryman traveled northward to Japan, where the creeping hand of fascism led to a few uncomfortable interrogations at the hands of petty customs officials. A decision was made to visit China, despite the increasing chaos brewing in that country. Nationalist forces under Chiang Kai-Shek were faced with the prospect of battling Mao Tse-Tung and the communists to the west and invading Japanese troops to the east, but the situation was still stable in the major cities. Herb spent four months there in the village of Ba Ta Chu, in the hills outside Peking.

Herb's time in China would be productive artistically as well as socially; it would also leave him with a full portfolio of artwork, which led to an exhibition at the Chouinard Art Institute in Los Angeles and, subsequently, his career at Disney.

Many years later, after the completion of Epcot Center, Herb left Imagineering for another adventure in the wilds of Africa. His paintings from the trip evoke the majestic landscapes of the continent, with which Herb became infatuated while working on the Equatorial

Africa pavilion for Epcot. Before he left, though, Herb was the guest of honor at an Imagineering "bon voyage" party. From the *WED/MAPO Imaginews* from February 25th, 1983:

> *Herb Ryman left last January 21, for an extensive trip to paint and observe peoples and cultures of different nations. All of Herb's friends at WED & MAPO got together to wish him a "bon voyage".*
>
> *Recently, "Herbie's" friends told the* Imaginews *that Herb will be traveling extensively throughout Africa, spending time in such places as Nairobi and Lake Naivasha, Kenya, East Africa. He is presently at Lamu Island. Later, Herb will continue his travels to such far-off and exotic locales as Singapore, Hong Kong and Japan.*

While on the aforementioned Lamu Island, Herb continued his lifelong habit of encountering fascinating people with remarkable connections. There, he paid visit to Frank Maurice "Bunny" Allen, a former big game hunter. Allen had served as a consultant on MGM's *Mogambo*, and in earlier times had worked as a gunbearer for both the husband and the lover of one Karen Blixen. Blixen would eventually be better known by her pseudonym Isak Dinesen, under which she wrote the memoir *Out of Africa*.

Of course it was Herb's work on the Equatorial Africa Pavilion that brought him together with another well-known writer, *Roots* author Alex Haley. Haley was a consultant on the pavilion and the two became such close friends that Haley later spoke at Ryman's memorial service. In fact, one of the last portraits Ryman painted was of Haley. It was a fitting cap to a life of extraordinary voyages and remarkable connections.

III.
The Vacation Kingdom

.12

In the Beginning, There was Project Future

Long before the Pueblo Room was a glint in Dick Nunis's eye, planning was underway for Walt Disney World. Who knows how long Walt had mulled privately over his ideas for a mega-project in the east; but even before the scope of his plans for the Florida scrub became apparent to the public, work was underway at Walt Disney Productions to define what, exactly, this project would be.

A planning meeting for "Project Future" took place at WED Enterprises on June 14th, 1965, and the minutes from that gathering provide a tantalizing glimpse at Walt's early ideas for his Florida experiment. The meeting allowed Walt to present his ideas to the board members and legal staff of Walt Disney Productions, lawyers and consultants from the state of Florida, and Disney's legal staff from New York City. This would, in turn, allow the staff an idea of the project's scope and needs so that they then could begin researching and crafting the necessary legal groundwork. This planning would eventually culminate in the special district legislation in the Florida legislature that led to the Reedy Creek Improvement District and the creation of Walt Disney World.

Walt's ideas for the property at this point were spelled out only in the roughest brushstrokes, but you can still get an idea of what he was driving at. While some of these ideas were clearly pie-in-the-sky, there are some interesting thoughts here about the underlying ethos of the resort. It's also amusing to see the concerns that faced the early planners, and how those concerns still rear their heads today.

Walt's first emphasis was the need to figure out what manner of project would "do well" in Florida. He suggested a study similar to those done by various research companies to prepare for Disneyland, which could be combined with the operational experience they had since gained at Disneyland to answer key questions such as what kind of facilities would be needed, to whom they would cater, and how big "Project Future" would need to be at the start.

Another core concern Walt expressed at this early date was something that has been foremost in the minds of Disney executives ever since – how to persuade guests to stay on-site for an extended period. The Orlando area at the time lacked a large population of permanent residents, which concerned Walt; from the very start the company was aware that the Florida market posed a very different set of circumstances than did Disneyland, with its heavy dependence on locals.

To draw these guests, said Wait, there would be many things "like Disneyland", but also lots of new offerings. Pointing to the success of Disney attractions at the 1964/65 New York World's Fair as an example, he emphasized the appeal of Disney experiences in the major population centers of the east.

Also drawing visitors would be a number of hotels, which Walt emphasized as necessary to keep visitors in the area for an extended period. The theme park would be the key to driving attendance, he said, but they must also provide "reasonable prices" and "complete facilities" ranging from trailers to sleeping bag areas. Providing reasonably-priced lodging was a key point for Walt – he pointed to the success of ski lodges, where skiers didn't pay much for their room but then felt free to spend heavily on facilities and equipment.

Long part of the Walt Disney World origin myth is Walt's desire to avoid the urban sprawl which enveloped Disneyland after its 1955 debut. Indeed this issue comes up at the 1965 meeting, with Walt emphasizing the need to control the area to avoid "the jungle of signs, lights and fly-by-night operations that have 'fed' on Disneyland's audience." If they could control the area, Disney could also enforce high standards on operations and maintain a certain level of prestige. Disney hotels, said Walt, would be priced competitively with other off-site lodging, but would be better places to stay "in every way".

Everything in Project Future would be its own attraction, according to Walt. The lake, the hotels, and any recreational facilities were to be as much of a tourist draw as the theme park, and would help in feeding park attendance as well as retaining guests for longer stays. Walt knew that the public would expect him to duplicate certain parts of Disneyland, as many guests to the Florida park would never be able to travel to Disneyland; this would make Imagineering's task easier, as those attractions were already proven, engineered, and ready to be installed into the new park.

One major consideration that Walt underscored was the need to plan for rain – a concern practically unknown at Disneyland. Areas would need to be enclosed so that guests could stay active – and keep spending money – even in a downpour. Walt offered the Houston Astrodome as an example of enclosing a large area, and suggested that a park enclosed in such a manner would require much less maintenance. Perhaps it was these early discussions that inspired later unfounded rumors of plans to enclose the entire Walt Disney World complex!

Intriguingly, Walt points out than an enclosed park facility could be built anywhere – close to major cities in the east and Midwest, for instance. "Therefore," the memo proposes, "there could even be more than two Disneylands." This was not an entirely new concept, as Disney had tinkered with an enclosed recreational facility in St. Louis in preceding years, and was obviously thinking of ways to present themed attractions in climates different from California's.

What's interesting is that so far in this memo, nothing has emerged relating to EPCOT; in the next year EPCOT would seemingly become Walt's sole focus in the "Disney World" development, but it makes no appearance here. Instead there's mention of an industrial complex, to be built along the road leading into and out of the theme park area – roughly the equivalent of today's World Drive. This, said Walt, would give participating industries "tremendous billboard exposure."

So at the end of the meeting the new resort was envisioned thus: a theme park, motel and residential areas, an industrial complex, and recreational facilities. "We're ready to go!" said Walt, first with the necessary research studies, then Imagineering, and finally engineering.

And so it began…

.13

A MODEL KINGDOM, 1968

One hallmark of Walt Disney World since its very inception has been the ambitious master plan; the sweeping, grand vision which finds its Blue Sky ambitions diminished once the practicalities of construction take their toll.

While the construction of the resort in the late 1960s involved a massive amount of terraforming and infrastructure creation, which resulted in miles of new drainage canals and the dredging of an entire lagoon in front of the Magic Kingdom, there were other major landscaping projects that never came to be.

This is apparent as far back as Walt's "EPCOT film" from 1966. The large map of property, which Walt stands in front of during the film, depicts a Bay Lake that has been artificially expanded so that it reaches all the way to where Epcot now stands. Had this plan come to fruition, it could possibly have covered the area now occupied by Fort Wilderness, Port Orleans, and Dixie Landings.

Over the years, other plans were hatched to enlarge and link the small natural bodies of water on property. At one point, what is now the Sassagoula River was to be widened so as to link a series of recreational areas north of the Lake Buena Vista Village; even Epcot Center's World Showcase Lagoon was once designed to extend beyond the current row of pavilions into a larger lake beyond.

It's not unusual to take a look at early plans for the Florida project and find obscure, forgotten zoning details like a "future lagoon extension" penciled in to wrap around what is now the Grand Floridian Beach Resort. That site was originally reserved for a planned "Asian" resort, one of three hotels in the original Walt Disney World master plan that were never built.

This model of the Vacation Kingdom comes from January of 1968 and represents one of the earliest models that I can recall seeing of Walt Disney World in a form similar to how it was finally realized. In the first publicly-revealed version of Disney World's theme park area, seen in the "EPCOT film", the resort hotels were located in front of the Magic Kingdom and there was no lagoon in between. This model shows a theme park area featuring a lagoon and a number of resort hotels. The hotel configuration seen on the model is completely different from any with which we are familiar from later pre-opening publicity artwork. Let's take a look.

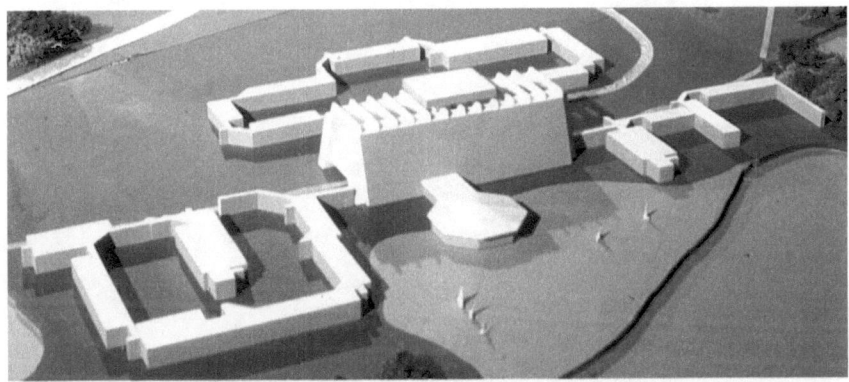

First, here's a familiar face to get our bearings. The Contemporary hotel is located much where we expect it to be, although its environs have been altered. Located between Bay Lake and the still-unnamed lagoon, the Contemporary is connected by monorail and roadway – although the famous "water bridge" has yet to appear and the road southward merely crosses a conventional causeway.

The core of the hotel itself looks much as it would continue to be depicted during the construction process. The octagonal dock seen here would continue to appear on Imagineering models, although the extensive garden wings shown winding around the building would soon vanish.

The next resort is also a familiar name, but with a different face. This is the Polynesian hotel, as originally conceived. Unlike the current "longhouse" design, this resort was originally envisioned as a high-rise hotel very indicative of the era in which it was created. This concept would last another year or so, before evolving into the hotel we know today.

As you can see, a much larger area would have been carved out of the lagoon to provide water-facing views and marina space. Multiple docks would have allowed access to a variety of watercraft and – who knows? – maybe that top floor would have featured a themed venue just as swanky as the Contemporary's Top of the World! You can bet your bottom dollar that, at the very least, there would have been glass-walled elevators in abundance.

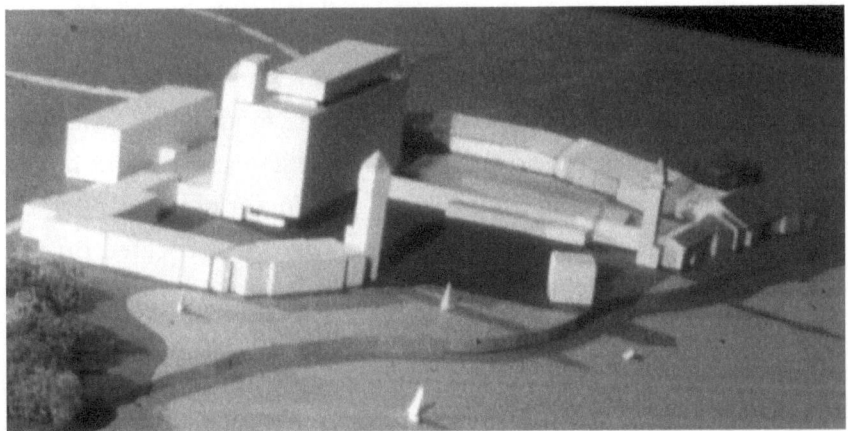

The last resort on this model which can be identified is in an unexpected place; the proposed Venetian hotel appears here where I've never seen it before. It is shown to the east of the Magic Kingdom, on a site facing Bay Lake which would be given a year later to the planned Persian theme hotel.

The design shown here seems familiar, though, and changed very little when it was moved to the Seven Seas Lagoon. The Venetian, themed to northern Italy, was composed of a central building with outlying wings, a marina, and two campanile "belltowers".

The biggest surprise of this model, however are two resort hotels that we've never seen before. These two anonymous hotels would be replaced over the next year or so with the Asian and Persian hotels, but they appear here and their themes remain, for now, a mystery.

Both hotels face the Seven Seas Lagoon; one is located on the expansion site where the Venetian would eventually be moved in 1969, while the other is sited on a spit of land somewhere between where the Grand Floridian exists today and the Magic Kingdom.

The first hotel is very reminiscent of other luxury hotels of its era, such as Miami's Fontainebleau. Its semicircular tower overlooks a circular pool and arcade, and several outbuildings provide added guest rooms. Note that it is also on the monorail line.

The second mystery hotel also features a "modern" design but might actually be a precursor to the Asian hotel which would replace it on the master plan. Note the odd shape of the central tower, as well as the somewhat traditional-looking pyramidal roof on the marina structure and the outbuildings. The size of the cabanas, and something about the slope of their roofs, make me think that this was an early attempt to give a vaguely oriental flair to a standard luxury hotel. This is pure speculation on my part, but it would explain the somewhat unconventional structure of the hotel tower.

So that's the Walt Disney World Resort, as conceived in early 1968. It's a world of endless recreational opportunities, but let's not forget what's sitting across that vast lagoon… It is, of course, the Magic Kingdom. A Magic Kingdom that is, perhaps unsurprisingly, as alien as it is familiar.

There are many major differences. Large, winding waterways sit both west of Frontierland and east of Tomorrowland. Space Mountain is the original, larger, quadrilateral design seen during the 1960s and known as "Space Port", and the black line of the Skyway can be seen extending from one of the Space Mountain spires, making a ninety-degree turn, and passing over Fantasyland.

There's a large show building one would see directly ahead after passing through Cinderella Castle, as well as an enormous show building guests would actually pass under upon entrance into Tomorrowland.

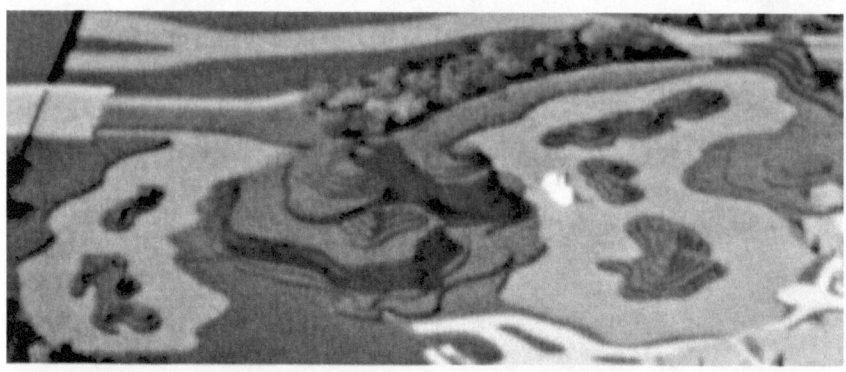

A prominent feature of this model is the legendary unbuilt attraction in Frontierland called Thunder Mesa, home of the *Western River Expedition*. Occupying a huge show building on the west side of the park, it was to be located where Splash Mountain and Big Thunder Mountain currently sit. The Walt Disney World Railroad would actually pass through the mountain after departing the Frontierland station.

The hulking mass of Thunder Mesa would loom over the area, facing the Rivers of America on the right, and the mysterious river area to the left. Look out, though – the steamboat is driving in the wrong direction!

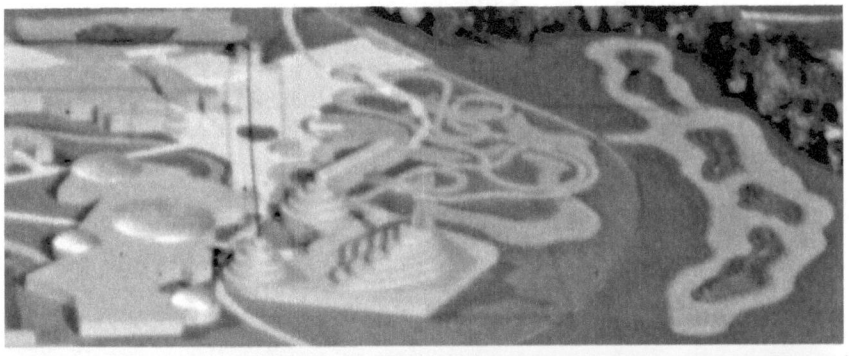

Other differences can be found on the eastern side of the park, in a Tomorrowland far different from today's. For instance, a monorail line enters the park and passes between Space Port and the building which straddles the entrance to Tomorrowland. It travels northeast to a station which would have allowed guests to exit the monorail inside the park itself. Passing over an Autopia area, the monorail would leave the park before looping around to the Venetian and Contemporary hotels.

You can see how the Magic Kingdom's version of Autopia was once planned to be much more elaborate – as well as water-laced. There's another one of those mysterious water ride areas to the east of the Autopia, and along the path of the Walt Disney World Railroad is a once-planned Tomorrowland railroad station. This was never realized, but twenty years after this model was built a station was finally erected in that spot to service the new Mickey's Birthdayland.

So that's a glimpse at Walt Disney World in its earliest recognizable days. Within a year, the design would have evolved; renderings from 1969 show that the additional lagoon idea had been abandoned and the resorts had taken their "traditional" locations. The Polynesian remained the funky, 1960s tower, but was correctly sited, and the Asian hotel sat on the square piece of land which would – again, twenty years later – play host to the Grand Floridian Beach Resort.

What a difference a few years and a few hundred million dollars made…

.14

The Lake Buena Vista STOLport

> *At its ultimate development, [Walt Disney World] is planned to include ... An "airport of the future," offering service to private and executive aircraft as well as commercial "commuter" service...*
> - *Preview Edition, Walt Disney World (1970)*

Part of Walt Disney's original plan for his newly-purchased acreage in Florida was an "airport of the future" that would service both the industries and residents of his planned city, EPCOT, as well as the guests to his new resort and theme park. The airport can be seen in early diagrams of Walt Disney World; its location, at the southernmost end of property, corresponded roughly to the current site of the town of Celebration. The airport would be linked by a central monorail line to a transportation hub and entrance plaza, a planned industrial park, EPCOT city, and the resort area and theme park.

The desire for Walt Disney World to have its own airport wasn't as arbitrary as it might seem today. In 1971, when the resort opened, what has now become the bustling Orlando International Airport was known as the Orlando Jetport at McCoy – a small commercial airstrip that operated out of a portion of the much larger McCoy Air Force Base. For a passenger terminal, the Jetport had inherited an old missile hangar from the Air Force; even after the government decommissioned the base in 1975 and transferred the entire site to the city of Orlando (leaving as a legacy its IATA code, MCO, which the airport uses to this day), air travelers arriving at the newly-named Orlando International Airport were greeted by the same primitive Quonset hut terminal until more modern facilities opened in 1981. It's easy to see how Disney, who expected guests to arrive by air from across the world, might see a need for an advanced and modern airport of their own.

Part of the legislation that created the Reedy Creek Improvement District did indeed grant Disney the powers to build and operate its own airport, but like so many of Walt's other dreams it never came to pass. For a brief time in the early 1970s, though, it *was* possible for the jet set to wing their way to the Vacation Kingdom of the World courtesy of Disney's very own landing strip – the Lake Buena Vista STOLport.

This facility, a private-use airport designated "DWS" by the IATA, was essentially a featureless 2000-foot landing strip and taxiway. For Disney fans, though, it's a mysterious glimpse into a long-lost era and a future that might have been.

In the late 1960s and early 1970s, there was a movement to mitigate the growing traffic problem on America's highways by building a national network of STOLports to provide inter-city regional transportation. STOL, or Short Take-Off and Landing, refers to small aircraft that can land on or take off from shorter airstrips than standard commercial jetliners. This would, theoretically, enable STOL facilities to be built on a wider scale and in more developed areas than typical airports. People would then be able to avoid traffic jams on the roads in their area by making short trips on a variety of commuter airlines.

In the early 1970s, this approach was being strongly encouraged by both the Florida Department of Transportation and then-Governor Reuben Askew. The state had proposed a demonstration route from Miami to Walt Disney World in March of 1971, with the eventual goal of fifteen to twenty STOLports in central and southern Florida to alleviate inter-city traffic.

As part of their effort to become an example of cutting-edge city planning, a STOLport was added to the master plan for Walt Disney World. Located to the eastern side of World Drive across from the Magic Kingdom's parking lot, the facility would allow for

The Lake Buena Vista STOLport 107

A rare photograph of the Lake Buena Vista STOLport in operation, 1971. © Disney

regularly-scheduled daily service to a number of regional airports, as well as providing connector flights to the main Orlando jetport at McCoy and Tampa International Airport. True to Disney's desire to innovate, the resort's STOLport was the nation's first. Intended as the nexus of a Florida-wide network of similar facilities, it would not only provide a convenience to arriving travelers, but also hoped to allow Disney guests "greater opportunities to visit all areas of the state."

The Disney company announced their plans for the airstrip on June 28th, 1971, with construction to commence immediately. The Lake Buena Vista STOLport, as it was to be known, would eventually consist of the 2000-foot runway and a terminal building. Donn Tatum, at the time president of Walt Disney World, said that the STOLport would be open only to commercial air traffic, with a second airport for corporate and private flights to be built later. Neither the STOLport terminal nor this second airport were ever built.

Disney had high hopes for the STOLport, with Tatum stating, "We believe the service will help demonstrate the effectiveness and economic feasibility of STOL aircraft." Tatum also announced that plans were underway with Eastern Airlines, then the official airline of the resort and consultant on the STOLport project, so that guests could buy their plane tickets to Walt Disney World anywhere in the world and have their luggage checked directly through to the resort.

Disney also announced an agreement with Shawnee Airlines to provide service to the STOLport from a variety of locations in the area. The small commuter airline would ferry passengers on its fleet of de Havilland DHC-6 Twin Otters. These reliable planes, carrying nineteen passengers per flight, remain in production to this day and are favorites of commuter airlines and bush pilots alike (possibly because they have one of the greatest airplane names of all time). Disney would soon add service by another regional outfit, Executive Airlines.

Executive, flying their own fleet of Twin Otters, announced in July of 1971 that they would begin service that September from St. Petersburg's Albert Whitted Airport to Tampa. This route, billed as "the first operating portion of the Disney World STOLport network," would be extended to Walt Disney World upon its October opening.

Inaugural service to Walt Disney World by both Shawnee and Executive began on the morning of Friday, October 22nd, 1971. The occasion was marked by a luncheon ceremony, where the state of Florida presented Disney with STOLport license No. 1. An array of local and state politicians and officials were on hand, as well as executives from the airlines and companies involved. With the array of officials, stewardesses, reporters, and others, there was a level of pomp

THE LAKE BUENA VISTA STOLport

In their bright orange livery, the Shawnee Twin Otters delivered ritzy vacationers directly into the Vacation Kingdom.

STOLport FLIGHTS

Shawnee Airlines operates 11 flights daily to and from the Walt Disney World STOLport (Short Take Off and Landing). Schedule is as follows:

Departs From:	Time	Flight No.	Arrives Walt Disney World
Daytona Beach	7:55 am	71	8:45 am
Orlando-Herndon	8:30 am	71	8:45 am
Fort Lauderdale	8:30 am	78	10:00 am
Palm Beach International	9:00 am	78	10:00 am
Tampa	9:35 am	72	10:05 am
McCoy Jetport	11:30 am	51	11:45 am
McCoy Jetport	12:30 am	53	12:45 pm
McCoy Jetport	2:05 pm	55	2:20 pm
McCoy Jetport	3:50 pm	57	4:05 pm
Orlando-Herndon	4:30 pm	73	4:45 pm
McCoy Jetport	5:20 pm	59	5:35 pm
McCoy Jetport	6:10 pm	61	6:25 pm
Tampa	7:00 pm	74	7:30 pm

Departs To:	Time	Flight No.	Arrives
Tampa	8:50 am	71	9:20 am
Orlando-Herndon	10:10 am	72	10:25 am
McCoy Jetport	11:05 am	52	11:20 am
McCoy Jetport	12:05 pm	56	12:20 pm
McCoy Jetport	1:35 pm	58	1:50 pm
McCoy Jetport	3:25 pm	60	3:40 pm
McCoy Jetport	4:45 pm	62	5:00 pm
McCoy Jetport	5:45 pm	64	6:00 pm
Tampa	6:00 pm	75	6:30 pm
Palm Beach International	6:30 pm	79	7:30 pm
Fort Lauderdale	6:30 pm	79	7:55 pm
Orlando-Herndon	7:35 pm	74	7:50 pm
Daytona Beach	7:35 pm	74	8:20 pm

This flight schedule appeared in the Fall 1971 edition of the Walt Disney World News, distributed to resort guests. © Disney

and circumstance rarely warranted by a 2000-foot strip of tarmac in the middle of the central Florida scrub.

Charles Bragg, president of Executive, said that he believed that day's trip from downtown St. Petersburg's Albert Whitted Airport to Walt Disney World to be the first-ever STOL to STOL flight. Col. John W. Dregge, director of the Office of Community and Congressional Relations for the Civil Aeronautics Board, proclaimed that STOL would be the "next breakthrough in air transportation." Even the president of de Havilland Aircraft of Canada, Ltd. was present to help promote the Twin Otters.

Disney announced that STOL service would commence with around 26 flights daily. Guests were to be transported to the airstrip by shuttle bus; at the time, the facility consisted solely of the runway, taxi ramp, and a four-plane parking lot. Disney re-iterated their plans to expand the STOLport in the future with a passenger terminal, baggage-handling facilities, full instrumentation, and lighting for around-the-clock operations.

But while Executive announced plans for limited service through October 30th, with service expanding again throughout November, the excitement was short lived. On December 9th, 1971, Executive eliminated their Southern Region which included service within Florida. A day later, on December 10th, they filed for bankruptcy. Shawnee stepped in to fill the gap, taking over Executive's service to Sarasota-Brandenton Airport. Shawnee's president David C. Latham said at the time that there hadn't been room in the Florida economy for two commuter airlines, and the demise of Executive would improve his own airline's bottom line.

Even then, though, the writing might have been on the wall for Disney's commuter service. Latham's optimistic economic prediction was that Shawnee would "come close" to breaking even in 1971 and might possibly turn a profit the next year. He indicated that the Disney route, while promising, would not make money for at least a year and was dependent on joint-fare arrangements with major airlines to succeed.

Can you guess where this is going?

By 1972, Shawnee was struggling to restore service to Walt Disney World from St. Petersburg in the wake of Executive's bankruptcy. The airline planned to restore unscheduled daily service to the city by mid-June, following an "intensive advertising campaign". Apparently, officials in St. Petersburg blamed Executive's failure on a lack of advertising, and Latham hoped to sell residents on the convenience of the half-hour flight to Disney World.

The airline's plan for the new route was to price flights on a sliding scale from $19 to $28, with the cost depending on the number of passengers aboard; they hoped to spur group sales with a package deal that included admission to the Magic Kingdom and a book of attraction tickets. Flights would remain unscheduled until Shawnee determined local demand; they had recently started regularly-scheduled flights out of Tampa, but that forced them to fly with empty seats. This kept ticket prices high ($28, roughly $165 in 2015 dollars). Another ominous quote from Latham: "We think this is the best way... any other and it would be a huge cash expense – possibly catastrophic."

To help promote the exciting possibilities provided by owning your own airstrip, even cast members got in on the act with Walt Disney World's Springtime STOLport Getaway – an opportunity for lucky employees to win a flight to the Bahamas directly from Disney property!

Shawnee Airlines now serving Sarasota, Miami, Tampa and Walt Disney World

8 Daily Flights

(We don't have our phones yet!)
For reservations and information call collect:

(813) 895-2116
(813) 229-7201

After Dec. 27 call Information for our new number.

SHAWNEE AIRLINES

The convenient commuter

Not inspiring confidence: This Shawnee ad appeared in the December 19th, 1971 Sarasota Herald-Tribune

And entering was so easy! Cast members were to clip a coupon found in the cast newsletter *Eyes & Ears of Walt Disney World* and deposit them in one of ten "Stowaway Suitcases" located in backstage locations across property. But don't get any funny ideas – people who submitted duplicate entries were disqualified. Dick Nunis will not abide cheaters!

The first winner was lucky nineteen-year-old Kathie McGuire, whose name was pulled from a basket by Mickey Mouse, with an assist from Shawnee Airlines official Al Porter. Kathie was a Reception Hostess at the Contemporary Resort, where she handled resort mail and messages; she was hard at work when Mickey "sauntered up" (according to *Eyes & Ears*) to present the winning ticket. Winners received a two night/three day holiday in the Bahamas courtesy of Shawnee.

But try as they might, Shawnee couldn't make their commuter service profitable. The tourism boom resulting from the opening of Walt Disney World led major carriers to increase their flights to and within Florida, and their higher capacity forced the local airlines out of business. Shawnee discontinued their service to Sarasota, Miami, Daytona Beach, Fort Myers, and Pensacola in November 1972. By the end of December, Shawnee went out of business. Latham blamed the new-found success of the major airlines in Florida, claiming that small commuter routes would never work without government subsidies. Perhaps most tellingly, Disney officials said at the time that the loss of STOL service would have "no significant effect" on attendance.

The last scheduled STOL flights took place Thursday, December 28th, 1972. Latham kept a skeleton crew at Shawnee to honor a commitment to provide service for a convention of the International Newspaper Advertising Executives Association at Walt Disney World from January 16-24th, but after that all STOL service ceased.

I can find no reference after this time of Disney attempting to restore service to the route; given its lack of profitability and the absence of any thriving regional carriers that's probably not a surprise. By this time, the political and economic troubles of the 1970s had begun, and

Mickey Mouse and Shawnee's Al Porter draw the name of the lucky STOLport Stowaway. © Disney

the company's expansion plans for Disney World began to be scaled back. By the time of the oil crises, the idea of affordable short-range air routes became completely impractical. Add to that the fact that by the end of the decade Orlando was well on its way to expanding its own International Airport, and it starts to seem that it was simply never in the cards for the Lake Buena Vista STOLport.

Any future thoughts of using the facility were precluded when monorail service was expanded to Epcot Center in 1982. The track's route, which runs southward along World Drive from the Transportation & Ticket Center, passes perilously close to the former STOL runway and any further aircraft landings were prohibited (whether this is due to FAA regulations or the concerns of Disney lawyers, I don't know). For well over a decade now, the airstrip has been used for a variety of purposes from providing a staging area for construction equipment or shipping containers to a parking lot for buses and, more recently, trailers housing Walt Disney Imagineering field offices.

It's been paved over with concrete, but it's still there – most guests probably don't even notice it as they're headed to the Magic Kingdom.

Amusingly, the STOLport was not eager to go quietly – at least in the realm of government maps and charts. It appeared on USGS surveys and maps throughout the 1980s and 90s, sometimes still labeled by its original name and sometimes just as "landing strip". This seems to have changed in the wake of the September 11th, 2001 terrorist attacks; since 2003 the FAA has, at the behest of Disney, imposed a mandatory no-fly zone over the property in Florida. It appears that all references to the airport have finally been removed from official charts – so much for the dream of flying into the Vacation Kingdom, pulling up to the terminal, and taking a short ride to your Disney resort.

The idea of what could have been is rather appealing, if you think about it. I picture a low-slung, air-conditioned terminal straight out of the 1970s… Eastern Airlines posters everywhere… muzak from *If You Had Wings* playing in the background… and possibly complimentary orange juice from the Florida Citrus Growers. Look, there's the Orange Bird! Straight from the Sunshine Tree!

There is one last tale from the Lake Buena Vista STOLport before we go. The facility was not without its controversies; before it opened, officials from Kissimmee protested Disney's plans, claiming that "skies are just too crowded." More likely, the politicians from other cities were concerned that Disney's new airstrip would hinder their efforts to build a $350,000 expansion to their own airport.

But the best story I've found about the STOLport comes from the *Lakeland Ledger*, on November 7, 1971. It's a story by someone named Don Emerson, who appears to have had a regular column called "Air Scoop". I reprint it here in its entirety:

> *Disney World Warns Pilots To Avoid STOLport*
>
> *This week's mail brought us this letter from Walt Disney World. We were hoping it contained an invitation to do an imitation of Grumpy, Sneezy, Sleepy or even Dopey in which we*

have had a little experience in each characterization at one time or another. Instead it read as this. "Dear Sir: This letter is to request your assistance in informing all AIRMEN of the status of the Lake Buena Vista STOLport located at Disney World.

"The STOLport is a private facility open only to the air carriers that have contractual agreements with Walt Disney World Company. Any landing by an unauthorized aircraft will be considered a violation of private property and the appropriate civil action taken.

"I will appreciate your assistance in informing fixed base operators, flying clubs, and airmen in your area of this information." There it is. No landing at Walt Disney World STOLport (Short Takeoff & Landing airport). Recently a pilot made an unauthorized landing there, parked his Lakes Amphibian aircraft. He spent most of the day savoring the wonders and excitement of the fabulously fantastic funland. Returning to the landing strip, he did not see his aircraft. Asking where it could possibly be, he was told it was at a nearby airport. He said this couldn't be as he had the ignition keys. Oh yes, it could be for aircraft mechanics were called, the wings removed and it was trucked off to a public airport and reassembled and there was his bill to prove it. This may seem to be drastic measures but when an airport is marked "Private" on the air charts, that's exactly what it means and a landing is trespassing. Many have had the experience of having their auto removed by a tow-truck from a no-parking area but few ever thought of aircraft being in the same category.

Another regulation pilots are breaking at Walt Disney World is the FAA requirement of 1,000 feet minimum altitude. You can understand the Disney people's concern with aircraft circling low overhead of thirty thousand visitors. A mid-air collision or engine malfunction would endanger hundreds of people. For their protection, personnel are stationed in Cinderella's Castle tower whereby accurate readings, altitude and aircraft registration number are recorded and violations are reported to the Federal Aviation Administration for corrective action. Another thing to bear in mind is its private airport is directly under Airway Route V-152S that is heavily traveled between Lakeland

and Orlando. This means even airlines using the Lakeland Omni Range are moving back and forth along this line or radial. So, a pilot really has no business to jeopardize aircraft in this flyway or the visitors on the ground by circling the area, for he will be probably looking down and not out and around to see if other craft are doing the same as he. Usually, a pilot circles to the left as he sits on that side of the aircraft and can see better when banking to the left. But, and here's where the real problem is, the passenger on the right wants to get a few pictures so the pilot banks or turns to the right… You just picture it. Half the cars on a racetrack racing in the opposite direction and everybody looking straight down! Stay safe near Walt Disney World and stay out of trouble.

Buzzing the castle? Spotters above the Magic Kingdom, looking for hostile aircraft? Those are stories I'd like to hear. Actually, that column might do a pretty good job of illustrating why Disney was so willing to shut down the STOLport and why the no-fly zone might not be so draconian after all. Imagine the damage that people can do in crowded park traffic with their strollers and ECVs and transpose that to the skies above. Yikes. But taking apart an entire airplane and having it moved to another airport? Wow. Don't ya just miss those days when Disney was willing to go the extra mile?

.15

Take the auto-train!

From the very beginning, Disney theme parks have been closely tied to their corporate participants. This was born of necessity; Walt had to rely on those sponsorships to get Disneyland built in 1955, and it's a tactic that the company has used ever since.

The effect of this heritage on Disney fans is rather odd when you stop to think about it, and it shows in the end just how successful these deals were for the sponsoring companies. For those of you who are long-time park goers, think about it: how many of your perceptions of specific corporations were shaped by their sponsorship of Disney attractions? In many cases, there's a friendly nostalgia among generations of fans for corporations or products that they never use or that might not even exist anymore.

How many young visitors from Walt Disney World's past now have a powerful affinity for the defunct Eastern Airlines because of *If You Had Wings*? How many long-time Disneylanders harbor a love for Monsanto, despite that company's dark history of injurious behavior, because they brought us the Mighty Microscope of *Adventures Thru Inner Space*? When I first started driving a car, I only bought gas at Exxon stations because they sponsored the Universe of Energy. Think of the others – Dole, Kodak, Kikkoman, or Bass. And how many of our ears perk up when we hear the name United Technologies, because they sponsored The Living Seas? Now raise your hands if you actually know what United Technologies does. A soft spot for a company whose products you have no idea if you ever even used – that's the power of Disney participant deals.

But outside of all the famous sponsors from years past, there are some that remain less well-known. There are several obscure participants who were only briefly involved with the Disney parks, and many lost to the mists of time that no longer exist even outside of the berm. One less-known sponsor, which came as a surprise to me when I found its ad in an old guide to Walt Disney World, was the auto-train. *auto-train!*

Instead of driving all the way to Florida, why not eliminate all that hassle? In 1970, a 33-year-old lawyer and civil servant named Eugene K. Garfield founded the auto-train Corporation. Building on a federal study from the 1960s that indicated a market for rail service for passengers and their vehicles (similar services existed already in Europe and Canada), Garfield purchased some used equipment and began a route from Lorton, Virginia to Sanford, Florida in December of 1971. The service was incredibly popular, allowing Garfield to upgrade the company's rolling stock, and was considered to be such a success that auto-train sought to expand its service to other routes.

It was during these flush times that auto-train became, as they advertised, the "official family railroad of Walt Disney World." The sponsorship ran only from roughly 1976 to 1977, but for that one brief year, Disney had its first and perhaps only official family railroad. But that's not all!

As a Disney participant, auto-train sponsored the Walt Disney World Railroad. I never knew that the WDWRR ever even had a sponsor, so this was quite a surprise, but a closer look at the old posters for the attraction do indeed reveal a tiny logo for the auto-train. And what better sponsor for the grand-circle tour of the Magic Kingdom than the official family railroad of Walt Disney World? And, when you're done, don't forget to stop at City Hall or the Travel and Tour Desks at the Contemporary Resort, Polynesian Village Resort, or Lake Buena Vista Hotel Plaza hotels to book your tickets home on the auto-train!

Sadly, things didn't work out for auto-train. The expanded service to new destinations was unsuccessful, never matching the popularity of the Virginia to Florida route, and an added route to Louisville, Kentucky proved a critical drain on the company's finances. An ensuing

All aboard the Walt Disney World Railroad, presented by "auto-train,ᵗᵐ" for a grand-circle tour of the Magic Kingdom.

"Auto-Train,ᵗᵐ" the train that carries you and your car to and from Walt Disney World, also sponsors the Walt Disney World Railroad, the old-fashioned steam train here in the Magic Kingdom.

So get on board. Because it's the ideal place to begin your Magic Kingdom visit. Riding along on this authentic, 1800's steam train, you get a glimpse of each of the Magic Kingdom's six themed lands. And at the end of your grand-circle tour, you'll be more familiar with the whereabouts of everything you'd like to explore.

One more suggestion. At the end of your day, stop by City Hall at the end of Main Street, U.S.A., to learn more about "auto-train,ᵗᵐ" the official family railroad of Walt Disney World. Or, use our direct-dial phones at the Travel and Tour Desks at the Contemporary Resort, Polynesian Village Resort or Lake Buena Vista Hotel Plaza hotels.

Have a wonderful stay.

P.S. After you've enjoyed your Walt Disney World vacation, read the back cover of this guide to find out how you can have a wonderful time going home, too.

1977 ad for the auto-train sponsorship. © Disney

drop in maintenance and service quality, along with several prominent derailments and accidents, led to the company's bankruptcy and the end of auto-train service in 1981.

Despite its problems, the auto-train service to Florida had remained popular until the end and demand for a similar service continued. Thankfully, in 1983 Amtrak recognized the market demand for such a route and purchased the former auto-train depots and much of the existing equipment and rolling stock. The revived Auto Train service is still in operation today, where it continues to be Amtrak's highest grossing and most profitable train. A new depot has since been built in Lorton, Virginia, and the outmoded facilities on the Florida end were replaced in 2010 thanks to $10.5 million in federal stimulus funds. So while no long a sponsor, unlike with Eastern Airlines you can still head to Walt Disney World on the Auto Train.

Auto Train!

IV.
Looking Back at Tomorrow

.16

The Tripartite Plan, 1975

By 1975, Walt Disney Productions had given up any pretense that it was ever going to build Walt's city of the future in Florida. The stirring images of Progress City had disappeared from their promotional materials, and by July of that year a Disney spokesman publicly stated that "the concept that was originally envisioned is no longer relevant."

Yet Disney executives still planned to go forward with an EPCOT project; after all, most of the concessions that Walt Disney World had obtained from the Florida government in the 1960s were predicated on the assumption that they were necessary for the specific purpose of bringing EPCOT to reality. Outside of the legislature, the public was clamoring for information on EPCOT as well. The vision of Walt's futuristic city had been well-publicized in the run-up to Walt Disney World's opening, and the people of Florida would not forget it easily. With this constant pressure from the outside, it was clear that despite Disney CEO Card Walker's back-pedaling, EPCOT was not going to go away.

As the original EPCOT concept of an actual working city faded, Disney slowly began to promote the narrative that the Walt Disney World property itself, with its innovative use of technology and new systems, was EPCOT made real. EPCOT was never meant to be an actual city, the story would go as the decades passed, but instead it was the set of values upon which the Florida property was modeled.

In 1975, however, the memory of Walt's EPCOT film with its soaring skyscrapers and swooping peoplemovers was still too fresh in the public consciousness for this story to have worked, and the company was fairly candid in its admissions that they were changing EPCOT into a form with which they were more comfortable – that of themed entertainment.

Disney still planned on incorporating many of EPCOT's ideas into its Florida property, they said, but instead of permanent residents it would now house and service a transient population of tourists and corporate personnel. The elements in and around Walt Disney World derived from the EPCOT philosophy would then be made accessible to the public through a series of themed attractions that would inform guests about the various EPCOT initiatives and allow them to experience the innovations firsthand.

How, exactly, Disney intended to do this remained vague until halfway through 1975. Prior to that point, Walker and others gave several clues as to what the Imagineers were working on, but it's clear from reading contemporary reports in the press that the media and public tended to interpret Disney management's vague clues to EPCOT's future in the context of their expectations of an actual futuristic city. This is despite the fact that in 1974 Disney had revealed that EPCOT would now take the form of a series of "satellites"; these would be demonstration sites within and without Walt Disney World that would display or promote new technologies or ideas. The first of these satellites, Disney announced in 1974, would be The World Showcase. This separately-gated attraction was to be "the first major step in the evolution of EPCOT."

The major turning point for EPCOT, though, was to come in 1975. Disney announced in its 1974 Annual Report that the new year would "mark the first period of concentrated planning and design" for the "centers of activity" within EPCOT itself. Said Disney:

> *Wide ranging discussions will be held with representatives of world governments, leading businessmen, engineers, scientists and artists, for only through their cooperation will the Company be able to bring this immense concept to life.*

Card Walker reiterated this intent in February of 1975, telling the *Christian Science Monitor* that "this is not double-talk ... It's serious.

We are really getting it off the ground." EPCOT, said Walker, would address "what is the best method of solar energy … new types of crop rotation … the whole field of solid waste disposal."

But why 1975? According to Walker, that year would officially mark the end of Phase I of Walt Disney World's development. The metric for this was the theoretical rides-per-hour capacity of the Magic Kingdom; with the addition of several new attractions the park had reached a theoretical capacity of 70,000, which matched that of Disneyland.

It seems that the pre-determined endpoint of "Phase I" might have been a bit of a moving target; prior to Walt Disney World's 1971 opening, the company gave themselves five years to achieve an annual attendance of ten million guests, at which point they claimed they would feel comfortable in proceeding with EPCOT. When the resort surpassed that attendance benchmark in its first year, a timetable recalibration was in order.

According to Walker, the result of Walt Disney World's success was that the start of their EPCOT studies was announced two years ahead of schedule. By early 1975, Disney was working with General Electric, RCA, the National Science Foundation, and the Jet Propulsion Laboratory to develop concepts for EPCOT. Said Walker, "We think we can do it, and if we can, it'll be one of the most exciting things the company has ever done. It's bigger than us, but because we're us we might be able to get it done. We're communicators; why not be able to communicate technology as well as entertainment?"

Disney made their intentions more clear on July 14th, 1975, when Walker and Disney Board Chairman Donn Tatum unveiled the company's plans for EPCOT for the media and around seventy guests and visiting dignitaries. The concept shown that day was very different from what Walt had originally announced in his famous EPCOT film; as the headline in the *Miami News* put it, "Disney's 'City of Tomorrow' will be built – without residents." As Walker would later report, talking about their "dynamic and achievable" approach to EPCOT, "We believe that in order to attain Walt Disney's goals for EPCOT, we must avoid building a huge, traditional 'brick and mortar' community which might possibly become obsolete, in EPCOT terms, as soon as it is completed."

"We believe," Walker continued, "we must develop a community system oriented to the communication of new ideas, rather than to serving the day-to-day needs of a limited number of permanent residents."

"EPCOT's purpose, therefore, will be to respond to the needs of people by providing a Disney-designed and Disney-managed forum where creative men and women of science, industry, universities, government, and the arts – from around the world – can develop, demonstrate and communicate prototype concepts and new technologies, which can help mankind to achieve better ways of living."

The plan which Walker announced in 1975 divided EPCOT's various activities into three categories. EPCOT, which Walker hoped to complete by 1980, would first consist of The EPCOT Institute, "an independent organization which will provide the administrative structure necessary to facilitate participation in EPCOT and its 'satellite' research activities by all interested parties."

The goal of the EPCOT Institute would be to guarantee that benefits from research taking place at EPCOT facilities would make their way to not only corporate sponsors but also the public at large. The Institute would ensure the credibility of EPCOT-related research by assembling expert advisory boards for each project.

Key to EPCOT's development would be the participation of outside entities, and the EPCOT Institute would facilitate this. As Walker said, "no one company, no one nation alone could accomplish the goal of EPCOT."

EPCOT's second planned component was to be the EPCOT "satellites" or activity centers, which Disney claimed would "be engaged in researching, testing, and demonstrating prototype products and systems in such fields as energy, agriculture, education, medicine, and communications, in locations best suited for the particular program."

The EPCOT satellite sites would comprise a loosely-defined variety of projects meant to publicly demonstrate innovations in EPCOT's fields of study. These could include any of the innovations already used for the working infrastructure of Walt Disney World, such as solar power installations or waste recycling facilities, or they could be sponsored, off-site research projects. At these centers, "experimental systems in the fields of transportation, energy, education, health and medicine, agriculture, outer space, oceanography, communications, and the arts [could] be designed, tested, and demonstrated."

The satellites would be open to guests, allowing them to see cutting-edge research and development in progress:

> *At each satellite, dedicated men and women will work to develop new technology in their field, seeking solutions and exchanging ideas in broad areas affecting the quality of life for people throughout the world.*
>
> Disney News, Spring 1976

As Disney had announced in 1974, the first of the satellite sites planned to open was the World Showcase, accompanied by the International Village in which the Showcase's cast members would reside. It appears that by the time of the 1975 announcement the Showcase had been moved from its previously-designated site; originally intended to sit adjacent to the Transportation and Ticket Center on the shore of the Seven Seas Lagoon, World Showcase was now to be built south of the Magic Kingdom's toll plaza on a 100-acre plot closer to the eventual site of the actual Epcot Center. The International Village, home to the young foreign cast members which would staff this new attraction, seems to have been slated for construction near the then-underway Lake Buena Vista development.

The final element announced in 1975 was the EPCOT Future World Theme Center, "a high-capacity visitor facility which will employ advanced communications techniques, including motion pictures, models, multi-media exhibits, and ride-through experiences, to inform millions of people each year about what is being done in the creative centers of science and industry around the world."

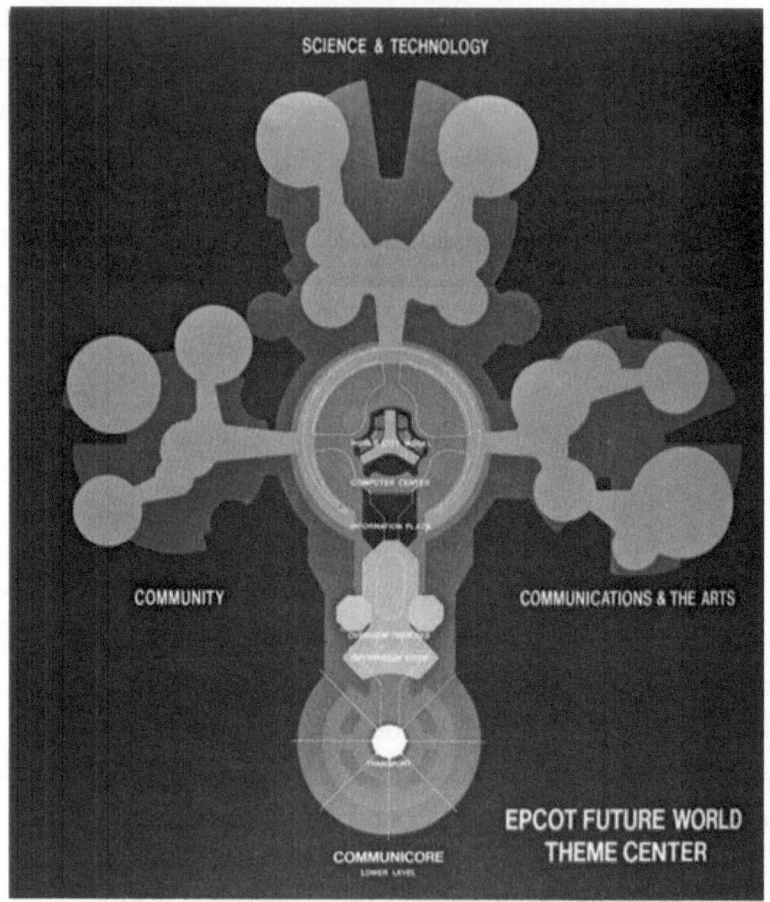

A layout of the EPCOT Future World Theme Center as seen in the 1975 Walt Disney Productions Annual Report. Aside from the three large theme pavilions, features included the World City Model, Computer Center, Information Plaza, Overview Theaters, Information Store, and a Transportation hub. © Disney

The Future World Theme Center was the real innovation of the 1975 plan; it was a single site in which all the ideas and fields of study being explored in the EPCOT satellites would be accessible to guests, and it would provide a nexus of sorts for the various EPCOT initiatives. The Theme Center represented the first emergence of ideas which would evolve into the Future World section of the Epcot Center theme park; it was even planned for approximately the same location on Walt Disney World property.

The Theme Center marked the first proposed appearance of pavilions themed to specific fields of study; these pavilions would, in this concept, tie into individual EPCOT satellite sites operating elsewhere. According to the Spring 1976 *Disney News*, inside the Future World Theme Center "360-degree movie screens and various displays will offer guests an overview of current EPCOT projects. Guests can then visit the areas, called satellites, of particular interest to them."

The Theme Center was called the "heart" of EPCOT, and in many ways that was true; its three major pavilions based on science and technology, community, and communications and the arts would "feature displays, shows, and information centers on ... various fields and disciplines." It would "keep abreast of scientific and industrial research around the world and make that information available to visitors."

The most important role of the Theme Center was to carry on Walt's hope that the systems seen in EPCOT could inspire other cities. It would, said Disney, "demonstrate how these new technologies and ideas can be applied in a practical way to improving the environment for living in existing communities throughout America and the world."

The plan, in 1975, was for there to be no fee for guests to visit the Future World Theme Center; Disney would, however, charge for admission to the World Showcase and the other satellite sites. Resort guests would be able to reach the Theme Center and World Showcase via an expansion of the monorail system. Other future satellite sites would be tied into the resort transportation system as well.

To publicize the new project and coordinate the recruitment of outside participants, Disney announced two prominent new executives to act as the figureheads and public faces of the EPCOT initiatives. L. Gordon Cooper, scientist and celebrity astronaut due to his membership in the fabled Mercury 7, would lead the technological aspects of the project as Vice President of Research and Development for

EPCOT. C. Langhorne Washburn, the Assistant Secretary of Commerce for Tourism, resigned his position in the Nixon administration to join Disney as the World Showcase Vice President. Washburn would coordinate the diplomatic efforts required to ensure international participation in the EPCOT project.

Construction on World Showcase was announced to begin in 1978, with opening day planned for 1980; later in 1975 Disney would claim that there had been so much interest in the project that they were moving up the timetable, with construction to commence in 1976 and a targeted opening day of October 1st, 1979. In reality, ground would not be broken on Epcot Center until 1979, with opening day coming in 1982.

As to cost, officials stated that World Showcase by itself could "reach dimensions and expenditures similar to that of the current Magic Kingdom theme park." Another spokesman said that the Florida property currently represented "an investment of $650 million now. We don't have a figure on how much money is to be involved in the new attractions, but it's possible that it could involve the same amount." Over time, that would prove an understatement.

Perhaps the greatest impetus for the EPCOT project can be found in another statement by an unnamed Disney spokesman on the occasion of the project's announcement: "It will give the public the incentive to spend at least a second day with us and possibly relieve us of some of the overcrowding that now occurs at peak times in the park." It was explained that EPCOT would contain so many trade pavilions, scientific and technical exhibits, and rides and theaters that visitors could spend an entire day.

The EPCOT of 1975 is very different from the Epcot Center that opened in 1982, but in its details we can see the germination of many ideas that would develop into that later park. For the very first time, we had early versions of both Future World and World Showcase, and at some point over the next year those two concepts would be combined into a single gated attraction that slowly evolved into Epcot Center.

What's interesting is how this earlier version of EPCOT was a very functional environment for active research and development. Instead of just addressing themes relating to the future, the EPCOT satellite centers would feature working installations of cutting-edge systems and the latest developments of public and private institutions and corporations.

The new momentum behind the EPCOT project could be seen in the increasingly aggressive marketing of the concept throughout 1975. In September of that year, Disney took advantage of the annual conference of the Southern Governors' Association to help promote EPCOT. The conference, which not coincidentally was held on Disney property at the Contemporary Resort, brought a number of notable politicians to Orlando, where they were a captive audience for Disney's presentations.

Aiding Disney's plans was Florida Governor Reuben Askew, who assisted the company in making their EPCOT presentation to Secretary of State Henry Kissinger, Senate Majority Leader Mike Mansfield (D-MT), and EPA Administrator Russell Train. The dignitaries were said to have "expressed their enthusiasm" for the concept. Governor Mills E. Godwin, Jr., of Virginia said, after witnessing the presentation, "The depth of planning and the vision that went into the concept, I am certain, will assure its success." Georgia Governor George D. Busbee said that "it is a concept that I feel certain will do a great deal for our own country and for the cause of world peace."

Secretary Kissinger assigned two of his top aides to view the presentation, and the State Department arranged meetings for the Disney marketing department in Amsterdam, Athens, Copenhagen, Brussels, and Paris. Additional presentations were made at Walt Disney World in July and October of 1975, and Disney opened an office in Washington, D.C. where World Showcase Vice President C. Langhorne Washburn could more easily present the EPCOT concepts to diplomats and politicians. In December 1975, Disney executives made a presentation on EPCOT to members of Congress in the theater of the Rayburn House Office Building.

EPCOT was underway. As Walker would say in the 1975 annual report:

> *It is my firm conviction that the need for EPCOT and the World Showcase has never been greater, that the timing is right, and that, in Florida, we have the right location. I am hopeful that by the time we celebrate our Bicentennial on July 4, 1976, we will be confident of enough foreign participation in the World Showcase to make the decision to proceed. If we do, it will become the focal point of our second phase of development at Walt Disney World.*

.17

Master Plan 5, 1977

As we've seen, Epcot Center's path from idea to execution was, in many ways, more tortured than it would later be portrayed. Instead of a simple conceptual transformation from Walt's notion of a futuristic city to the eventual realization of a "permanent World's Fair" (or, as modern revisionists would have it, a straight shot from Walt's mind to the park that opened in 1982), Epcot's development occupied the full span of the 1970s. In that time, the vision of what might constitute "EPCOT" took a number of different forms.

"EPCOT", in one form or another, was announced on several different occasions – often with great fanfare. But as disjointed as this development process might seem, it follows a clear evolution. While the overall concept and planned physical layout of EPCOT changed often, certain core themes remained throughout.

The ideals that underpinned Epcot Center were formulated early in the 1970s and grew fairly organically from Walt's ambitions for EPCOT the city; each variation of the EPCOT concept derived its mission, in some fashion, from these ideals. The first recurring point was that Walt Disney World itself was, in a way, EPCOT, and would provide a living laboratory for a number of innovative technologies and systems. A second goal for EPCOT centered on the international community, and on ways to bring various cultures together in one place. Plans for a World Showcase were, in fact, the first elements of EPCOT announced for construction in the early 1970s.

The other key aspect of EPCOT, of course, involved the creation of a futuristic "community" that would allow the public to encounter new technologies and to see how these ideas and innovations would shape their lives in the future. An important element of this would be the involvement of major American corporations, as the Disney organization under Card Walker believed that American free enterprise held the answers for problems facing our communities and, when given free reign (as Disney itself had been in its self-governed Reedy Creek Improvement District), these corporations could and would address those problems head-on.

EPCOT's futuristic aspects took longer to develop, only truly emerging with Card Walker's EPCOT Center announcements in 1975, and the so-called "EPCOT Future World Theme Center". Here, and at the EPCOT satellite sites mentioned in the previous chapter, public and private researchers could interact with the goal of addressing society's ills – all under the watchful eyes of thousands of daily visitors. Outside of the Theme Center, the EPCOT satellites would stretch beyond the borders of Walt Disney World and to various research locations nationwide. It was with an eye towards this goal that Disney held a number of academic conferences under the EPCOT name during the 1970s, focusing on subjects ranging from energy technology to health care.

Obviously, something happened between these early visions and the announcement in 1978 of a theme park that is recognizably Epcot Center. There's always been the famous story of Marty Sklar and John Hench, staring down the barrel of an impending visit from Disney executives, pushing the World Showcase and Future World models together to form a single park. But even that tale belies a more complicated truth.

The first time the World Showcase and Future World ideas were combined into a single gated attraction appears to have been sometime in 1976. At the time, the park's layout was far different, and reversed – guests would enter the park through World Showcase, which would serve as a sort of international Main Street before guiding visitors

RIGHT: This 1977 model shows Future World connected to a World Showcase which spans two lagoons. Clockwise from Spaceship Earth and Communicore, the Future World pavilions include Life and Health, The Land, Transportation, U.S.A., Space, The Seas, and Energy. © Disney

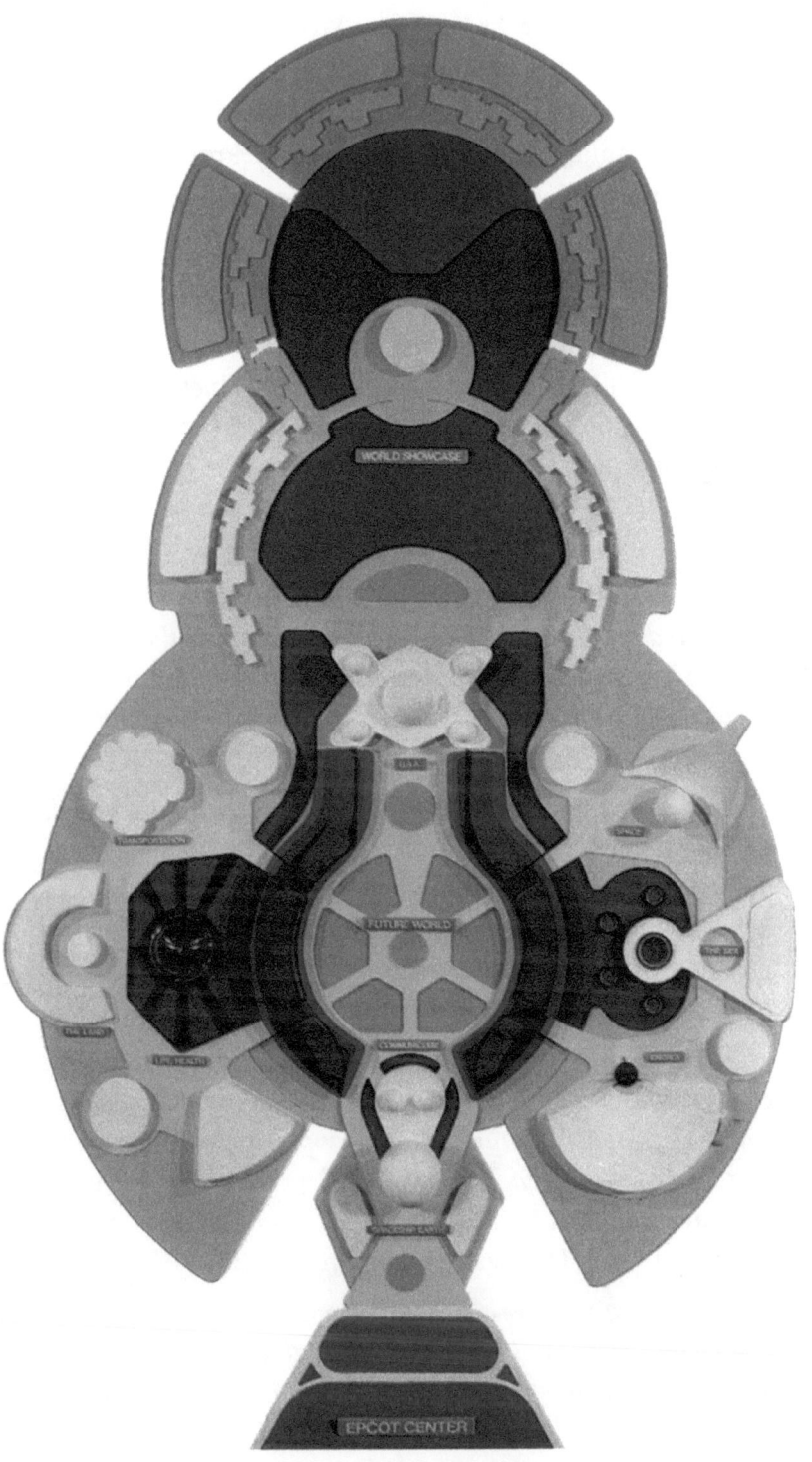

into the technological realm of Future World. Looking at plans from the period, it's clear that Disney was still trying to work out a defined vision for the park. In 1977, things would start to click into place.

With great fanfare, the 1977 Walt Disney Productions Annual Report rather breathlessly heralds the "conceptual breakthrough" of Master Plan 5 – their newest vision of what EPCOT Center would be. To quote CEO Card Walker's letter to shareholders:

> *There has never been a greater need for the communication of information about the diverse peoples of our planet, the new systems and technologies evolving to meet the needs of those people, and the alternative decisions we face. Our future depends upon it. For the better we understand today, the choices for tomorrow, the better decisions we will make.*
>
> *This is what EPCOT Center and its two major themes, Future World and the World Showcase, will be devoted to: the advancement of international understanding and the solution of the problems of people everywhere – through the communication of ideas.*
>
> *Our dedication to this concept will not be limited to the EPCOT Center site in Florida. It will extend as far as the Disney ability to communicate can reach, including films, television, educational materials, and even the licensing of concepts and products. For this reason, we believe, EPCOT Center can open an exciting new dimension for Walt Disney Productions.*
>
> *At this writing, for example, a series of five television specials exploring each of EPCOT Center's wide-ranging themes is under development. Our preliminary plans are to inaugurate this series with a gala "Disney Week" on television, recreating the career and dreams of Walt Disney, culminating in a major special on "Walt Disney's Greatest Dream: EPCOT".*
>
> *However, as we have consistently pointed out, EPCOT Center cannot and should not move forward on the financial or creative strength of any one organization. It requires the best thinking*

and financial support of American industry and the commercial and government interest of other nations as well.

Therefore, while our creative people have been developing the conceptual breakthrough for EPCOT Center, we have continued to seek support for the first phase of World Showcase from foreign industry and governments around the world. Our efforts have included Canada, Costa Rica, England, Israel, Japan, Mexico, Morocco, Poland, Saudi Arabia, South Korea, United Arab Emirates, Venezuela, West Germany, and other countries. Several of these have already indicated their intention to participate as sponsors of pavilions and exhibits in the World Showcase. Others are in varying stages of negotiations which we feel will lead to their participation.

Over the past few months, we have begun to emphasize our concept for EPCOT Center's Future World. We have discussed the first phase development with such major American corporations as American Telephone & Telegraph, ARCO, Borden, Coca-Cola, Exxon, General Electric, General Motors, IBM, RCA, Sperry Rand, Standard Oil of Indiana, Westinghouse, and others. The initial response from these corporations has been most enthusiastic. And we have entered into negotiations with a number of them which we feel will result in their participation as sponsors of pavilions and exhibits in Future World. We believe EPCOT Center has stimulated many of America's leading corporations because the EPCOT dynamic is really the America dynamic. It is founded on the principles of American enterprise – and a belief that an informed public can, and will, make better decisions for tomorrow if they understand and believe accurate and relevant information today.

So, you know, no pressure.

Walker's statement is interesting, even aside from the historical curiosity of his list of nations and sponsors who would never actually join the EPCOT ranks. He makes sure to adhere to core EPCOT talking points, including the fundamentally important belief that when presented with accurate and truthful information, the public could better make decisions in their best interest. As the Disney report would later state:

> *As conceived here, EPCOT will be a "Showcase for prototype concepts", demonstrating practical applications of new ideas and systems from creative centers everywhere. It will provide an "on-going forum of the future", where the best thinking of industry, government, and academia is exchanged to communicate practical solutions to the needs of the world community. It will be a "communicator to the world", utilizing the growing spectrum of information transfer to bring new knowledge to the public. Finally, EPCOT will be a permanent "international people-to-people exchange", advancing the cause of world understanding.*
>
> *In addition, we are convinced that EPCOT will provide a much needed symbol of hope and optimism that our major challenges can, and will be met. It will provide outstanding family entertainment from which people may draw enlightenment, as well as enjoyment. And it will, of course, represent a major new extension of our business activities around the world.*

It is clear from the 1977 report that Future World entered development much later than World Showcase; surprisingly, though, the vision described for that area in the report hews very closely on a pavilion-by-pavilion basis to the park that opened in 1982. This is as opposed to World Showcase, which can be seen in models to take the form of a double promenade, which provided far more open space for potential national pavilions than the final layout. The American pavilion, labeled on the model as "U.S.A.", sits not at the far end of the World Showcase lagoon, but instead straddles the path from Future World to World Showcase. It would remain in this spot until 1979.

Disney, proud as they were to promote the success of Master Plan 5, acknowledged that things remained in flux, assuring readers that "the specifics of this plan will, undoubtedly, change time and time again. This is a natural result of the Disney creative process which continually probes for the best alternative."

Despite a great deal of shuffling in the years to follow, however, the basic layout of the 1977 plan would remain substantially the same. "'Future World' and the 'World Showcase,'" said Disney, "together with the 'American Adventure', which acts as a gateway between the world of today and tomorrow, provide what we believe are the best opportunities for meeting the four major objectives we have established to bring Walt Disney's last and greatest dream to reality."

It seemed, at last, that Imagineers had found a concept that they liked. So let's take a look around EPCOT Center in 1977; a familiar yet strangely different park, which is still strongly defined by the divide between its two sections: Future World and World Showcase.

Future World, promoted as "a community of ideas", took a recognizable shape even at this time. Spaceship Earth was situated in its proper place, as was CommuniCore. Going clockwise from where today we'd find the Universe of Energy were "Life & Health", "The Land", "Transportation", "U.S.A." (The American Adventure), "Space", "The Sea", and "Energy."

If you remove The American Adventure, that's the same number of pavilions that Epcot Center would feature in its actual phase one, although only Spaceship Earth, CommuniCore, and "Transportation" – later World of Motion – would remain in their designated spots throughout development. The fact that General Motors signed on as Epcot's first sponsor in 1978 meant that the Transportation pavilion got a big head start, and if you look at Epcot construction photos from 1979–1982 you'll note that the World of Motion is always much farther along in construction than other pavilions.

Future World was described as "an American enterprise forum", meant to pose challenges and preview alternatives for the future. The park's central icon, then as now, was Spaceship Earth. The grand mirrored orb had yet to sprout legs, though, and was not a geosphere – merely a gold-hued geodome. A great deal of the attraction would have taken place in a show building behind the dome, not in the dome itself.

As the park's "major introductory theme show", Spaceship Earth was meant to provide an introduction to the concept and meaning of EPCOT. It would, said Disney, focus on "the relationship between communications and humankind's continuing dynamic – survival." The attraction's story would hit many of the same beats of the final attraction:

> *A time machine journey into the past to trace man's progress as he acquires and utilizes new knowledge. Surging forward through time, guests will see historical milestones unfold as man records, communicates more broadly, and finally uses computer technology to process ever increasing amounts of information.*

Spaceship Earth would provide "an optimistic statement recognizing our enormous challenges and concluding strongly that creative men and women of the world can develop a viable 'instruction book for Spaceship Earth.'" Its emphasis was that access to accurate and relevant information, along with the ability to craft new and better tools for survival, have been "the real dynamic of our voyage aboard Spaceship Earth." It would conclude with an exhortation for guests to go forth into Future World and explore the topics presented in its various pavilions.

The first of these pavilions, CommuniCore, was said to be "a global marketplace of new ideas bringing the public into direct interface with industry." Intended as a much more vibrant and vital section of Future World than it ever was in actuality, CommuniCore was the community – and communications – core of EPCOT, and it would be the place where guests would synthesize the information from the various theme pavilions and interact with these new futuristic concepts in relatable ways.

A series of attractions and exhibits would allow guests to interact with industry and "participate in a 'hands on' exchange of new and exciting ideas, systems, products, and technologies." A handful of

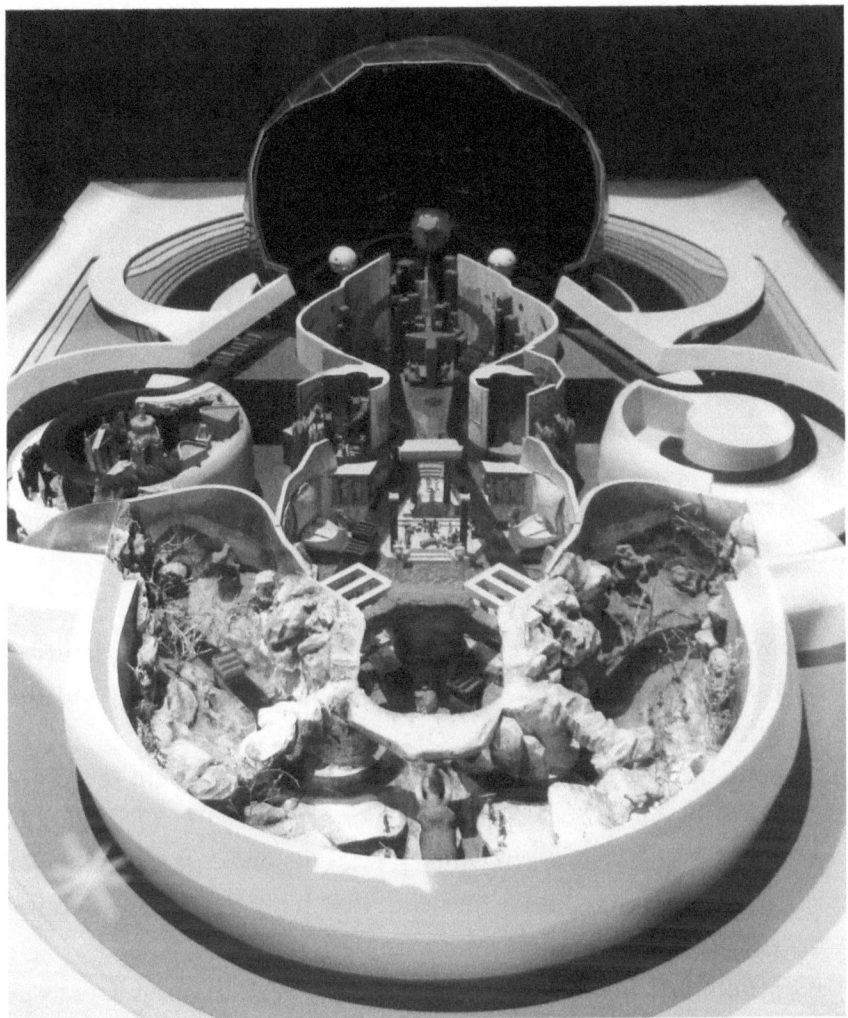

This early model of Spaceship Earth shows how the majority of the attraction was originally to be housed in an external building rather than inside the dome itself, which is cut away in this view. Scenes in the foreground depict prehistoric man, while those in the central area would take riders through the classical age and Renaissance. The show scenes in the far background, taking guests into and out of the domed section of the building, were to feature the modern information age and mankind's future in space. © Progress City

Concept art for the Travel Port, where guests could electronically preview their vacations. Note the old Disneyland-style Mark III monorail depicted in the background. © Disney

these would survive in some form in Epcot Center's eventual attraction roster, but a great many more would never pass beyond the conceptual stage.

Among the ideas for the "information marketplace" were Telstore, a Future World "video bookstore". This is one of those EPCOT concepts which underscores the era in which it was conceived, as it would offer an area where guests could "experience first-hand the newly emerging world of video information for the home."

One item that would actually appear in the real CommuniCore was described in 1977 as the "Future World Travel Port", a place where guests would electronically provide their travel interests and desired itinerary in order to receive an "instant preview" of their next vacation. Another area, FuturePlan, was to be a career center providing information about up and coming careers for young people as well as "the newly developing field of second careers for retiring citizens."

EPCOT was developed during the era in which video game technology was first developing, so a number of ideas were floated over the years to add some sort of advanced arcade to the new park. In

"The study model of the Life & Health Pavilion includes an area offering guests a ride through the fantastic wonders of the body and The Great Midway of Life, where they will learn their personal responsibility for good health habits."
© Disney

the Informat Arcade, the idea of gaming would be combined with "providing new experiences for the public in information retrieval" to create a "casino of information" in video game format. It would, in Disney's words, "[take] the penny arcade of the past into the information age."

Other potential CommuniCore exhibits included "The Good Health Emporium, the drug store of tomorrow, and The Future World Office, a paperless place of business." The drug store of tomorrow? A career center? The penny arcade of the information age? As you can see, CommuniCore would have been a much different place had these plans gone through; it would have certainly served more as a futuristic mirror to Disneyland's Main Street, U.S.A., as seems to have been intended.

Moving on, we reach the Life and Health pavilion. Though long planned, it would also be a long time coming for Epcot fans. A health-themed pavilion would not actually open in the park until 1989, when Wonders of Life debuted. Still, as you might be able to tell, that pavilion drew a great deal of inspiration from these early concepts.

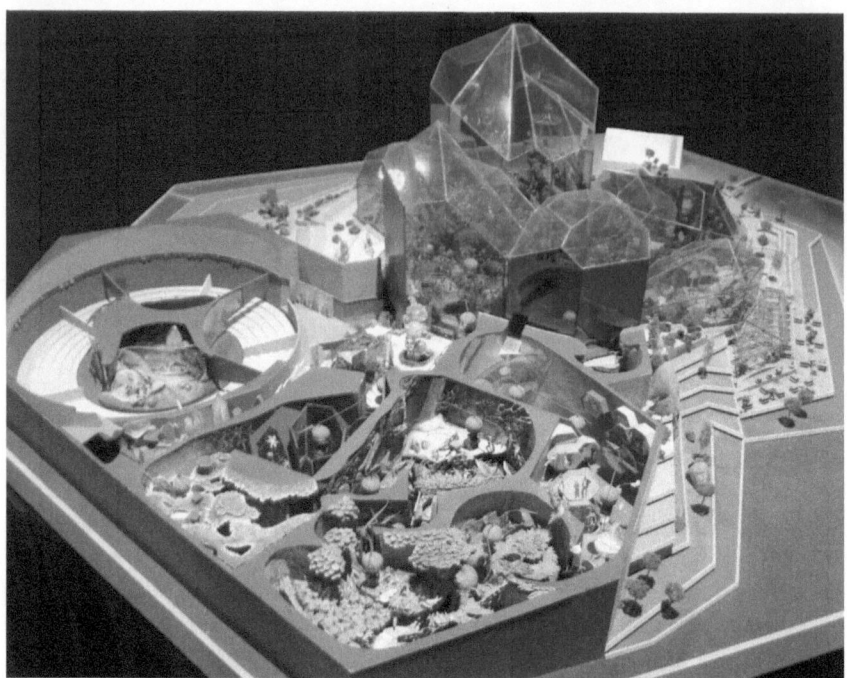

This cutaway model of The Land shows not only the large crystalline structures containing a variety of ecosystems, but also the carousel theater show (left) and dark ride (foreground) which would comprise the pavilion's major attraction.
© Progress City

The interior of this pavilion would have had a whimsical design, courtesy of veteran Imagineer Rolly Crump. Guests would enter "The Great Midway of Life" in the central circular area, around which would be a number of shows and experiences. Some of these would later have analogous attractions in the similarly laid out Wonders of Life building.

Guests would enter the pavilion through the plaza seen to the right of the model pictured on page 143. Moving clockwise around the pavilion's interior, guests would encounter *The Joy of Living*, a multimedia show said to "extol the beauty, the dignity, and strength of man from birth to the golden years."

Continuing around the pavilion would be a sensory funhouse, the *Tooth Follies* (a theatrical show with animatronics set inside a giant mouth), *The Head Trip* (a precursor to the later *Cranium Command* show), Good Health Habits (a "casino" of health-themed games), and, in the large angular show building at the top of the picture, *The Incredible Journey Within.*

This massive dark ride would have transported guests into the human body, where they would board red blood cell–shaped vehicles in a trip past giant animatronic replicas of a beating heart and breathing lungs. Eventually guests would encounter a "brain storm", where sparking neurons would send them careening to the end of the attraction.

The Land pavilion, occupying here a spot in Future World that would eventually go to Horizons, was originally a much different pavilion than that one we would come to know in 1982. Designed by rookie Imagineer Tony Baxter – I wonder whatever became of him? – this attraction focused more on the natural world around us than on the cultivation of crops.

"TRANSPORTATION PAVILION: A concept for 'hands-on' experience with working prototype vehicles of the future will be a part of this guest experience."
© Disney

Housed in a series of large, crystalline structures would be a diverse group of biomes based on ecosystems from around the world. These would range from tropical swamps to temperate grasslands to alpine meadows. Guests could explore these different habitats on foot or, aboard an attraction called *The Blueprints of Nature*, via a hot-air balloon. The animatronic show that would serve as introduction to this ride would focus on "harmony between man and his environment", as well as "man's role as a 'protector' of this finite resource, as well as his alternatives and choices in maintaining, and even enhancing, the delicate balance within the natural environment."

The original sponsor for The Land, a lumber company, eventually fell through and was replaced by Kraft. This switched the focus of the pavilion from ecology to food and farming, and Baxter's concept was abandoned. Happily, he would go on to create Journey into Imagination, which would be housed in a crystalline pavilion similar to his concept for The Land's glass biomes.

Unlike The Land, the 1977 version of EPCOT's transportation-themed pavilion bears many similarities to its eventual successor, the World of Motion. The round building is familiar, as is the open central courtyard. This design is a lot busier, though, with a full-scale Space Shuttle orbiter hanging over the courtyard as well as a vehicle track in the area outside the pavilion.

The dark ride shown here appears similar to the actual attraction; visitors, Disney said, would "see man's earliest and most humble designs grow and change as he reaches out to explore the world around him." It seems that there was to be an additional attraction where guests were allowed to ride some sort of "futuristic" prototype vehicle; not only does a secondary ride track appear in the model, but Disney promised at the time that visitors would "be treated to simulated trips aboard some of today's modes of transportation ... and have a glimpse at future transportation systems ... including a 'hands-on' involvement with working prototypes of tomorrow's vehicles."

If anything puts a wistful look in the eye of an Epcot geek, it's a mention of the Space pavilion. This massive attraction was announced

Master Plan 5, 1977

Rendering of the massive "space vehicle" that would be the feature attraction of EPCOT's fabled Space pavilion. © Disney

"SEAS PAVILION: This WED study model includes a dramatic 'ride beneath the seas.'" © Disney

for EPCOT early on, but later slipped to "phase II" status along with the Life & Health pavilion. It never saw the light of day.

Produced with the assistance of author Ray Bradbury, the centerpiece of this pavilion would have been a massive simulator attraction that would have moved an entire theater in sync with outer-space visuals. It would, according to Disney, "transport passengers to the outer frontiers of the universe, highlighting man's efforts to reach out for the stars around him ... from the early pioneers who looked and wondered ... to modern-day space travelers and their triumphs ... to the challenges and possibilities of future space technology and exploration."

While The Living Seas did eventually open in 1986, years behind schedule due to difficulties in finding a suitable sponsor, it lacked the elaborate dark ride that would have served as a highlight of the version described in 1977. Here, the sea lord Poseidon would appear and challenge guests to brave the ocean depths, from the Continental Shelf to the Great Coral Reef. The destination, then as in 1986, was Sea Base Alpha, where guests would experience "an authentic ocean environment with live marine life, an undersea restaurant, and a showcase of oceanographic exhibits and displays."

This early version also contains an entirely separate attraction; guests would board the clipper ship *Spirit of Mankind*, "to sail through moments of peril and triumph with seven legendary mariners ... the great explorers who charted the seas for civilization."

Note, too, that the alternate concept for the pavilion's exterior, seen on page 147, was much more organic and roughly textured than the final design.

Compared to some of the other pavilions described in the 1977 report, the Energy pavilion presents a comfortingly familiar face. That angled, reflective wedge would survive the development process to become well-known to generations of Epcot visitors. What's funny, though, is that the park model shown earlier depicts an entirely different version of the Energy pavilion design – a semi-circular bank of mirrors facing a central solar collector. That design would be shown

MASTER PLAN 5, 1977   149

"PRACTICAL APPLICATIONS: The Energy Pavilion will feature demonstrations of solar energy applications." © Disney

Concept art by Herb Ryman shows a much different idea for the entrance to The American Adventure. © Disney

prominently in various EPCOT promotional films during 1978, but the competing concept shown in this rendering would win out in the end. Look closely, though, and you'll see some details shown here missing from the final design: various solar collectors, what appears to be a greenhouse, and a wind-powered turbine.

According to Disney, the Energy Pavilion would depict the formation of fossil fuel energy, "climaxed by a sudden energy storm of wind, lightning, rain, fire, and volcanic eruptions, demonstrating the almost endless potential of raw energy available for man." Guests would see how man overcame energy crises in the past, and the choices humanity faces today – "racing against the clock in a search for new energy, and finally harnessing tomorrow's vast new sources for 'The Future World of Energy.'"

While The American Adventure as described in 1977 sounds familiar, its show building certainly wasn't. Conceived as the "Gateway to World Showcase", the American pavilion would span the bridge between EPCOT's two areas. Instead of a Georgian mansion as found in the park today, the edifice proposed in 1977 was a circular modernist design.

This was seen as a symbolic representation of an America standing at a crossroads – facing both the future, embodied by Future World, as well as playing "host" to the nations of the world in World Showcase. The following quote, by Herman Melville, was cited by Disney as inspiration for The American Adventure:

> "America has been settled by the people of all nations, all nations may claim her for their own. We are not a narrow tribe of men ... No: our blood is as the flood of the Amazon, made up of a thousand noble currents all pouring into one. We are not a nation so much as a world..."

This was roughly the sixth concept pitched for the American pavilion, but it's similar to the show as it exists today. Famously, Will Rogers was slated to be the attraction's third host alongside Benjamin Franklin and Mark Twain, as a representative of the twentieth century. Fearing (sadly) that Rogers would be too obscure for audiences,

Unlike earlier proposed versions of World Showcase, the design revealed in Master Plan 5 featured highly-themed national pavilions encircling two large lagoons. © Disney

Imagineers eventually relieved him of his hosting role and relegated him to a cameo.

The show, said to take guests on a journey through "the remarkable three-century story of the American people, from the first step onto Plymouth Rock, to the first step onto the moon," was intended to present a sense of optimism for the future. It would show how Americans of the past dreamed of a better tomorrow and how the country, founded in liberty, "gives its citizens the opportunity and incentive to build on the great foundations of the past."

Despite having been in development longer than Future World, little is said in 1977 about World Showcase. This is most likely due to the unsuccessful scramble at the time to sign up national participants. Although this conception of World Showcase was rather optimistically designed to have two rows of countries, with plenty of room for several dozen national pavilions, in the end this was not to be.

The big breakthrough in Master Plan 5 was an idea that seems obvious today – that the national pavilions would be housed in separate buildings around the lagoon, and that they should all have highly themed exteriors to match their national sponsors. This plan was the brainchild of Imagineer Harper Goff, and it flew in the face of the original plans for World Showcase. Initially, national pavilions were to be housed adjacent to each other in very modernist, featureless, semi-circular structures. The pavilions would be well-themed on the inside, but to all outward appearances they would be identical.

Goff hated this idea, and envisioned a highly-themed area that would use well-known visual icons for each country, much like World Showcase does today. Try as he might, though, he couldn't get it past Card Walker. Goff knew he was right, and one day when a number of potential international sponsors and investors were to tour Imagineering, Goff made sure to leave a number of his elaborate paintings of the forbidden World Showcase concept lying around in plain sight. Needless to say, the money men were smitten with Goff's detailed and lush paintings and he won the argument by default.

Disney heralded this "exciting new concept" in the 1977 report, describing countries standing "side-by-side in friendship" around the lagoon. The lagoon itself would be "symbolic of the waters that bind together the diversified peoples of the world."

In this new "community of nations" would be found the "first permanent international exposition of its kind anywhere." Each pavilion would showcase the culture, history, tourism, and accomplishments of participating nations. "Here," said Disney, "guests will visit a wide variety of exciting shows and ride through attractions, restaurants, and shopping streets unique to the individual nations, and areas presenting travel and products of industry."

Disney often advertised World Showcase as a "people-to-people concept" where, as today, young adults from participating nations would travel to Florida to staff the various pavilions:

> And these young people will not only work together, they will also live, play, and learn together. Many of these young adults will be future leaders of their countries. Their association and work experience in EPCOT Center could be a significant step

toward generating greater understanding among the peoples of the world.

This is something that Card Walker mentioned often during these years – the hope that the international students coming to work at EPCOT would return as friends to lead their own nations. Walker often referred to his hopes that some day Israeli and Palestinian leaders, or U.S. presidents and Soviet premiers, could defuse global tensions as they reminisced about their days at EPCOT. It seems funny now, but it was a big part of how EPCOT was promoted in the 1970s.

EPCOT in 1977 feels for the first time like a fully-formed idea, and you can see the roots of many attractions that were to become fan favorites. Within the next year, Disney executives would commit to the idea, sponsors would come aboard, and throughout 1978 the idea of what Epcot Center was to be became clearer and more real. And it all started with Master Plan 5.

.18

IRAN SO FAR AWAY

It's January of 1978 and Disney is desperately trying to sign up governments to sponsor pavilions for World Showcase, which was still in the conceptual phase. Epcot Center's groundbreaking was still almost two years away, its development slowed by the inability to line up sponsorship deals. Later, Disney would give up on recruiting governmental participants entirely and go directly to individual corporations from desired nations for funding. But in 1978 Disney executives continued to wine and dine diplomats and envoys from around the world.

"Last weekend, Bob Allen and Carl Bongirno hosted Her Imperial Majesty Shahbanou Farah Pahlavi and her official party for a briefing and update on World Showcase. The Empress of Iran and her party visited the Magic Kingdom early Saturday evening before departing for a formal dinner on the *Empress Lilly* where she was joined by Governor and Mrs. Askew." ©Disney

And so here's the Empress of Iran in the Magic Kingdom, the mere fact of which is almost as entertaining as Minnie's little hat. Why'd she lose the hat? I think it works. Anyway, what the happy empress doesn't know is that in about a year she and her husband would be fleeing their country in the wake of Iran's Islamic Revolution.

Although it might seem bizarre today, Iran was a prime target for participation in World Showcase. Imagineers spent quite a lot of time designing a pavilion for Iran while shuttling back and forth to Tehran to seek the support of the Shah.

Renderings from the time are impressive; they depict a large, airy lobby of mirrored glass framing a pavilion entrance decorated with elaborate bas relief carvings drawn from ancient Persian architecture. Giant Assyrian winged bulls framed the entryway, while an enormous carpet draped from the ceiling to serve as a marquee was embroidered with the names Iran and Persia.

Imagineer Marty Sklar tells an amusing story of how he and Disney marketing maven Jack Lindquist had traveled to Iran to try and secure an official agreement for participation in World Showcase. They spent days sequestered in an opulent palace waiting for an audience with the Shah. They kept getting delayed, and delayed, and delayed by various royal underlings, but eventually they did get to do their presentation and it went very well. Iran seemed a lock for EPCOT's lineup.

The Imagineers came back to Glendale, happy with their success. But then almost immediately after their return came the aforementioned Islamic Revolution, the regime in Tehran crumbled, and for some reason the Ayatollahs were less willing to sponsor a theme park attraction.

So it goes…

.19

Ahead of the Curve

With the focus of the automotive world ever-so-slowly shifting towards more sustainable vehicles, and the increasing popularity of hybrid-electric vehicles, this news from Disney came as a welcome reminder of Walt Disney World's ambitious origins:

> About two months ago, Walt Disney World began participating in a special Electric Hybrid Vehicle Program with the federal government. This program involves using a special test vehicle in an area usually served by a gasoline powered vehicle... in this case a pickup truck operated by the Facilities area.

Welcome news indeed. Except for the fact that – oh wait – this news is from way back when in 1979. Oh, it's true.

With all the talk about how the entirety of Walt Disney World was intended as an extension of the EPCOT ideal, we've yet to look at any actual examples of Walt's futuristic ambitions that actually came to pass. But in the 1970s there were a number of cutting edge technologies put to use in the Vacation Kingdom, ranging from prototype transportation systems to innovations in the fields of communications and energy.

Energy, in particular, was of prime interest during this era; with the nation beset by a series of oil crises, Disney management worried that gasoline prices would continue to rise and lead to a permanent change in American vacation patterns. With a perceived threat to the future of the American road trip, a number of expansion plans for Walt Disney World's first decade were postponed or eliminated entirely.

Pedro Arcia and Larry Danielson, Walt Disney World Machine Shop Cast Members, examine the Electra-Van 1000P while thinking of new verses for "Convoy" incorporating references to fuel cell technology.
©Disney

While these fears would prove unfounded, they would lead to a number of intriguing energy conservation projects at the resort, many in concert with the United States Department of Energy. These included a solar power demonstration site at Disney's main energy production facility, as well as a pyrolysis plant intended to turn the resort's waste products into electricity.

Another of the collaborations with the federal government involved the use of these hybrid vehicles, decades before similar technology would hit the mainstream marketplace. Disney was one of hundreds of companies that expressed interest in participating in the program, and were one of the five selected alongside Consolidated Edison, Long Island Lighting Co., AT&T, and EHV Distribution Inc. The goal was to examine the use of hybrid technology under real-world conditions; after receiving the required specifications for testing, Disney decided that the pickup trucks used in maintenance areas would be a suitable venue to utilize the electric vehicles.

That sweet ride above is an Electra-Van 1000P – a Chrysler pickup converted to run on 24 six-volt lead acid batteries. According to a

Disney report from September 1979, the truck drove and handled "very much like a regular truck." "It has a three-speed shift," they added, "and an engine response similar to a gas-powered truck. The chief difference is obvious when you raise the hood to find it full of batteries … and not the engine."

The pilot, which lasted two months, was such a success that Disney agreed to buy twenty additional electric vehicles – fifteen pickups, three cargo vans, and, most impressively, three converted AMC Pacer Wagons!

It was a little slice of Progress City in the real world. "No waiting in line at gas stations for the owners of vehicles like this," said Disney at the time, "but beware the person who forgets to plug his truck in overnight!"

.20

Your Very Own WorldKey

The field of information and telecommunications was a critical element of the early plans for Walt Disney World and EPCOT, and another way that the resort helped introduce cutting-edge prototype systems in its early years. One of the very first corporate partners announced for the resort before it opened was RCA, which was to have sponsored an elaborate facility in Tomorrowland where guests could have viewed Walt Disney World's advanced digital telecom system at work.

This never happened, of course; RCA decided to get out of the computer business in 1971 and sold its computer division to Sperry – which, ironically, would become an Epcot Center sponsor several years later. But that's another story entirely. Disney stayed in the telecommunications business, creating its own telephone utility for Walt Disney World. Vista-United Telecommunications would be the first commercial telephone utility to provide fiber-optic service and to utilize buried cables, and it was the first phone system in Florida to offer 911 service.

For a young techie in the early 1980s, one of the many highlights of visiting Epcot Center was getting to use the WorldKey Information System. Developed by the Bell Labs in concert with Disney, the WorldKey was an interactive guidebook to the park, which guests could access from kiosks in both Future World and World Showcase. Video content highlighting the various pavilions was streamed over fiber optic cable from centrally located videodisc players, and guests could also connect via a live closed-circuit video system to Guest Relations hosts in order to make dining reservations or ask other questions. The simple, touch-screen interface seemed sleek and futuristic, and was the first time that most Epcot guests had probably experienced the now-commonplace technology.

Sadly, the WorldKey is now long-gone. Since its content was not generated dynamically, but instead had to be created by hand and recorded to videodisc, it was not easily updated or reprogrammed. Its content grew stale, with patchy latter-day additions painfully obvious, until it was removed. Planned upgrades, like the promised inclusion of French and German language options, were never realized.

Bell Labs, which had become AT&T soon after the park's opening, didn't give up on the idea so easily. Witness this ad, from February of 1986, for AT&T's Ariel system – the commercially available version of the WorldKey technology. It offered a "centralized source of information in a variety of public locations," and promised applications as diverse as "a tenant directory in office buildings, an entertainment guide in hotels, a product and service guide at retail locations, and a point-of-information terminal in financial service institutions."

AT&T's Ariel technology was originally developed by **AT&T Bell Laboratories** for Disney World's **EPCOT** Center as an experimental video information communication system to demonstrate new technologies in information retrieval.

All for the low, low price of $11,000! (Potted plants sold separately)
© AT&T

This truly is an example of the intended purpose of EPCOT – testing and prototyping new systems and technologies that would then be introduced to the free market. The Ariel system, released four years after WorldKey debuted, advanced the design and increased its flexibility. The 3B2/300 computer which sat at the heart of the system and provided centralized administration of Ariel terminals came onto the consumer market in 1985; it was a 32-bit UNIX-based system and was priced at around $10,000 for a model with 512K of RAM and a 10 megabyte hard drive, and $15,500 for the deluxe version with 1 megabyte of RAM and 32 megs of hard drive space. Networking hardware and software, of course, would cost a few thousand dollars extra. The 3B2 series would stay in production into the 1990s, and many remain in use today.

The 3B system could push new content and operating system updates to terminals, as well as conduct remote diagnostics and collect terminal usage data. Ariel terminals could also operate independently of their host, especially for applications that did not require frequent content updates.

If you wanted to set up your own home WorldKey installation, a stand-alone Ariel system 1500 unit would set you back $11,000; a network-enabled unit was $12,000. If you actually wanted to create your own content, you'd need an AT&T Frame Creation System Series 300/350, which was used to created graphic and video content – only $18,500!

What's funny, of course, is that the technology inside any given handheld device today would wipe the floor with the Ariel; technology has come so far that a high school student could probably whip up in a long weekend what most likely cost millions in 1982. This begs the question – where's today's version of the WorldKey?

.21

Welcoming Our New Go-Bot Overlords

One oft-repeated element of early Epcot Center lore is how, when the park opened in 1982, it was completely devoid of any of Disney's signature characters. Disney executives thought it important that the new theme park create its own unique identity, and feared that taking Mickey and the others outside the borders of the Magic Kingdom would dilute their impact and make that park less special. Instead, Disney hoped to rely on its stable of artists and Imagineers to create a whole new generation of Epcot-specific characters that could capture the imagination of young visitors and, of course, sell lots of merchandise.

This task was made easier when Journey Into Imagination was added to Future World's roster late in Epcot's development, as that attraction's host Dreamfinder and his pet dragon Figment would be highly sought photo opportunities for years to come. For World Showcase, it was decided to repurpose the eight-foot-tall "dolls" from the 1976 Bicentennial's America on Parade, and to dress them in various country-specific costumes. Needless to say, the effect was somewhat terrifying and these towering international golems didn't prove as endearing to children as Mickey and Donald. They were soon removed, and when new CEO Michael Eisner arrived in 1984 he mandated the addition of classic Disney characters into the park.

But what's widely unknown is that Disney's attempt to create Epcot characters went far beyond Dreamfinder and the Showcase dolls. In an internal Imagineering publication from January of 1983, cast members were allowed a sneak preview of Epcot's cuddly, robot future – The Go-Bots!

Go-Bot sketches by Imagineer Chris Runco. © Disney

Apparently recognizing the need for additional Epcot-specific characters, Imagineering held a contest among WED and MAPO employees to develop a "concept for a walk-around character with the charm of Mickey Mouse and the unique feeling of EPCOT Center." At the end of April 1982, thirty-seven designs were submitted from far and wide for "a new generation of Disney walk-around characters." As Disney pointed out at the time, this was no small task "considering that we were entering the last six months to our October opening day and time and imagination were at a premium."

The next January, WED's Creative Development Division announced that Imagineer Chris Runco from the Special Effects department had submitted the winning idea, which would be sent on to Walt Disney World's Entertainment department for further development. Chris also won a trip for two to – where else? – Epcot Center. Said Disney:

> Chris' idea was for a group of "Go-Bots" each with his or her own unique personality and each made of "squeezable" padded cloth and sponge rubber, with big molded plastic buttons. When the "Go-Bots" are hugged, patted, or otherwise interacting with guests, they would beep, buzz, or make "pocketa-pocketa"

sounds with electronic noisemakers controlled by the person inside. As Chris says, "my main thrust was to create a technological character as warm and as friendly as our Magic Kingdom Characters." The result – huggable "Go-Bots."

Spoiler alert: They never made the Go-Bots. Chris Runco, however, went on to have a long and illustrious career as an Imagineer, which continues to this day.

One side note - those of you who are, like me, children of the 1980s will remember Tonka's lame Transformers knock-off GoBots; they starred in a brief cartoon series and were sold in stores from 1983–87. Not very "squeezable", though.

.22

To GYRO and GERO in the Wabe

While Chris Runco's Go-Bots never made it to Epcot, park managers continued to seek out interactive entertainment to join the likes of Dreamfinder and Figment. Traditional Disney characters would remain completely absent from the park until 1984, but with its vast, open areas, Epcot Center still needed something happening to enliven the sprawling plazas between the pavilions.

Someone, apparently, also thought that it needed robots. Lots and lots of robots.

At the very beginning there was SICO, who appeared in Epcot Center's premiere television special in 1982. Created by International Robotics Inc. and its founder Robert Doornick, SICO appeared on the program to introduce hosts Danny Kaye and Drew Barrymore to Epcot's own Dreamfinder and Figment – an incident that encapsulates everything one really needs to know about 1980s television.

SICO wasn't under an exclusive contract to Disney, however; he went on to a memorable yet inexplicable appearance in 1985's *Rocky IV* and, bafflingly, guest starred for an *entire season* on the television soap opera *Days of Our Lives*. Disney needed their own robot and, with all high-profile androids apparently busy in major early-80s media projects, Epcot was forced in a pinch to go the organic route with the "robot" IB4E in early 1984.

Who, you might ask?

Early Epcot is fondly remembered for its legendary lineup of classic attractions, but even the most devout fan could be forgiven for being unaware of the short-lived entertainers "Mr. Intelligence" and "IB4E". This new comedy duo was introduced in the February 2nd,

The first production run of Bill Nye was a dismal failure. © Disney

1984 issue of *Eyes & Ears of Walt Disney World*, which described a fifteen-minute show that took place every half hour from 10:30 a.m. until 5 p.m., Saturday through Wednesday, on the bridge between Future World and World Showcase.

Mr. Intelligence was described as "a young, studious-looking chap, sporting the attire of a gentleman scientist – silver bow tie-and-vest, pinstripe pants and lab coat." Take note, in case you ever become a "gentleman scientist" and need to know what to wear. IB4E, on the other hand, was said to be "a lovely young lady with the frozen pose of an android."

It does, perhaps, sound a touch creepy in retrospect:

> *The fun begins when "Mr. Intelligence" puts his pretty "robot" creation through her paces. The "robot", named IB4E (i before e, get it?), then engages in a number of delightful demonstration exercises "programmed" by "Mr. Intelligence" via a remote*

GYRO greets Epcot guests. © Disney

control device filled with colorful, blinking lights: Waving "hello", walking, shaking hands ... even flirting!

Later, "Mr. Intelligence" selects a youngster from the audience to help operate IB4E. The youthful volunteer unwittingly programs IB4E to snatch purses and unleash a physical attack on "Mr. Intelligence" himself!

If you have to explain the pun, it's not worth it.

In any case, these shenanigans apparently bought Disney enough time to create a real robot, as GYRO made his debut at Epcot Center in 1985.

"What's 4 feet 10, weighs a portly 150 lbs., has a blue body, and a golden head encasing a computerized brain that controls its electronic senses?" asked *Disney News* in fall 1985. The answer was GYRO, "the very latest in electronic robots." GYRO made the rounds in Future World, conversing with guests in a "robotic" voice.

(One thing that amuses me about GYRO is that he's always seen wearing one of those military-style Epcot caps that they used to sell in the Centorium. In the old Epcot catalogues you could get them either with or without "scrambled eggs" on the brim; I was strangely fascinated with this terminology when I was a kid. But I digress…)

After GYRO came GERO, the "G.E. Robot", and perhaps the best known of Epcot's "walkaround" droids. Unlike GYRO, who wandered throughout Future World, GERO is most closely associated with Horizons and its sponsor General Electric; he could be found in the vicinity of the pavilion's exit area riding around on his large custom scooter and interacting with guests.

GERO was conceived to address a problem that General Electric often expressed in the early years of its Horizons sponsorship; namely, that guests weren't associating the company with the blockbuster attraction that it had underwritten. The creation of a "G.E. Robot" with which people could interact would reinforce the company's link to Horizons, as well as adding an additional draw to the pavilion and helping to create a friendly, warm public face for the company.

"GERO" was the early favorite for the new robot's name, as it met the desired criteria of identifying G.E. as the sponsor as well as being memorable yet not too cutesy. While GERO was the top recommended name, other proposed options included GENIUS, GENIE, RND, PROTEUS, and, amazingly, G. ERNEST NEWBY.

In the summer of 1986, Imagineer Tom Fitzgerald wrote a story for *Disney News* entitled *Disney's Exotic, Robotic Cast*. Fitzgerald mentioned several notable Epcot robots, from *The Bird and the Robot*'s Tiger to Jason from The Living Seas and SMRT-1 from CommuniCore, but his focus is on the debut of GERO, the "most sophisticated robot to join the Epcot Center cast." In fact, General Electric's Dave Fink claimed that GERO was "probably the most sophisticated

GERO bares his soul. © Disney

entertainment robot in the world." Fitzgerald himself felt certain that the robot was "destined to become one of Epcot's most beloved characters."

As Fitzgerald told it, GERO's design began at Walt Disney Imagineering, based on inspirational artwork and sketches by Disney Legend X. Atencio. Designer Gil Keppler refined the robot's look, adding details to give it "a machined, hi-tech look". The result, according to the article, was "a fun-loving, friendly teen-ager – complete with a sporty scooter with room for riders!"

Imagineering artisans sculpted the robot in plaster, and then shipped it to Walt Disney World for fabrication. GERO's body was crafted from Lexan, a polycarbonate thermoplastic formerly manufactured by General Electric, and the same material used to fabricate the Horizons ride vehicles. In this way, GERO and his sister attraction were shaped from the same material.

GERO's exterior was finished up with a metallic silver and gold paint job, and his battery-powered scooter was painted a sporty red. Meanwhile, his innards were being assembled by scientists and technicians at the General Electric Research & Development Center in Schenectady, New York. Said Fitzgerald:

> Included in the 900-pound mountain of electronics are linear stepping motors, field effect transistor brakes, pulse-width modulated drives, incremental optical shaft encoder, fiber optics, laser disc player, 160 watts of biamped audio power and nine batteries – all controlled by 19 microcomputers!

The four-feet-tall GERO was able to operate for up to eight hours on a single charge of his nine lead-acid batteries. His scooter was roughly six feet long and thirty inches wide, and could reach a top speed of four miles per hour while carrying a 200 pound passenger, or group of small passengers (a function envisioned for use in parades). GERO's typical speed when interacting with guests ranged from a slow creep up to 1.5 mph.

Controlled by an operator dressed as a tourist and concealed within the surrounding crowd, GERO was highly maneuverable. Each of his scooter's three wheels had a computer-controlled drive motor, allowing for precise steering and control; it could even rotate in place. GERO himself could move at the waist and neck, tilt his head, and had articulated shoulders, elbows, and wrists. His large eyes featured more than 200 controlled fiber-optic lights that could convey a range of emotions.

Complicated, coordinated movements were pre-programmed into his onboard computers, allowing GERO to be controlled by a simple

wireless device concealed in his operator's pocket. This allowed for a wide variety of possible interactions, such as shaking hands, waving, pointing, or driving his scooter. Many of these were hard-coded into his programming to simplify operation; for instance, if his scooter started moving beyond a slow crawl, his hands would automatically return to the handlebars and his eyes would track the direction of the vehicle. The operator could, in turn, override these built-in commands to allow for spontaneous interactions with guests.

GERO's operator also provided the robot's voice, speaking through a microphone concealed in his hand. The speech was then altered by synthesizer to create an electronic voice that was still intelligible. An onboard CD audio system provided additional sound effects, background music, and a pre-recorded singing voice for when GERO conducted his guests in a sing-along.

But who *was* GERO? Who was the man behind the circuits? Described as witty, and as sharp as any educated adult, his personality was liked by Fitzgerald to "that of a bright, polite, well-brought-up teenager." He was never mean or stooped to "insult-humor"; he was helpful but not abrasive; he liked small children and was respectful to adults.

GERO even came with a detailed biography, full of electronic puns. Born in lower Manhattan (near the Battery), he went on to attend "Particles Elementary School", "Junior High-draulics", and "Tech High" before enrolling at "Solid State". His father was an engineer and a general (General Electric), and was descended from Newton, Copernicus, and Archimedes. His mother was a mathematician and a major (a major appliance), and claimed Benjamin Franklin, Michael Faraday, Thomas Edison, and "Cousin Charlie Steinmetz" among her family tree.

All of GERO's family worked for G.E. His sister, the brightest member of the family, worked in the lamp business. His brother worked in microwaves, and another sister was a robot on the G.E. jet engine assembly line (a steady job, it was said, but she didn't get out much).

GERO holds court amongst his admirers. © Disney

Among GERO's interests were science and math, and the three R's: "reading, riting, and robotics". It was claimed "he was very much into electronics even before electronics were into him." He was working his way through school doing opinion-research polling, and hoped to grow up to be R4-D4 – that is, R2-D2, "only twice as well paid".

As for likes and dislikes, he always enjoyed reading the G.E. Annual Report, and liked to eat chips – "but only a byte or two at a time". He didn't care for long lines or short circuits, or being overcharged, but he was a fan of G.E., Horizons, the future, singing, and Mickey Mouse.

While their memory is mostly lost to history, GYRO and GERO received commemoration in a very unlikely place – Innoventions at Disneyland. During a 2009 visit, I was shocked to come across these Epcot friends in a series of pictures showing robots from Disney's past. In the display were animated robots from various Mickey and Donald cartoons, GARCO from *Wonderful World of Color*, and, shockingly, GYRO and GERO.

These long-ago efforts are the root of so many things we see in the Disney parks today – from talking trash cans and water fountains to Lucky the Dinosaur and other creations. But remember, as Walt always said, it all started with SICO.

.23

Tomorrow's Windows

For those who love the Epcot Center that once was, nothing better conveyed the themes of that park than Horizons. Other Future World pavilions examined individual topics, but it was Horizons that tied them all together to show how advances in those fields would lead to better lifestyles in the future. Horizons represented a thesis statement for the park, and of all the pavilions it best evoked the ethos of Walt Disney's own vision for EPCOT. For this reason and many others, not the least of which were the ride's technological wizardry, style, and humor, Horizons remains beloved to fans long after its closure.

Horizons' roots go back to at least 1958 when Walt and his Imagineers proposed an expansion to Disneyland called Edison Square. Although never built, the concept evolved into the Carousel of Progress, which debuted at the New York World's Fair in 1964.

By the time of Epcot Center's groundbreaking in October 1979, the only committed sponsors for the park were G.M., Exxon, and Kraft. Talks were underway with General Electric, which had continued to sponsor the Carousel of Progress after it moved to the Magic Kingdom in 1975. In late 1979, G.E. announced they would sponsor a pavilion called "Science and Invention".

G.E. hoped the new pavilion would show how their products could improve guests' lives. Their slogan at the time was "we bring good things to life", and that's what they wanted for the new show – something forward looking and progressive. G.E. advisors thought it critical to emphasize that the future will provide individuals many options for how to lead their lives.

The designers assigned to the pavilion in 1979 were George McGinnis and Collin Campbell, who proposed something called the "Edison Lab". Much like the old Edison Square plans, this would have looked back at Thomas Edison and the origins of G.E., before surveying the company's technological feats over the years.

This concept was rejected by Reginald Jones, then the chairman of G.E. As Marty Sklar would later say, "They told us our idea stunk." The sponsor wanted something forward looking and spectacular; in their words, the new show "must not dwell on the past, it must be dedicated to the future." With a mandate that "the future should be exciting and thus the G.E. presentation should be a ride – a thrilling ride – to and through an exciting tomorrow", the Imagineers returned to the drawing board.

Several G.E. team members had worked with Disney since the World's Fair, and after some feedback the idea emerged to make the pavilion a follow-up to the Carousel of Progress. Whereas that show followed a family from the 1890s to the present, the new attraction would start with a humorous look at the futurism of yesteryear before meeting up with the Carousel family in the next century – following them into a world of space colonies, undersea cities, and desert farms.

Family was important to the Horizons story. McGinnis said at the time, "We kept 'people' details in mind, too. We're convinced that even though environments will change, people won't. Teenagers in our show still monopolize the phone; kids and dogs still exasperate mom and dad. We believe one of the main differences high technology will make is that it will give us more choices."

Early designs were hashed out by a large team from both Imagineering and G.E., including McGinnis, Campbell, and Claude Coates. Coates, who took an early pass on many Epcot attractions, served first as show designer, before later turning over the role to McGinnis. It was also Coates, along with architect Bill Norton and industrial designer Bob Kurzweil, who hammered out the preliminary layout for the attraction. After the design team determined the final storyline and layout, writer Tom Fitzgerald honed the narrative to add

Horizons art director George McGinnis examines a model of the attraction's iconic "Omnisphere" centerpiece. © Disney

humanizing detail to the overarching themes established by McGinnis, Sklar, and John Hench.

Ned Landon, a thirty-year G.E. veteran, joined the team as the company's representative in 1979. As sponsor, General Electric did more than just cut a check; several of its divisions contributed technical expertise in relevant areas. Advice ran the gamut from pavilion lighting and what a kitchen of the future might look like, to input from the Medical Systems division on how diagnostic equipment might be used in outer space.

The contributions didn't end there. Ride vehicles, made from Lexan polycarbonate, were operated with G.E. motors and drive systems. The company provided everything from wiring to transformers, infrared control systems to mobile radio applications. A G.E.-made robot, combined with their "Gemlink" video transmitter system, provided a live aerial view of the park to the pavilion's corporate lounge.

The pavilion was originally to be called "Century 3"; with America fresh off the excitement of the 1976 bicentennial, the pavilion intended to show what America could achieve in its third century.

From a 1980 press release:

> *The Century 3 Pavilion, presented by General Electric, will celebrate the envisioned technological achievements of America's third century ... the years of the 21st Century leading to the U.S. Tricentennial in 2076 ... and what these advances will mean to each of our lives.*
>
> *Visitors to the pavilion will see the ever-expanding opportunities and choices for tomorrow's world ... and the important role their decisions will play in making those visions come true in Century 3.*

Imagineers eventually realized that "Century 3" might prove cryptic to foreign visitors; Landon said that "the allusion to our own nation's history seemed too parochial." When G.E. finally signed on in October 1980, the name of the pavilion had been changed to Future Probe.

Renderings of the pavilion's exterior from 1980 appear indistinguishable from the building's final gemlike design by architect George Rester. The pavilion was called Futureprobe as late as April 1981, when it was decided that another renaming was in order. As Ned Landon famously said about the Futureprobe name, "We always thought it had a rather uncomfortable medical connotation." Several new titles were proposed, including "Great Expectations", but in late 1981 the team settled on Horizons. As Landon would go on to say, "We thought Horizons was just right. There always is a horizon out there. If you try hard enough, you can get to where it is – and when you do, you find there's still another horizon to challenge you, and another beyond that."

Site work on Horizons began August 5th, 1981; construction commenced in January 1982 with opening day scheduled for October 1st, 1983. The show's specifications were daunting; with a ride time of 14 minutes 35 seconds, Horizons featured 35 scenes in its three-acre show building. Its 1,346-foot track could carry 2,660 guests per hour past the show's 49 audio-animatronic figures, 17 sets, 583 props, 456 plants, and 110 lighting effects which required 177 miles of fiber optics. The 78-foot high pavilion needed 3,700 tons of structural steel to enclose its 137,000 square feet of show space.

A trip aboard Horizons began in the FuturePort – a transportation hub of tomorrow. Kaleidoscopic travel posters, using artwork by futurist Robert McCall, depicted potential destinations. There was the magnificent floating resort of Sea Castle in the Pacific Ocean; Mesa Verde, a flourishing city reclaimed from the desert; and Brava Centauri, the latest of the Centauri class of space stations.

The FuturePort, designed by Gil Keppler, also featured the pavilion's theme song – "New Horizons", by George Wilkins. Legendary songwriters Richard and Robert Sherman were originally assigned to write the ride's theme, but their compositions were never used. One example, for Century 3 in June 1980, was entitled "Tomorrow's Windows". In October of that year, they wrote "Tomorrow is the Rainbow"; it seems to have also been called "New Horizons". Another, "Reach for New Horizons", circulates amongst fans; several versions are known to exist.

Ultimately, the Shermans' material was rejected by G.E., who desired something that felt more fresh. They thought the songs seemed like traditional Disney fare, which was incongruous with their mandate for the show.

Aboard the attraction, on "Horizons Flight 83", riders sat four abreast in a unique variant of the time-tested Omnimover. Unlike other rides, Horizons' vehicles faced only the left side of the track as, hanging from an overhead rail, they moved horizontally through the attraction. The ride's soundtrack, recorded digitally, was transmitted to receivers in each vehicle via infrared light.

After Mission Control signaled that "Horizons One" was ready to depart for the twenty-first century, a pair of narrators chimed in over the in-car loudspeakers to promise a look at the future, complete with desert farms, floating cities, and colonies in space. Passengers then entered a "time travel" tunnel designed by WED Special Effects

Manager Dean Sharits. Layers of hand-sculpted, sandblasted acrylic clouds concealed and diffused 22,000 points of shifting colored light – an effect requiring forty miles of fiber optic cable.

Horizons' first act, "Looking Back at Tomorrow", examined the future through the eyes of past visionaries. Said Tom Fitzgerald, "The technologies that men like Verne and Wells envisioned were 100 years ahead of their time, but the designs remained rooted in their own time." These scenes were developed by Campbell and McGinnis before McGinnis became the attraction's show designer. A series of projections resembling woodcut illustrations introduced the concept; here was the Icarus of ancient legend, a man flying with the assistance of caged birds, Verne's own ship to the moon, and other improbable aviation schemes from antiquity.

Verne appeared next, aboard his ballistic craft from 1865's *From the Earth to the Moon*. Seemingly ill-prepared for zero gravy, the author's pet dog and an uncaged chicken floated freely in his lavishly-appointed Victorian spacecraft. Verne succeeds in reaching the moon, in a gag referencing the story's 1902 film adaptation by Georges Méliès.

The whimsical Paris of 1950 as envisioned by French author and illustrator Albert Robida (1848–1926) came next. Robida's future was a busy place; the sky filled with soaring craft shaped like fish or birds, while streams of nattily-attired tourists boarded "les Tubes" – air-propelled cylinders providing mass transit service to Madrid.

Around the corner appeared a vision more distinctly American – the Art Deco future of the 1930s and 40s, where easy living was guaranteed via automatic labor and push-button convenience. A leisurely gent stood, long-stemmed cigarette at his side, gazing out the window at an atomic-powered metropolis while a robotic butler vacuumed behind him. Above, a fashionable blonde soaked contentedly in a bubble bath as she watched television – a mammoth, black-and-white model which bore a close resemblance to the radios of the era. Onscreen, a dapper fellow in a tuxedo crooned an adaptation of the classic Disney anthem "There's a Great, Big Beautiful Tomorrow".

Disney Legend Wathel Rogers programs the Jules Verne animatronic for his flight to the moon. © Disney

Originally penned by Richard and Robert Sherman for the Carousel of Progress in 1964, "There's a Great, Big Beautiful Tomorrow" had long since been replaced in that attraction by another composition when Horizons opened. Even after the song returned to the Carousel of Progress in 1994, its inclusion in Horizons remained a sly nod to Disney history. As performed by actor Larry Cedar, the Horizons adaptation was a pastiche of big band–era crooners.

The Art Deco scene also featured two of Horizons' best-remembered visions of retro-futurism. An older gentleman relaxing in a recliner received a haircut and shoeshine from robotic arms, while he enjoyed a tropical breeze from a device that could recreate everything from balmy trade winds to arctic gusts. A sunlamp overhead was adjustable to provide tans from Hawaii, the Bahamas, or Florida.

Unnoticed, in the kitchen, was a glimpse at how the conveniences of the future might not prove foolproof; a robotic chef had gone haywire and was wreaking havoc. As the smiling automaton's head spun wildly around, its many arms flailed at stacks of dirty dishes and ruined food. The only beneficiary of this chaos was the cat of the house, who lapped happily at the constantly-replenishing pool of spilt milk on the floor.

The next "look back at tomorrow" came through the films of the past. Black-lit theatre marquees, giving the appearance of multicolored neon, advertised science fiction films from the early years of cinema – *Metropolis* (1927), *Things to Come* (1936), and *Modern Times* (1939) were among those featured. As stylized theater marquees gave way to mid-century ranch houses and television aerials, 1930s sci-fi was replaced by televised futurism of the 1960s as seen in Disney's Ward Kimball–produced *Mars and Beyond* and *Magic Highway USA*.

The Neon City's visual style – dark ride techniques of fluorescent paint lit by ultraviolet lamps – continued in a scene depicting the "future from the 50s". The far-out panorama represented a jet-age futurism familiar from *The Jetsons*, complete with personal hovercraft and rocket packs.

This scene's minimalist look owed to budget cuts late in Horizons' development; early plans called for fully dimensional sets and animatronics, but it was decided to instead use black-lit wire frames to save money. These savings were somewhat offset, though, when John Hench decreed that the scene wasn't using its allocated space well. Hench thought the cavernous area needed a large spire to draw the eye upward, and so the towering "Sky High School" was constructed to use the full height of the building.

Leaving the past behind them, Horizons passengers then entered the Omnisphere for a look at cutting-edge technologies of the current day – circa 1983. To create this most memorable element of the attraction, Imagineers placed two Omnimax screens together for the first time anywhere to create a massive projection surface 240 feet wide and 80 feet high.

The idea of using an IMAX screen in Horizons was first raised by Imagineer Dave Burke. Marty Sklar, then Executive Vice President for Creative Development at WED, brought the concept to McGinnis and

The Horizons Omnimax screens under construction. © Disney

asked him to incorporate it into the attraction. McGinnis, who had tinkered with curved Omnimax screens for a previous unproduced project, selected that process instead. McGinnis's original plans called for the Omnisphere – formed by three adjacent screens – to serve as the ride's grand finale; it was later moved to the attraction's midpoint by the story team.

Filmmaker Eddie Garrick was in charge of shooting the Omnimax scenes. Using 70mm film, he captured subjects ranging from undersea divers to a space shuttle launch. When the equipment required to film other desired subjects did not exist, Garrick and his team helped design the necessary technology themselves. The result was innovative in several ways; the spiraling DNA chain and the wireframe space station represented the first use of computer animation in an Omnimax film. The micro-photography of growing crystals was another Omnimax first, as was the computer-enhanced Landsat satellite photography.

A booming score by George Wilkins rounded out the experience, with synthesizer work by Michael Boddicker and a grandiose solo on the pipe organ by Richard Bolks. For added kick, low-frequency sonic transducers were placed in ride vehicles near the base of each passenger's spine to add a rumbling effect during the film's space shuttle launch.

The ride reached its maximum height of 65 feet in the Omnisphere, placing guests at the "sweet spot" for viewing in the center of the screen. With walls three feet thick, the enormous theater was the largest single element of the pavilion and its placement greatly determined architect George Rester's final design for the building.

In Claude Coates's original layout for the attraction, vehicles were to approach the Omnisphere by rising along a spiraling track past a montage of artwork from pulp science-fiction magazines. McGinnis and Campbell researched these publications at the University of Redlands Science Fiction Library, and had a wealth of material from which to draw. The plan was for riders to enter the Omnisphere on the second floor where, surrounded by three screens, they would make two complete downward circuits around a central column before exiting. On the ground floor once more, vehicles would rise back to the second floor and enter the third act of the show.

During development, the Horizons team was asked to cut $10 million from the project's budget. One of the three Omnimax screens was eliminated, as was 600 feet of ride track comprising the upward and downward track spirals. In the final ride, vehicles rose to the second floor via one single, 90-second pass of two Omnimax screens. The pulp magazine montage was removed, and that space was instead used for the "future from the fifties" scene.

Imagineers John Hench, Tori Atencio, Kathy Knutson, and George McGinnis gather 'round the "symphosizer" as they celebrate the completion of the "Urban Habitat" scene. It was the first of the Horizons show scenes to be finished and approved for installation. © Disney

The third act of Horizons, "Tomorrow's Windows", jumped ahead to showcase life in the 21st century. While the future suggested by the Omnisphere might seem fantastic, the narrators assured that it wasn't science fiction; after all, they said, they lived there.

The tour of the future began in the "Urban Habitat" – home to the attraction's unnamed narrators. The ride's story shifted here to the family; Tom Fitzgerald said at the time, "We wanted to emphasize the family unit. Some people think that it may not exist in the future, but our feeling was that advances in transportation and communication will bring families closer together." Of course it's no coincidence that the narrator and his family strongly resembled the cast of the Carousel of Progress – right down to the familiar family dog.

The Nova Cite apartment overlooked soaring skyscrapers and swooping maglev trains. Our host, playing a tune on his "symphosizer", welcomed guests while his wife conversed with their daughter on the holographic telephone. After passing through the couple's hydroponic garden (designed, by the way, so that it could actually work in the real world), the next stop was the desert farm of Mesa Verde where the narrators' daughter and her family lived.

As riders entered the citrus grove, a puff of scented air was blown towards the track by the Imagineering "smellitzer" scent cannon. The rich perfume of oranges brought the desert orchard to life and quickly became a hallmark of the attraction. To this day, fans continue to track down the elusive chemical formula from its original manufacturer in an attempt to evoke – if ever so slightly – the Horizons experience.

Mesa Verde, once desert, had been converted into a lush oasis thanks to advanced technology. Fields of generically engineered citrus stretched into the distance, monitored by the woman previously seen via hologram. Robotic harvesters farmed the fields in the background, while helium lifters loaded the crops for transport to market. The scene, developed by Claude Coates, used forced perspective to great effect in making the small show space appear to be a vast desert.

The technologies depicted, fantastic though they seemed, were developed with the help of expert consultants. Said McGinnis, "Both Disney and G.E. were anxious to show that desert, sea, and space could be interesting and practical places to live and work. We got some concepts and models together and tried them out on the experts." Assisting with the desert farm was Dr. Carl Hodges, founder of the Environmental Research Laboratory at the University of Arizona, and a key advisor on Epcot's The Land pavilion.

Alex Taylor created the genetically engineered plants and trees that occupied the farm, although at first he encountered some difficulties. "Every time I designed something I thought was totally new, I would take it over to our horticulturists and they would tell me it

Imagineer Alex Taylor shows off a batch of Flavor Grapes and a hybrid Pinana. © Disney

already existed," said Taylor. "I began to despair of coming up with something nature hadn't already done." Eventually he got the hang of it. Perhaps his most famous creation was the "Lorange", an elongated hybrid citrus fruit engineered to grow on the outside of the tree for easier harvesting. There were also "Pepcumbers" (a red pepper/cucumber hybrid), "Flavor Grapes" (clusters of multicolored grapes with different flavors), Siamese Apples (a "triple apple"), and Pinanas (a pineapple/banana hybrid). Said Taylor, "I designed a whole bunch of different kinds of these vegetables and then invited people in to look at them and decide which ones looked good enough to eat."

Inspiration came from many directions. From the electric eel came the idea for the "Golden Glow"; from an ancient musical instrument came the "Aeolian Harp", which produced music from passing breezes. The kinked patterns of the circuit board inspired "Circuit Egg Ivy".

Explained Taylor, "Carl Hodges told me that using the principles of genetic engineering, I could let my imagination run wild, and I did."

Back at Mesa Verde, the farmer has received a video call from her husband to warn that a storm is approaching. Passing her personal hovercraft, guests found the couple's desert home tucked into a natural landscape among desert rocks and a garden of tropical flowers. By a waterfall's pool, a housecat pawed hopefully, yet unsuccessfully, at a jumping fish.

The habitat, with its glass floors and large windows, was designed and detailed by Gil Keppler, who had also helped McGinnis design the desert farm's control room. In the kitchen, the man of the house was trying to decorate an elaborate birthday cake, but his son seemed more interested in misdirecting the voice-activated cabinets. Meanwhile, a teenaged girl in the next room was supposed to be doing her chemistry homework (on her "Athene 2500" microcomputer) but, to her grandfather's chagrin, she's actually talking to her boyfriend on an enormous wall-sized videophone. The boyfriend, whom the narrator pejoratively refers to as a "beach boy", is studying marine biology on a floating city; his girlfriend's main concern seemed to be his potential tardiness for the upcoming family festivities. Tom Fitzgerald portrayed the boyfriend on film; the ride's designers dubbed his animatronic counterpart in the next scene "Tom II".

Slowly descending, riders entered the undersea world of Sea Castle. In the "solosub" bay, Tom II worked to repair a single-passenger submarine while chatting with his girlfriend. On the deck below, a class of young children – and their pet seal Rover – impatiently prepared for a diving expedition as their teacher reviewed the safety rules one last time. Two of the students were modeled on show designer McGinnis's own children; Scott (then 5) appeared as the boy getting licked by the seal and Shana (7) became the young blonde girl who sat tapping her toes impatiently.

Outside the floating city, in a scene detailed by Tom Scherman, residents could be seen enjoying dinner through a row of bubble-shaped windows. The young divers from the classroom then re-appeared, swimming underneath the vast city in a projected effect. As the narrators touted the wealth of riches available in our oceans, riders passed robots harvesting manganese nodules and kelp from the seafloor.

Horizons' final destination was space station Brava Centauri. Originally, a special effect designed by Don Iwerks was to bridge sea and space; the submarines of Sea Castle and shuttles of Brava Centauri were designed with similar profiles, allowing for a projected submarine to morph into a space pod as viewers transitioned between the two scenes. Ultimately, the projector built for the effect proved susceptible to the vibrations of passing ride vehicles, rendering the concept impractical.

Once in orbit, construction workers were seen building a series of stations that rotated in the distance. Consulting on their design was Princeton physicist Gerard K. O'Neill, a staunch advocate for space colonization and designer of the "O'Neill Cylinder", on which the designs for Brava Centauri were heavily based. Inside the colony, past the airlock and shuttle bay, was a zero-g gymnasium where station inhabitants could exercise in rowing or bicycling simulators, or perhaps enjoy a game of low-gravity basketball. Outside a long, windowed tunnel rotated the interior of the cylindrical colony. An eight-foot spherical model was built for this effect, which was filmed from inside with a 19mm Kowa lens. It required 8,000 miniature lights to bring life to Shim Yokoyama's painting of the homes, green space, and recreational facilities of the station interior. Sharp-eyed guests might have even noticed a hidden Disneyland among the station's features.

In the next scene, the shuttle *Santa Maria* had arrived in the docking port and its passengers were adjusting with some difficulty to their new habitat. As little Tommy floated around the room with his dog Napoleon, his father tried to retrieve the child's stray magnetic boots. Meanwhile, the family's baggage had slowly started to drift away. Tom Fitzgerald's story team had proposed adding the family to introduce warmth to the scene; young Tommy was modeled after McGinnis's son Reed, then 5.

Input from NASA and the Jet Propulsion Laboratory inspired a facility where giant crystals grew in microgravity, but riders could not linger – it was time for a party. Everyone had gathered to wish a happy birthday to the narrators' grandson, living with his parents on the space colony. Appearing via holophone were the narrators, their granddaughter from Mesa Verde, and her "beach boy" boyfriend. Always a stickler for authenticity, Disney actually had to pay the copyright holder for the rights to the song "Happy Birthday to You".

In the pavilion's early design process, a show writer at WED named Marc Nowadnick had developed a post-show area called "Future-Fair" to highlight G.E. products and services. Jack Welsh, who had become chair of G.E., actually vetoed the idea of a post-show because, remarkably, he thought it seemed too commercial. The post-show's $28 million budget was instead funneled into the ride itself.

One proposal for the post-show was for a tunnel through which guests would pass on a moving belt. Inside, they would be followed by images highlighting the businesses that comprised the G.E. empire. The concept was inspired by journal articles McGinnis had read describing the projection of advertisements in subway tunnels alongside moving trains. Having studied the mechanics of synchronizing projections to ride vehicles, McGinnis salvaged his idea when the story team moved his Omnisphere finale to the ride's midpoint. Sklar asked McGinnis for a new ending, so the idea from the rejected post-show was adapted into Horizons' famous "Choose Your Tomorrow" sequence.

It was originally proposed to use the ride's finale to poll guests on various issues about their future, but G.E. rejected that idea. Claiming they could just as easily get meaningful polling data from surveying a small sample of guests as they exited, they decided instead to use the interactive technology to allow guests to select the ride's finale. After leaving Brava Centauri, "Horizons One" passengers were to return home via transportation of their own choosing.

Marty Kindel took McGinnis's idea for moving projections and developed it into a 50-foot-long traveling picture that, combined with

The massive Mesa Verde model, rigged for filming with its custom camera gantry in a hangar at the Burbank Airport. © Disney

tilting vehicles and low-frequency vibrations, provided a primitive simulator experience. Riders chose one of three destinations via a console in their vehicle; the result with the most votes would be the return route to the FuturePort. Options included a hovercraft flight over the desert, a solosub from Sea Castle, and an intercolony shuttle to Omega Centauri. Plans originally included a fourth film, a maglev train ride through Nova Cite, but that was scrapped.

Special effects veteran Dave Jones, who had worked on *Star Wars*, spent two years designing, constructing, and filming the miniature

Artist Robert McCall with his masterpiece, *The Prologue and the Promise*, in his Arizona studio. © Disney

sets. According to Jones, the desert film was the longest continuous sequence ever done with miniatures, and required an 86-foot model – all for 31 seconds of video. Disney's ACES computer-guided motion control camera provided the precise camera movements needed, and a special gantry was built so that the camera wouldn't cast a shadow on the model as it filmed. The desert scene was staged in an enormous hangar at the Burbank airport, while the space sequence was shot on Soundstage 3 at the Disney lot. The undersea scene was shot dry; smoke was blown onto the set to create the illusion of oceanic haze.

The 35mm films were transferred to videodisc and rear projected onto screens in-ride with G.E. Talaria PJ-5055 light-valve video projectors. These projectors were capable of the resolution needed to project large video images on screens close to the viewer. Concerned about visual intrusion from neighboring vehicles' films, G.E. team members requested that flaps be added between ride vehicles.

After riders unloaded, they originally passed by an enormous 19-by-60 foot mural by renowned artist Robert McCall. McCall, who had done conceptual artwork for *2001: A Space Odyssey* and *The Black Hole*, spent three months at his Arizona studio developing the concept, which he called "The Prologue and the Promise". This was followed by six months at the Disney studio in Burbank painting the actual mural with the help of his wife Louise, finishing in March of 1983. McCall originally created a sketch of his idea, and then a 10-foot master image. This was sectioned off into one-inch grid squares, which were projected onto a large canvas to allow McCall to create a perfectly scaled final image.

According to McCall, the mural represented the "flow of civilized man from the past into the present and toward the future." The result was spectacular – a vast panorama of human achievement beginning with prehistory and culminating in a towering space-age metropolis. Unfortunately, exit polls showed that guests weren't associating sponsor G.E. with the attraction, and McCall's masterpiece was replaced just a few short years after its debut. In its place was a rainbow-lit, mirrored hallway leading to a G.E. logo, casting off sparks as it rotated behind a giant lens.

G.E. eventually abandoned the pavilion it helped create when its sponsorship ended on September 30th, 1993. Horizons continued to operate without a sponsor, but with no one coming forward to fund a much-needed refurbishment, the pavilion closed in late 1994. Thought was given to converting the building into a new space-based attraction, but Disney balked at the cost. Horizons re-opened in December 1995, after delays pushed back the new Test Track attraction's opening, and it continued to operate until it entertained its last guest on the 9th of January, 1999. The pavilion remained intact until March of 2000; it was then slowly emptied and demolished over the span of several months.

While Horizons is now long gone, its memory lives on in generations of fans – some of whom were never even able to experience it in person. It lives on in countless online tributes, fan-produced videos, and homemade t-shirts. Most importantly, it lives on in a vision of the future that, regardless of outdated color schemes or polyester outfits, remains just as distant, elusive, and inspiring as it was in 1983.

V.
The Wonderful Weird of Disney

.24

Little Orange Memories

The longer one is a fan of anything, the more likely they are to pine for past glories, and those of us interested in the history of the ever-fluid theme park industry are no different. Wonders large and small have been lost over the years, and the Disney parks are no exception to this wistful truth.

The Orange Bird used to belong squarely in the realm of the obscure. Designed by Disney as a mascot for their sponsorship deal with the Florida Citrus Growers, Orange Bird dominated Adventureland with his citrusy presence in the 1970s but had mostly disappeared in the park by the time Epcot Center opened.

He remained nearly forgotten until he began to appear on merchandise at Tokyo Disneyland – a park where he had never been featured during his glory days – after the turn of the 21st century. As the Disney online community grew, his existence became known to more recent fans, and the company finally began to exploit Orange Bird's burgeoning cult status with a line of merchandise leading up to Walt Disney World's 40th anniversary.

This resurgence culminated in 2012, when the plucky little character made a triumphant return to the Sunshine Tree Terrace in Adventureland, along with a signature citrus treat – and a personal favorite – the Citrus Swirl.

This was an exciting turn of events. Nostalgia for these little things speaks to one of the key philosophies often cited as a secret for Disney's success – a focus on detail. Anyone who grew up going to the parks knows how easily one can become fixated on some bizarre, out-of-the-way detail. With so many fascinating design elements populating the parks and resorts, it's not hard to find something that enthralls you and becomes "your" personal, private touchstone. It can be something as remarkably mundane as an eye-catching staircase or a hexagonal bathroom tile, but it's something you look for every time you visit; it draws your eye, and it becomes almost ritual. And this is why, when things like this are lost, it detracts from the overall experience and the reaction from fans can be highly personal.

And it's no wonder that the Orange Bird had such fervent supporters, seeing as he had deep ties to the very earliest days at Walt Disney World. According to a 1972 article in the *Los Angeles Times*, Disney had its first meetings with the Florida Department of Citrus on July 3, 1967 – several years before Walt Disney World's 1971 debut. On October 1st, 1969, the citrus industry became the first entity to sign a participation agreement with Walt Disney World.

Through the years of negotiations, the two parties had attempted to find an exhibit or attraction for the citrus industry to sponsor that would reach their desired audience at a price they could afford. The desire for a "completely family-oriented, high-volume traffic entertainment exhibit" led them to the Enchanted Tiki Room, to be housed in Adventureland's Sunshine Pavilion.

One particularly fortuitous meeting between Disney marketing staff and the Department of Citrus led to the Orange Bird, who would play host to visitors at the Sunshine Tree Terrace snack stand. Disney had been asked to look at Department of Citrus advertising materials and recommend ways to blend their existing ad campaigns with Walt Disney World's own promotions, when Disney marketing maven Vince Jefferds came up with the idea of the Orange Bird. He subsequently helped develop the character's backstory.

A pre-notoriety Anita Bryant, already a spokesperson for the citrus industry, came aboard to record an album about Orange Bird, featuring songs by Disney stalwarts the Sherman brothers. Orange Bird went on to appear in animated television ads and on a wide array of promotional material and merchandise.

But the citrusy Florida goodness couldn't be confined to just the shade of Adventureland's Sunshine Tree. As part of the sponsorship deal, a full harvest of Florida citrus products were featured in restaurants across the resort.

It really cannot be understated how different the Walt Disney World of the 1970s was from the resort today. Early Disney World seems to have had this bizarre schism in its personality; on one hand, it tried really hard to be a fancy, grown-up place with adult entertainment and restaurants with dress codes, where shrimp would be prepared in fascinating modern ways. On the other hand, the way in which it went about this often comes off as a kid dressing up in their dad's suit and playing grown-up.

Part of this was simply a function of the times; Card Walker and his executive buddies might have spent all day on the golf course, but I doubt they demanded anything fancier afterwards besides a well-done ribeye and a pitcher of martinis. This was the era when the height of exoticism was Chow Mein noodles. In the parks you could literally order franks n' beans and other delicacies that seem cribbed from a middle school cafeteria menu. Why, I'll have a sliced peach on a leaf with cottage cheese, please!

The sum effect of all this was an atmosphere that seems incredible today, but which I'm not sure it would be wise to revive in totality. Sure I want my Bob-A-Round boats and the *Eastern Winds*, but people also ate aspic back then. Aspic!

Many of the more insane elements of vintage Walt Disney World came from the realm of dining. Thankfully, the *Los Angeles Times* was kind enough to catalogue some of Disney's unique citrus creations for our revisionist palates to judge.

At the time, Florida citrus products were served, in one form or another, in each of the Magic Kingdom's lands. Citrus was on the menu at three locations in Main Street U.S.A., two establishments in Adventureland, and one location each in Liberty Square, Fantasyland, and Tomorrowland.

At the Sunshine Tree Terrace in Adventureland, orange and grapefruit juices were featured. But unlike today there was an enormous variety of other tangy treats; the *Times* mentions "tangerine soft freeze, a sherbet-like mixture of orange juice, tangerine concentrate, tangerine oil, and sweetener; an orange juice bar on a stick; and a jellied citrus salad composed of broken orange and grapefruit segments, grapefruit juice, sugar, and gel."

I'll admit, I think these concoctions sound incredible. As do the other confections once on the menu:

> *Also offered is tangerine cheesecake, comprising cake topped with tangerine and orange glaze sauce; citrus tarts of heavy cream in an open shell, topped with orange sections and glazed orange sauce; and crepes ambrosia, a delightful mixture of oranges, tangerines, marshmallows, and coconut dipped in heavy cream and rolled in a French pancake.*

A French pancake! So fancy. And, needless to say, I would have queued up for any of these.

At the now-defunct Adventureland Verandah, guests could order the somewhat unappealingly named "Fiji Chicken Orange Chunk", "made up of fried chicken breast, Cantonese rice, Polynesian vegetables, egg roll, grated orange rind, and parsley, topped with orange or tangerine segments."

The Tomorrowland Terrace served a hamburger plate with sides of French fries and Florida citrus jello. They also featured citrus tarts and a citrus salad "containing orange and grapefruit segments topped with orange sherbet." Because nothing makes a salad pop like some orange sherbet. These same offerings were featured at the Pinocchio Village Haus in Fantasyland.

At the Crystal Palace on Main Street U.S.A., diners could order an orange Waldorf salad, as well as a "Cottage Cheese Jubilee Salad", a very 1970s-sounding concoction of "cottage cheese mixed with tiny bits of oranges and pineapple". But it was at Liberty Square's Liberty Tree Tavern that perhaps the most remarkable citrus cuisine was available. The colonial establishment featured not only "Shrimp Florida", "utilizing pink Florida shrimp with diced oranges in sauce Louis", but also the breathtakingly 1970s-evocative "Pâté Maison

Florida", "composed of thin slices of homemade pâté, with orange rounds molded into each slice."

Yes, my friends, "Pâté Maison Florida". No amount of nostalgia can justify the resurrection of that. But citrus tarts and tangerine cheesecake? I wouldn't mind seeing a revival of those.

It's amusing how the insanity slowly escalates as you progress through this list of citrus dishes. At first you think, "Hey, this is valuable background information." Then suddenly you're in the land of "Fiji Chicken Orange Chunk" and "jellied citrus salad" and "pink Florida shrimp with diced oranges in sauce Louis" and all bets are off. Cottage cheese makes its mandatory appearance. So does the appetizing inclusion of "gel" as an ingredient in the citrus salad. Gel?? That is almost unnervingly vague. I'm not sure what "tangerine oil and sweetener" is but I'm pretty sure I'm for it, and I'm glad that they clarified that a crepe was a "French pancake".

When the Orange Bird and the Citrus Swirl returned, long-time fans rejoiced. After years of pining, it was exciting to revisit a favorite treat. But, as you see, there is an almost endless list of now-forgotten offerings just waiting to be revived.

Just not the Pâté Maison Florida.

.25

Experimental Prototype Callgirls of Tomorrow

As the eyes of the nation turned towards Orlando in October of 1982 for the grand opening of Epcot Center, they witnessed the arrival of a new theme park based – quite proudly and vocally – on the American free enterprise system. So closely was Epcot's development tied to some of the world's largest corporations, that I'm pretty sure Card Walker would mumble "free enterprise" in his sleep; he would certainly bring it up at the drop of a hat.

"Free enterprise" was indeed critical to Epcot's completion, because the park was such a large and expensive project. Walt Disney Productions, as it existed in 1982, certainly couldn't fund it on their own, and corporate participants were necessary to underwrite the massive pavilions. This meant nearly a decade of wining and dining doughy, rich old white guys with endless steak dinners and pitchers of cocktails; it meant countless private jet flights and limo rides to a range of corporate headquarters, with dinner, drinks, and a show afterwards.

And it also meant that when the park opened, all those doughy, rich old white guys headed down to Orlando to see what their millions had bought, and to check out their new corporate VIP lounges. And this is where the hookers come in!

"Epcot Draws Prostitutes" read the headline of the Associated Press wire story, one that no doubt drew the eyes of surprised readers in October 1982 just as it did a rather bemused researcher (who shall remain nameless) decades later.

"Prostitutes are traveling to Orlando from as far away as Philadelphia to cash in on the opening of Walt Disney World's new Epcot Center", proclaimed the article, in a lede that no doubt spoiled Card Walker's breakfast and probably made Dick Nunis punch through a wall. Surely this was the sauciest thing to happen in central Florida since the Lake Buena Vista key party pandemic of '76.

For the article the AP interviewed an agent from the Metropolitan Bureau of Investigation, the improbably-named Sgt. Richard Klawe. According to Klawe, arrests for prostitution during the first twelve days of October surpassed the number of arrests during any previous month that year. The twelve days saw 42 such arrests, whereas the previously monthly high was 33 arrests.

The entrepreneuring women told agents that they were visiting from Philadelphia, Atlanta, south Florida, and Volusia County to, in the words of Sgt. Klawe, "commemorate the opening of Epcot". It's nice to see that everyone was so excited for the 21st century to begin!

Free enterprise, after all.

.26

GREATEST. PRESS. RELEASE. EVER.

Modern corporate marketing is rather stale and predictable fare; any given press release today feels as if it had been spit out by the same robot with only a few key words altered to suit the occasion. Once marketing became something quantifiable that you could get a Master's Degree for, it became rather rote and derivative. Which is not to say that there has not always been an element of that in the field, but one feels that there is a sense of showmanship that has been lost. Back in the day, they had *ballyhoo*.

And no one had better ballyhoo boys than Disney. Walt Disney Productions had an ever-scheming team of marketing madmen like Jack Lindquist and Charlie Ridgeway constantly figuring out new events and gimmicks to draw attention to Disneyland and Walt Disney World. Disney became renowned for its lavish, multi-day media events, which drew coverage from across the country and around the world. Every park anniversary became more spectacular than the last; every character birthday was noted; every holiday warranted a television special. And some of these events were really out there.

It would be hard to find a better example of this than a certain press release from 1987 that I once happened to uncover. It embodies the grandiose, hodge-podge nature of the old Disney press events, which pulled in a bafflingly disparate range of people and concepts to celebrate seemingly unrelated topics. Perhaps the first paragraph of the press release will better illustrate:

> *LAKE BUENA VISTA, FLA., Sept. 29 /PRN/ — Beginning Sept. 30, Walt Disney World will introduce two new shows saluting the bicentennial of the U.S. Constitution, a daredevil circus starring international and intergalactic performers, Disney Dollars,*

a monkey-breeding program to aid quadriplegics, a joint experiment with NASA to find a way to grow food in space, and a Constitution-era exhibit including a Liberty Bell cast from the original mold, and the Brasher Doubloon, the world's most valuable coin.

With this roster of activities, one is not sure where to start. As your eyes scan the paragraph they pick up random keywords: Monkey. Constitution. Quadriplegic. Daredevil. Intergalactic. Doubloon. Breeding. Circus. NASA. On a percentile basis, I'd say that there are more words that I'd never expected to find than in any other paragraph written about Walt Disney World, ever. At least, I didn't expect to find them in this specific configuration.

So what exactly was on the slate of events for this rather remarkable event? Well, perhaps obviously, there was a Walt Disney Imagineering presentation about all the new attractions then under construction at Walt Disney World. It was a rather impressive list, including the Disney-MGM Studios park, the Grand Floridian Beach Resort, Epcot's Norway pavilion, the Pleasure Island complex, as well as Typhoon Lagoon.

Also debuting on September 30th was *America the Musical*, a stage show in the Magic Kingdom. In the release, Disney bills it as "unabashedly patriotic", which seems strange, as if we'd expect them to be abashed. Why so defensive?

At 2 p.m. on the 30th, in the Magic Kingdom's Liberty Square, Mercury astronaut Gordon Cooper, *Roots* author Alex Haley, and Walt Disney Attractions President Dick Nunis dedicated a replica of the Liberty Bell cast from the original mold. Alex Haley, Gordon Cooper, and Dick Nunis debuting the Liberty Bell? All that's missing from that scenario are a priest, a rabbi, Bette Midler, and Sir Edmund Hillary.

At 3 p.m. was the debut of the "All America Parade", a salute to the bicentennial of the Constitution "from sea-to-shining sea". This parade would see a lot of re-use over the years, becoming a salute to Mickey Mouse's 60th birthday "from sea-to-shining sea" in 1988, and appearing in several Disney Christmas and Fourth of July parade broadcasts.

Following the parade was the "raising by helicopter of the largest U.S. Flag"; the enormous flag, measuring 235 feet long by 104 feet wide, weighed three-quarters of a ton.

The next day, which was incidentally Walt Disney World's 16th anniversary, featured events held at Epcot Center. Premiering at 2 p.m. was the infamous *Epcot Center Circus Spectacular*, "featuring Jay Cochrane walking tightrope 180 feet above ground, Flying Rodriquez Family from the Moscow State Circus and the Winn Family, 1987 winners of circus' highest honor, the Gold Clown Award." The Flying Rodriquez Family of Moscow? I guess the Great O'Shaughnesseys of Shanghai were already booked. Also note that "circus' highest honor" is the Gold Clown Award. It's the only major award that will also haunt your dreams.

If the "raising by helicopter of the largest U.S. Flag" hadn't proved enough excitement for you, at seven that evening one could attend a demonstration of "Disney's futuristic transportable meal", the Handwich™, by the members of the "Walt Disney World Culinary Olympic Team". Having now long passed into legend, the Disney Handwich™ is probably the only sandwich in history worthy of having a "demonstration" for the public. "Gentlemen, behold!"

Friday, October 2nd began with the east coast introduction of Disney Dollars, when Scrooge McDuck greeted the Wells Fargo truck which delivered the bills to Epcot Center. It was followed with a "Kraft/NASA" press conference for food and science writers at The Land. How many Kraft/NASA press conferences do you think there have been in all of history? My guess – not many. Afterwards, Disney President Frank Wells, Kraft President Michael Miles, and space shuttle pilot Steve Oswald dedicated a NASA experiment designed to grow food in space.

So there you go - just a nice assortment of completely random and brilliantly obscure events tied up in a three-day period. And, don't forget, this was all to celebrate the bicentennial of the American Constitution. But that's not all! Lastly, the press release helpfully points out that from Wednesday through Friday, Boston University psychologist M.J. Willard would be available for interviews on "Helping Hands, Simians for the Disabled". Said Disney:

> *Walt Disney World is establishing the breeding colony on Discovery Island for capuchins (organ grinder monkeys) in cooperation with Dr. Willard who has developed a program in which the monkeys are trained to aid quadriplegics.*

Now, obviously, it's a noble cause with a good purpose, but… "Simians for the Disabled"? How about "Ungulates for the Obese" or "Cetaceans for the Deranged?" Capybaras for the Mundane?

The best part is that they felt the need to clarify that these were "organ grinder monkeys". I envision the grizzled news editor sitting in his office, chomping on his cigar, thinking he needed to spice up the press release a little bit: "Sure, sure, we got all this doubloon stuff but the rubes won't go for this! What kinda scientific bunk is that – 'capuchin'? Just put 'organ grinder monkey'! They'll get that out in the sticks!"

Now that's ballyhoo.

.27

THE BALLAD OF BISONTENNIAL BEN

Disney history is littered with characters once used for special events or who were tied to films, television shows, or other properties that are long gone from the spotlight; characters appeared in the park for every animated feature from the 1980s and 1990s, but when was the last time you saw llama Kuzco or the cast of *The Great Mouse Detective*?

While they're no longer marquee names, many of these characters are still loved by fans and are worth trotting out on occasion. Who wouldn't want their pictures taken with the Rocketeer, or the *DuckTales* crew, or any of a hundred long-abandoned walkaround characters?

The forgotten Disney roster doesn't end there, though. Aside from film and television stars, Disney has also created many one-off characters for specific in-park uses or for special events or outside sponsors. Dreamfinder and Figment, as well as the recently-resurgent Orange Bird are famous examples of park-specific characters; don't tell me there wouldn't be a meet-n-greet queue if they were to return. And what is obscure Disneyland history without the Kaiser Aluminum Pig or the Frito Kid? There were a slew of characters outside of the parks as well, many long forgotten, including Andy Anaheim and the 1984 Summer Olympics mascot, Sam the Eagle.

Occasionally, though, no matter how much of a nerd you are for these obscurities, you find something that you've never heard of. Something that somehow flew under your radar. Something so bizarre and amazing that it quickly becomes one of The Best Things Ever.

Something – someone – like Bisontennial Ben.

Bisontennial Ben. © Disney

Bisontennial Ben.

Bisontennial Ben.

But of course! Don't you remember Bisontennial Ben, the Disney-created mascot of the 1987 bicentennial of the American Constitution? The triple-pun combination of a buffalo and founding father Benjamin Franklin who appeared at a variety of events, including the 1988 Tournament of Roses Parade alongside Muhammad Ali and Buzz Aldrin? Of course you remember!

Ok, I totally didn't remember. But it blows my mind.

While most fans are aware that Disney threw a massive Bicentennial celebration at Disneyland and Walt Disney World in 1976, many people today have forgotten that they also tried to make an event of the 1987 Constitutional Bicentennial. The massive "Spirit of America" parade, mentioned in the previous chapter, appeared daily at the Magic Kingdom, and a series of events were held throughout the year to mark the occasion.

At a media event in 1986, which kicked off Walt Disney World's 15th anniversary, former Supreme Court Chief Justice Warren Burger appeared to speak about the upcoming bicentennial celebrations. Burger, chairman of the Commission on the Bicentennial of the U.S. Constitution, appeared alongside journalist Nicholas Daniloff, who had just been freed from a KGB prison in the Soviet Union. Again, I underscore that this all happened at a media event for Walt Disney World's 15th anniversary.

Burger even provided the pre-recorded introduction to *America the Musical Salutes the Spirit of America*, a stage show which was performed daily in front of Cinderella Castle. Starring Mickey, Minnie, Goofy, Pluto, Donald, Chip and Dale, and the Country Bears, alongside the usual lineup of singers and dancers, the show featured fireworks and the release of 200 doves, a salute to the armed forces, and, believe it or not, a recitation of the Constitutional preamble by the characters. It ended with Mickey, Donald, and Goofy appearing as the "Spirit of '76", a visual familiar from 1976's "America on Parade".

"Yes, yes," you say, "but what about Bisontennial Ben?"

Bisontennial Ben was created by the Creative Resources department of Disney Consumer Products, and offered to the national Bicentennial commission. When the federal commission passed on the design, it was adopted by the California Bicentennial Association for their own four-year celebration of the event.

The "robust" bison was chosen "because of his historic significance and air of dignity, strength, and endurance", according to Disney. The character was meant to resemble founder Benjamin Franklin, with his trademark (non-rose-colored) bifocals, and often appeared with a quill pen in hand, just in case there were any historical documents that needed signing. He was announced in 1987, with plans to appear "throughout the year at many of the events currently being planned by the California Bicentennial Foundation, including a number of corporate-sponsored activities." Further plans included his appearance on a variety of merchandise commemorating the event.

Bisontennial Ben was created at the behest of the improbably-named Peter Paul, an entrepreneur and, shall we say, "promoter", who was the executive vice president of the California Bicentennial Foundation. "We are making the Constitution user-friendly," said Paul at the time. "We have taken California innovation and creativity and directed them to selling an important message."

This impetus for showmanship had drawn a fair bit of criticism for the California commission. Initiated and funded by the state legislature, the Foundation had seen its state funding revoked in 1987 when three of its commissioners were forced to resign after they approved the publication of a book, *The Making of America*, which contained racist elements. State Senator Gary Hart, who had supported the creation of the Foundation in 1984, led the fight to defund it in 1987. Further attacks came from state officials and former commission members, who felt that the Foundation had lost its educational focus and had become fixated on showmanship and the sales of thousands of Bicentennial gold and silver coins, t-shirts, bumper stickers, balloons, and buttons.

Paul insisted it was all part of promoting the Constitutional message, although even his defenses drew criticism. "We're using the same people who sell soap to sell understanding of the Constitution", he told the media; this and other comments, as well as Bisontennial Ben himself, drew criticism from some of the more stodgy letter-writers to the *Los Angeles Times*.

The Foundation claimed that all the pizzazz was necessary to give California's celebrations their own unique identity, as the western state didn't have the deep ties to colonial times found in the east coast colonies. They intended to stray far from "fife and drum" type shows, as they coordinated with groups to sponsor speeches, parades, essay contests, concerts, and fireworks in more than a hundred California towns. "If you had a reenactment of 39 sweaty old men arguing in Philadelphia, how many of our children would be interested?" said Paul. "But put them in space suits, and the kids will really go for it."

No, seriously, he totally said that.
© Disney

This rather gonzo attitude can be seen in the events planned for September 17, 1987, the actual anniversary of the Constitutional signing. As described in the *Los Angeles Times*, the Foundation's events were to go something like this:

The day would begin at Seal Beach, where Bisontennial Ben and Apollo astronaut Buzz Aldrin would plant a Bicentennial flag in the sand while a live band played and an Air Force jet squadron flew overhead. Aldrin would then depart by helicopter for Beverly Hills, where he would tour local schools.

Later, everyone would travel to Knott's Berry Farm, where, at the park's re-creation of Philadelphia's Independence Hall, California Chief Justice Malcolm Lucas would symbolically sign a copy of the Constitution. Lucas would be joined by Aldrin and "celebrities, dancers, movie stars, and Olympians", as well as 100 "resident aliens". After the immigrants were sworn in as American citizens, Helen Reddy would sing *America the Beautiful* and, at 1 p.m., a replica of the Liberty Bell would ring for 200 seconds.

Peter Paul, Buzz Aldrin, Mickey Mouse, Muhammad Ali, and Bisontennial Ben appear alongside a model of "Communicating Freedom", the California Bicentennial Foundation's float for the 1988 Tournament of Roses Parade.
© Disney

The last widely documented appearance of Bisontennial Ben seems to be in January of 1988, when he appeared on the Foundation's float in the Tournament of Roses Parade, taking his place beside Aldrin and Muhammed Ali.

Two "civilians" also appeared on the float, selected from 3,000 submitted names. Sara Beth Heller, a 7-year-old from Lancaster, Pennsylvania, and 81-year-old Herbert Blackburn of North Las Vegas, Nevada, were picked to ride after, according to the *Los Angeles Times*, a "computer, a Boy Scout, and the organization's buffalo-robed mascot, 'Bisontennial Ben,' narrowed down the list on the *Big Spin* lottery show."

And so ends the tale of Bisontennial Ben... almost.

In researching this saga, what appeared at first to be a brief postscript to the story wound up tracing a bizarre series of events that, twenty-five years after Bisontennial Ben's celebration, wound up tying right back into modern day Disney-related news.

It all has to do with Peter F. Paul, the aforementioned executive of the California Bicentennial Foundation. A cursory look at his website,

Former Disney CEO Michael Eisner and Peter Paul.
© Disney

which remains online as of this writing, reveals that he seems to be one of those guys who is constantly getting involved with different causes and fundraisers in order to get his picture taken with various celebrities and politicians. One imagines his office is lined, wall to wall, with autographed photos of him with people who don't quite remember remember meeting him in any of a million handshake lines. He's a promoter, and an almost *Zelig*-like figure with quite a history.

A lawyer and "entrepreneur", Paul has been convicted several times on charges ranging from drug dealing to securities fraud. In the 1970s, he led a scam which sought to defraud the Cuban government, which he would later claim was intended to be anti-Communist activity. In reality, he sold agents of Fidel Castro $8.75 million in nonexistent coffee, and then sought to sink a cargo ship to cover up the crime and, incidentally, defraud the ship's insurer. The plan fell through when the erstwhile saboteurs literally missed the boat, and Paul was arrested. When police went to search his house, they found a garage full of cocaine; Paul was indicted and found guilty of federal conspiracy charges as well as possession of cocaine with intent to distribute.

After getting out of prison, Paul traveled to Canada in 1983 with a false ID; this was not only a crime but a violation of his parole, and he went back to prison. In 1985 he was out again, and wound up being an executive of the California Bicentennial Foundation for the Constitution and Bill of Rights. He tried to involve himself with politicians and celebrities; he also served for a time as Fabio's agent.

The many faces of Bisontennial Bill. Note his vanity plate: "BUDGET".
© Disney

In 2000, Paul became a major fundraiser for Hillary Clinton's Senate campaign. He put together a huge fundraising gala in Los Angeles, using money that he had fraudulently borrowed from Merrill Lynch. When the Clinton campaign found out about his background they returned his donations, and he spent much of the next decade in a series of nuisance lawsuits against Clinton, her campaign, and even the Federal Election Commission. He became a darling of the far-right fringe for his attacks on the Clintons, although he eventually turned on his arch-conservative backers and filed suit against them as well. These lawsuits found little traction, as most of them were filed while Paul himself was in Brazil, where he was fleeing extradition for a variety of federal criminal charges.

This is where it gets back around to Disney.

In 1998, the irrepressible Mr. Paul co-founded the internet startup Stan Lee Media, alongside legendary comic creator Stan Lee. The internet media company ran out of money during the dot-com bust of 2000; Paul blamed Bill Clinton for the failure, and filed suit against him, but it turned out that Paul and another of the company's executives had illegally tried to bolster the company's stock price by fraudulently buying stock with bad checks. Stan Lee Media went bankrupt in 2001, and Paul fled to Brazil.

He was finally extradited in 2003, and charged with securities fraud and a range of civil suits. As of this writing he resides in federal prison. But he continued to file a slew of lawsuits against Lee, Lee's family, Marvel, and other Marvel executives, claiming that he actually owns the rights to all of Lee's famous comic creations due to their former partnership in Stan Lee Media. He has even accused Lee of colluding with the Clintons. And, as you might have seen, he filed a multi-billion-dollar lawsuit against The Walt Disney Company in October 2012 stating again that he owns the rights to all of Lee's Marvel characters and is therefore owed for all of Disney's recent cinematic superhero successes.

After more than eight years and a torrent of lawsuits, never winning one, and losing time and again in various district and circuit courts to an increasingly annoyed array of judges, Stan Lee Media finally came to the end of the road when they were denied a chance at appeal by the U.S. Supreme Court in March 2015. Stymied by the American legal system, as so elegantly laid out in the Constitution.

And that, as the man once said, is the rest of the story.

Of course, the only obvious outcome which could square this circle of historical randomness is for Bisontennial Ben to become part of the Marvel Cinematic Universe. Maybe he could appear in a future *Avengers* film! He should at least get to audition for Rocket Raccoon if *Guardians of the Galaxy* gets a permanent in-park meet and greet. Hopefully, his costume is in the back of a closet somewhere, ready to be taken out of mothballs for a future round of "limited time magic".

Because... Bisontennial Ben.

Bisontennial Ben!!

VI.
A Disneyland Interlude

.28

A STROLL DOWN LIBERTY STREET

From the beginning, Disneyland smacked of pure Americana; Walt's original plans for a small "Mickey Mouse Park" across the street from his Burbank studio had a definite air of apple pie and small Midwestern towns. Disneyland was designed to take people back to Walt's roots in turn-of-the-century Missouri, to share the tall tales of America's creation in Frontierland, and to explore its final frontiers in Tomorrowland.

When Disneyland quickly proved a success upon its opening in 1955, thought turned toward expansion. Walt's Imagineers began to tinker with ideas for the large, empty plot of land sitting between Main Street, U.S.A. and Tomorrowland. Their first concept was for an area called International Street; while this plan never came to pass, it did eventually provide the basis for Epcot Center's World Showcase decades later.

In November 1956, it was announced that a new area called Liberty Street would be coming to Disneyland, connected to Main Street's Town Square adjacent to the Opera House. In this Colonial-era cul-de-sac, Imagineers would, according to promotional materials, "excitingly dramatize the events of the Revolutionary War period, and present them in such a way as to give us a better personal understanding and pride in our American way of life."

Perhaps it's no surprise that Colonial America was on the minds of Disney artists at the time. The studio had been working since 1955 on research for *Johnny Tremain*; that film would hit theaters in the summer of 1957. Also a factor in the development of this project was Walt's frequently-expressed belief that Americans needed to be more aware of and grateful for their heritage. In the words of a 1957 booklet

This doctored promotional photograph shows where Liberty Street would have been located, branching off from Disneyland's Town Square. Also note, along the top edge of the photograph, another planned-but-unbuilt area, "Gay Nineties Square". © Disney

discussing the expansion, "Liberty Street is the result of a personal philosophy that Walt Disney has long shared with many other Americans. It is a belief that we, as Americans, often fail to comprehend the tremendous significance of our heritage, as related to our personal lives and the growth and prosperity of our country."

Walt often made statements along these lines; when honored with the George Washington Award by the Freedoms Foundation in 1963, he declared that it was the only reward he'd ever received "for just being an American – a heritage we all take too much for granted."

Walt added, "Personally I don't understand why the heck it was given to me. I've just been going along doing what sort of comes naturally to me. I might say, I've been selfishly indulging myself as an American – as a United States Citizen… enjoying all the privileges that one has as a citizen, and it's only times like this that you sort of wake up to the fact that… what it really means to be a citizen."

Herb Ryman's concept art for Liberty Street from the perspective of a guest entering the area from Town Square. © Disney

Liberty Street, Walt felt, would be a reminder to park guests of their great heritage. In this new area, the company said, "Walt Disney intends to excitingly dramatize the events of the Revolutionary War period, and present them in such a way as to give us a better personal understanding and pride in our American way of life."

Stepping off of Town Square onto the cobblestone pavers of Liberty Street, guests would have found themselves on a winding lane lined by buildings reminiscent of those found in American cities around 1770. As they made their way up Liberty Street into its central area, Liberty Square, they would pass a series of shops and exhibits authentic to the time period.

Each of these establishments would be fully operational, and reports from the time suggested they could include a blacksmith shop, apothecary, glassmaker, weaver, print shop, silversmith, and cabinetmaker. Each of these, as well as the attractions housed in the theaters facing Liberty Square, would be "an integral part of the total free 'show'" and would not require guests to purchase a ticket.

Concept for an operating glassblower's shop on Liberty Street. The rear window looks out upon a diorama depicting George Washington's Mount Vernon home.
© Disney

To pay for this new expansion, and to offset the cost of presenting such elaborate attractions free to visitors, Disney sought out sponsors to fund the individual workshops. A glass company, for example, could sponsor the glassblower's shop; it would be fully period-authentic in the front, but behind a partition, a "modern" exhibit area would display the company's current products, methods, and advertising. Hoping to entice participants, Disney promised that these exhibits would "tell the story of how that small undertaking has grown and evolved into a major American enterprise, and how that enterprise serves the nation today."

While the shops all looked out onto Liberty Street, their back windows would face a series of historical dioramas depicting scenes of interest and import. Renderings by Imagineer and master artist Herbert Ryman show a glassblower's shop looking out upon an "evening at Mt. Vernon" and a silversmith's workshop overlooking Boston's Old North Church.

As visitors approached Liberty Square, they would see in the distance towering masts of sailing ships docked in some just-out-of-sight colonial harbor. This was the "Waterfront Diorama", a delightful bit

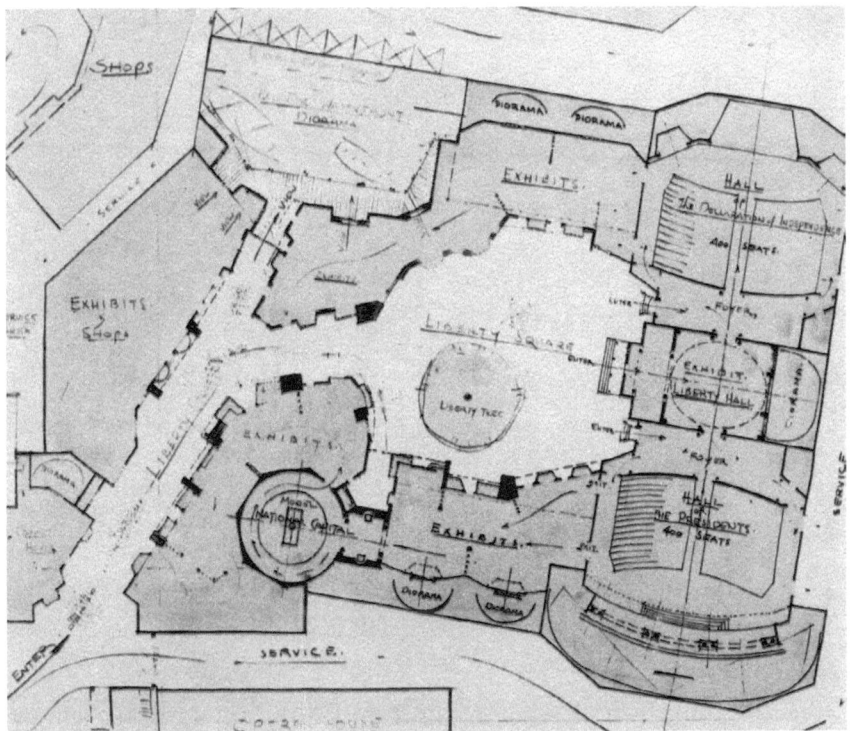

This overhead layout of Liberty Street and Liberty Square shows the various exhibits, shops, and attractions that would make up the area, as well as the path guests would take through them. © Disney

of illusioneering that would present the appearance of a bustling seaport. In the diorama, Imagineers said, would be "two life-size sailing vessels of the type which were used in trade with the Far East during the formative years of our nation."

Gracing the center of Liberty Square would be the Liberty Tree. This was a nod to the original Liberty Tree in Boston, which also played an important role in *Johnny Tremain*. In 1765, the first major protest against British rule occurred beneath this massive elm, when a group that became known as the "Sons of Liberty" burned straw effigies of British administrators to protest the new Stamp Act. So important was the symbolism of the Liberty Tree, that it became a centerpiece of Walt Disney World's own Liberty Square years later.

Past Disneyland's Liberty Tree was to be Liberty Hall, where guests would enter the area's keynote attractions. Through a central lobby

Concept art for the Hall of the Declaration of Independence, showing the three well-known patriotic paintings that would come to life as Audio-Animatronic tableaux. © Disney

featuring dioramas of scenes from the Revolutionary War, visitors would enter one of two theatrical attractions—the Hall of the Presidents or the Hall of the Declaration of Independence.

Seated on wooden pews inside the 500-seat Hall of the Declaration of Independence, and lit by 13 stars set into the ceiling, guests would witness the "stirring and dramatic story of the birth of these United States". Three scenes, based on famous paintings, would honor the Declaration of Independence by depicting the "framing, signing, and proclaiming" of a document that Disneyland's promotional booklet lauded as "the most important state paper ever written".

Curtains on a wall would part to reveal three scenes in sequence, each based on a painting but presented in life-size three-dimensional tableaux. These were essentially animatronic shadowboxes, set in gilded frames but designed in forced perspective with the intention of giving guests an "experience" rather than a "show". According to the Imagineers, a feeling of "life and reality" could be created thanks to "new techniques in stereophonic sound, lighting, narration, and staging".

Cutaway view of the shadowbox effect by which the Audio-Animatronics figures would appear, in perspective, to be staged as notable paintings from the history of the Declaration of Independence. This scene, showing Thomas Jefferson, Ben Franklin, and John Adams consulting on the document, would years later inspire a similar moment in Epcot Center's *The American Adventure*. © Disney

As a narrator told the story and significance of the events depicted, and quoted excerpts of the Declaration itself, guests would witness Benjamin Franklin and John Adams consulting with Thomas Jefferson as seen in J.L.G. Ferris's *The Drafting of the Declaration of Independence*. The signing of the Declaration itself was staged to resemble John Trumbull's well-known masterpiece *Declaration of Independence*, which hangs in the Rotunda of the United States Capitol. Finally, guests would see the proclamation of the signing, as depicted in Henry Mosler's *Ringing of the Liberty Bell*.

On the other end of Liberty Hall was to sit the Hall of the Presidents. Here, in a "mighty cavalcade" would be recounted the "trials, decisions, and formation of our heritage". Similar in content to *The Hall of Presidents*, which debuted at Walt Disney World in 1971, this show would feature animated figures of every president – 34 up to that point.

Housed in a 400-seat theater, with a script by James Algar, the show would begin as curtains parted to reveal only the silhouettes of Presidents Washington, Jefferson, Adams, and Madison. As music and narration began to play, the lights would come up on these first presidents and guests would hear portions of addresses given by Washington and the others.

As the story continued, the curtains would continue to part to reveal subsequent presidents until they were all on display. In a musical finale, a rear curtain would open behind the presidents to reveal a wide-format movie screen on which the Capitol dome would appear. Projections of clouds would appear to drift across the sky.

Upon exiting the theater, guests would pass a carved scale model of the Capitol building. Walt had come in contact with George Lloyd, a sculptor who had, in 1930, obtained photographs and blueprints from an architect who had worked on the actual Capitol building. Over the course of three and a half years, he carved the building in intricate detail from a single piece of Caen limestone. Disney eventually obtained the model, which would come in later years to be part of the pre-show display for Disneyland's *Great Moments with Mr. Lincoln*.

While Liberty Street wouldn't make that projected 1957 opening, the attraction would see continued development over the years; Imagineer Marty Sklar went on to prepare story outlines and treatments for the project in 1959. The concept of the Hall of Presidents was obviously important to Walt, as the studio continued to seek a sponsor who could underwrite the show. Imagineers developed a prototype Audio-Animatronics figure of Abraham Lincoln as a "proof of concept", and they continued to refine the technology while the sponsor search continued.

By 1961, the show had been retitled *One Nation Under God featuring The Hall of Presidents*. In a pitch for the project, Walt raved, "In all my forty years in show business, I can't remember anything that has created quite as much excitement around the studio." This version of the show was presented as theater-in-the-round, housed in a circular theater, and combined elements of the two separate shows originally developed for Liberty Street.

It was this show that Walt pitched for inclusion in the 1964/65 New York World's Fair – providing, naturally, that it could find a sponsor. With a cost estimated at $2.7 million in 1963 dollars, Disney needed someone to help foot the bill for the half-hour show. Fair impresario Robert Moses was transfixed by the idea; upon having shaken the prototype Lincoln's hand at the Disney studio, he declared that it must be part of the fair.

Even as time drew short, Moses refused to give up on the inclusion of Walt's show in the Fair's lineup. Writing in 1962 to Norman Winston, the man in charge of the Fair's official United States pavilion, Moses urged: "I renew the recommendation that you personally sponsor the so-called Disney Hall of Presidents. I still believe this is a terrific show, that it would be an enormous drawing card and that regardless of other exhibits, it would add to your own reputation."

But as a series of sponsors – General Foods, Coca-Cola, the American Petroleum Institute – balked at the cost of sponsoring the exhibit, Disney began to pare down the show's scope. Originally, elaborate filmed segments were to make up 27 minutes of the show's run-time. By eliminating those, and keeping the focus on the presidents, the price of sponsorship would be significantly lowered. The Fair offered to chip in and donate land for the pavilion rent-free, even as they continued to lobby businesses on Disney's behalf.

Eventually, Disney officials entered talks with officials from the state of Illinois with the thought of including, at the very least, the existing Lincoln figure in the state's pavilion at the Fair. Negotiations continued during the summer of 1963, and the Disney-Illinois partnership presenting *Great Moments with Mr. Lincoln* was announced that August. The state had continually lowballed the figure they were willing to pay for the exhibit, and while Walt had tried to play tough in negotiations, his instinct as a showman eventually won out and he proceeded with the project at a financial loss for the studio.

And while Disneyland never did see its own Liberty Street, the idea lived on. When Walt Disney World was announced just a few years after the World's Fair closed in New York, Liberty Square and *The Hall of Presidents* were among the very first attractions to be revealed to the public. The show, which hewed closely to many of the story beats from Algar's original *One Nation Under God* script, has been updated several times over the years, and continues to be an important part of the Magic Kingdom experience today.

.29

Pooh For President

In 1968, an unlikely Disney character threw his hat – or, rather, his honeypot – into the political arena when Winnie the Pooh declared his candidacy for president. Of the United States. No, really.

It all kicked off on July 14th, when a number of Disney characters turned up for Family Night at the Hollywood Bowl and the first "Winnie the Pooh for President" convention. In front of a crowd 10,000 strong, Snow White and the Seven Dwarfs, Mickey and Minnie Mouse, the Three Little Pigs, Peter Pan, and Mary Poppins were joined by a slew of other characters and the emcee, comedian Morey Amsterdam. Musical entertainment was provided by the Hollywood Bowl Orchestra and Disneyland's Kids of the Kingdom, and a local ice company provided twenty tons of ground-up ice for snowman building and snowball fights.

Pooh kicked off his campaign in style, joined onstage by his friends from the Hundred Acre Wood for a campaign musical number and the release of thousands of red, white, and blue balloons. Signs appeared in the crowd with such politically-charged – and almost unbelievably bizarre – messages as "Huny In Every Pot", "A Good 5-Cent Candy Cigar", "Yoyo a-go-go", "Export All Spinich", and, for some now-incomprehensible reason, "A Chicken in Every Poot". The evening was closed out with a group sing-along of "it's a small world" and "When You Wish Upon a Star".

Building on the success of this rally, Pooh moved his campaign to Disneyland where, at the Tomorrowland Stage, his "musical political convention" became part of the *On Stage U.S.A.* show. Throughout August, *Winnie the Pooh for President* was performed twice a day

Pooh on the campaign trail. © Disney

alongside celebrities such as songstress Peggy Lee, comedian Rich Little, and puppeteer Shari Lewis.

Pooh lost the 1968 campaign, although Democratic candidate Hubert Humphrey admitted to reporters that the bear made more sense than "any other candidate". It wasn't the silly old bear's last brush with politics, though. On October 1st, 1972, at a convention held at Walt Disney World, Pooh was nominated to run for president on the "Children's Party" ticket.

Drawings had been held at Sears, Roebuck and Co. stores across the nation to select delegates from each of the fifty states to be sent with their families to Walt Disney World. There, they nominated Pooh for president in the forecourt of Cinderella Castle. Another "nominating convention" had been held for Pooh in Chicago that July to coincide with the Democratic National Convention. Two days after the Walt Disney World event, from his "west coast retreat" at Disneyland, Pooh announced his platform and campaign strategy.

"Although scheduled to rest up from the convention proceedings at Florida's Walt Disney World," the media breathlessly reported, "Pooh took the microphone for some thirty seconds to address a large group

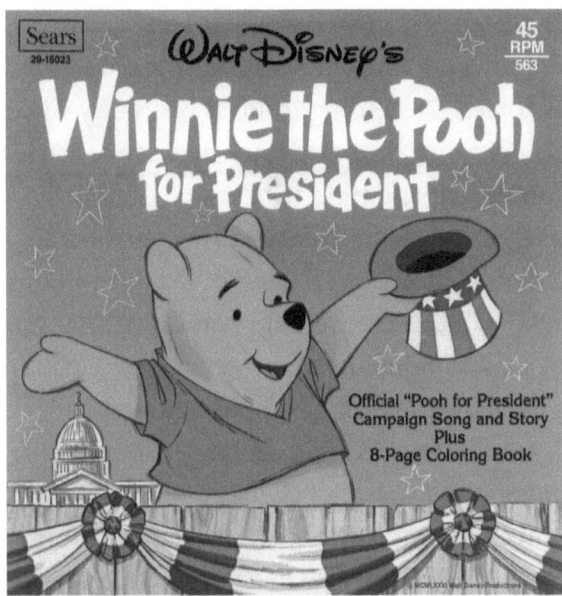

A 45 RPM single was released of Pooh's official campaign song in 1976. © Disney

of personal friends and enthusiastic supporters who had gathered near the park's Sleeping Beauty Castle."

What message did he have for his constituents? According to the media, among Pooh's policy platforms was a promise to put "hunny in every pot". He also "stressed his battle to 'lick' the high price of ice cream cones". "Hot fudge sundaes every Monday and banning spankings" rounded out his mostly pun-based proposals.

With a campaign staff consisting of Press Secretary Tigger and Political Advisor Eeyore, Pooh declared that he would soon depart on a whistle-stop train tour of California before opening his national campaign headquarters at Disneyland during a three day party from October 21st to October 23rd.

At the behest of his press secretary and "close personal friend" Tigger, Pooh unveiled a slate of proposals targeting the youth vote. "If elected in November, I will put two tricycles in every garage, provide free candy on holidays, and make sure everyone enjoys two Saturdays a week," announced the candidate.

Media speculated on just who would get the nod to become Pooh's vice presidential candidate, with insider buzz naming Eeyore and Owl as top choices. "According to Press Secretary Tigger," claimed one report, "Owl is on the inside track because of the learned bird's appeal to both the left and right wingers."

I would like to emphasize that these are actual quotes, taken from actual press reports, from actual news outlets.

"Pooh-litical" rallies were held up and down the west coast that month, with marching bands and free balloons, pictures, buttons, and posters for kids; there are no reports noting if this activity was monitored by the Federal Elections Commission.

From October 21st to 23rd, a tickertape "Pooh-rade" was held daily at Disneyland. Children were asked to gather in front of *it's a small world* at 11:30 a.m. to join in the parade and political rally. Three times a day, the *Pooh Revue* was presented on the Tomorrowland Stage, and free showings of *Winnie the Pooh and the Blustery Day* were held in the Fantasyland Theater. Pooh, Tigger, and Eeyore were available for meet and greets all day at their National Campaign Headquarters in the Carnation Plaza Gardens, and upon departing the park, each child received a free "Pooh for President" poster, pin, and coloring kit.

Pooh lost that election in the fall of 1972, polling significantly behind both sitting President Richard Nixon and even his Democratic challenger Senator George McGovern. He claimed to withdraw from politics in the years after, but also failed to publicly comment on rumors that he was spotted backstage with Nixon advisor Pat Buchanan when the president gave his infamous "I am not a crook" press conference at Walt Disney World's Contemporary Resort Hotel in 1973.

OK, that part I made up.

Pooh ran once again in 1976, and this time he had his own theme song. "Winnie-the-Pooh for President", penned by novelty songwriter Larry Groce, was released as a single which was sold in Sears locations. Once again, Disneyland played host to "Winnie the Pooh for President Days" on October 23rd and 24th. In addition to the daily

"Fun Raising" rallies and "Pooh-litical" conventions, a daily "Tigger-Tape" parade led kids through the park to a rally for "The Children's Pick in '76" on the steps of Main Street Station.

Pooh's 1976 bid was no more successful than his earlier outings, although his campaign song was nominated for a Grammy for Best Recording for Children. Perhaps this is what gave him the impetus for his final campaign in 1980, when Pooh for President Days were held one last time at Disneyland in October.

.30

THIRD THEME PARK - IT'S DOT COM!

What if Pooh's "100-Acre Wood" was in Anaheim? Or Ariel and Sebastian found their new undersea home here? What if Anaheim could be home to not two, but three Disney parks?

– Excerpt from thirdthemepark.com

Yes, what about that?

A particularly odd moment in Disney history came when, from 2000 until 2002, the company operated a website called thirdthemepark.com. It is an interesting piece of Disneyland lore, especially for those interested in the "neverland" of lost park concepts. Thankfully, although the site itself is long gone, one can still view elements of it courtesy of the Internet Archive.

The story of this historical oddity begins, as all good stories do, with a Japanese immigrant farmer and his family's strawberry fields. Hiroshi Fujishige's father arrived in America in 1915 and settled down outside of Los Angeles, where he began to farm and eventually married in 1918. The Fujishiges lived there until 1941, raising Hiroshi and his brother Masao, until the outbreak of World War II led to a number of U.S. policies unfriendly to Japanese-Americans. Seeking to avoid the internment camps, Hiroshi's family agreed to a government-directed "voluntary" evacuation and moved to live with a relative in Utah.

Hiroshi, who had just left high school after the completion of his third year, was eventually drafted into the army. Before he departed for Europe, however, he became violently ill with an infection, only to discover that he had been poisoned by a dentist who sought revenge for a relative lost in the Pacific War. By the time Fujishige had recovered, the war was over.

At this point Hiroshi and his brother moved back to California and started a farm in Norwalk. Several years later, in 1953, they traded that land for fifty-eight acres in Anaheim. The deal, worth about $2,500, allowed them to farm in peace without being hemmed in by development. Then, two years later, Disneyland opened and rural Anaheim changed forever.

Forty years later, Fujishige was still waking up at 5 a.m. every day to tend to his strawberries on the farm he owned with his wife of thirty years. He operated the fruit and vegetable stand from 7 a.m. to 5 p.m. daily, while raising his crops on land valued between $1 million and $2 million an acre. In 1994 he told the *Washington Post*, "If I had more schooling and knew what all these deals were, I might have been out of here a long time ago" and called himself "just a dirt farmer". Yet while Fujishige affected a folksy hayseed persona, he was obviously a sharp customer who knew exactly how valuable his farm was worth. It was this refusal to be bullied or bought that drove developers, and Disney management, crazy for decades.

Fujishige had already refused many offers, some upwards of $50 million, by the 1980s. In 1985 he was taken to court by the city of Anaheim, who sought in vain to build access roads for new development through his property. After an arsonist burned down the fruit stand in 1986, the Fujishige family agreed to the project, but the development eventually fell through. That same year Masao Fujishige killed himself, allegedly due to despair stemming from his slow recovery from a stroke. And then, into this mix of despair and determination, with his mind fixed on resort expansion, strolled Michael Eisner.

At the start of the 1990s Eisner had grand plans. He announced the Disney Decade, which would result in four fully-realized Disney resorts around the world. No longer would Disneyland exist only as a single theme park; rather, it would soon be the centerpiece of an entire destination resort along the lines of Walt Disney World in Florida. Eisner was focused on locking families in to an entire Disney vacation;

at no point should they have to leave property to spend their carefully earned cash. California would soon see a new Disney park – the only question was where.

Eisner decided to play the cities of Anaheim and Long Beach against each other to determine where Disney would build its new park. Dangling the possibility of building one, both, or neither of the parks, Eisner started a bidding war to see which city could offer the best sweetheart deal while also eliminating civic and governmental roadblocks in the shortest time.

The first volley came in July of 1990 when Disney announced plans for the Port Disney facility in Long Beach. This $2.8 billion, 414-acre seaside resort would be centered around the DisneySea park and feature five resort hotels, retail shops and waterfront dining, a marina, and a port for cruise ships. The complex would incorporate the *Queen Mary* luxury liner, which along with Howard Hughes's *Spruce Goose* had been obtained by Disney as part of their purchase of the Disneyland Hotel from the Wrather Corporation in 1989.

While Disney tried to overcome zoning and environmental hurdles in Long Beach, they continued to lay groundwork for the Anaheim resort. In February of 1991 they acquired twenty-three acres of land – a former trailer park – adjacent to the Fujishige farm for $1.3 million an acre. At the same time, they offered the Fujishiges $32 million for a 99-year lease to their strawberry field. Fujishige declined, but did not rule out future negotiations despite calling Disney's offer "insulting". He told the Associated Press that "it sure seemed to me that I was about to end up like those Indians who used to own Manhattan Island. When they came in with such a low offer, I was about ready to walk out of the meeting right then. Disney will do what they want to do, and I'll do what I want to do."

Things remained contentious throughout 1991. In May of that year, Disney revealed its new concept for Anaheim. An ambitious plan, it called for a $3 billion, 470-acre resort expansion that would add three new hotels, a nighttime entertainment district, and WESTCOT

Rendering of the proposed WESTCOT Center with its massive icon, Spacestation Earth. Disneyland can be seen to the left. A new retail and entertainment district would surround the lake in the center foreground, corresponding roughly to the current site of Downtown Disney. A completely new Disneyland Hotel, seen in the lower right corner, would replace the existing structure. © Disney

Center – a new theme park that sought to perfect many of the concepts that Disney first tried at Epcot Center in Florida.

It was a glorious plan, tying all the disparate pieces of the Disneyland Resort into a whole. All those small parcels of land occupied by abandoned motels and cheesy tourist traps that Disney had picked off over the years would be transformed into a lush resort with hotels, entertainment, and parks linked by monorail. The master plan even showed a large parcel of land to the southeast of the resort for future expansion – enough for a third theme park!

One problem – Disney's promotional materials for the master plan all labeled the Fujishige farm as the site of future expansion despite the fact that there was not, and had never been, any agreement for the family to sell their land to Disney. As part of the planning process for the resort, Disney included applications for permits to build a third park on the site. This did not go over well with the Fujishiges,

Third Theme Park - It's Dot Com! 245

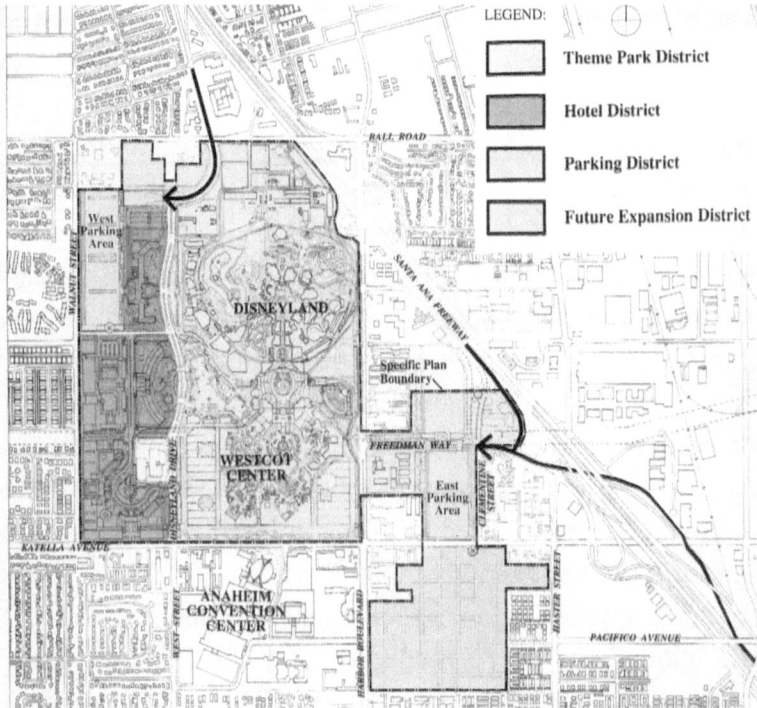

The Disneyland expansion map that touched off conflict with the Fujishiges. The area earmaked for future expansion overlapped their strawberry fields. © Disney

who famously pronounced in 1993 that they would never, under any circumstances, sell their land to Disney.

So, here we are in 1991. Disney Imagineers, at the behest of Michael Eisner, have created plans for two theme parks that, if built, would be the jewels in Disney's crown. Magnificent and highly integrated plans for resort areas had been created for the two cities, including plans for a third park in Anaheim. So, what happened?

Throughout 1991 Eisner and other Disney managers cut a swath through California, lobbying officials on the state and local levels for money and infrastructure improvements for the two projects. In Anaheim and in Sacramento they made few friends with their tactics, dangling offers from others cities over officials' heads.

In December of 1991, Disney announced that it was abandoning the Long Beach project and building WESTCOT instead. The legal and logistical issues involved with building on the Long Beach site, including the hundreds of acres of landfill that had to be dredged, continued to push up costs and delay timelines. WESTCOT could be built by 1999, while Port Disney could have taken until 2010 to be completed. Rather than deal with the hurdles that still remained in the halls of Sacramento, as well as the further cost of environmental reviews, Disney decided to play it safe and stay at home. Anaheim celebrated, and the wait began.

Then things took a turn. In April of 1992, EuroDisney opened near Paris and immediately began to hemorrhage money. EuroDisney only contained a single theme park and was a quick commute from Paris, resulting in mostly day-tripping visitors instead of the week-long vacationers Disney was used to seeing in Florida. The resort's many hotel rooms sat empty and, while the park itself was well-attended, the resort as a whole began to accrue massive debt.

The fallout from this resulted in cutbacks for Disney's other proposed projects, and the first casualty was WESTCOT. In April of 1993 Disney announced a redesign of the park with the 300-foot Spacestation Earth replaced by a lone white spire. Plans for Disneyland Center, the lakeside shopping district, had been eliminated from the plan and the hotel expansions had been scaled back as well. Disney instead planned to incorporate hotel rooms into the park itself, allowing guests to stay inside internationally-themed resorts. Downscaling continued throughout 1993, with Disney announcing in December that they were going to adopt a "smaller and slower" approach to WESTCOT. While they promised the park would be built, it would most likely be in slow and gradual phases. The EuroDisney problems led to a "wait and see" attitude, and construction continued to be delayed.

Negotiations continued, with Eisner continually threatening to pull out of the expansion while still demanding parking and infrastructure investments from the city of Anaheim. Then, with the fear of cost overruns at WDI still on Eisner's mind, 1994 arrived and changed everything at Disney. The death of Frank Wells and the departure of

Jeffery Katzenberg, Eisner's health scare, and the cancellation of Disney's America – these events took their toll, and management became cowed. Fearful of risk, Disney announced in June 1994 that they were putting off a decision on WESTCOT's future for a year. This, despite the fact that they had just recently signed an agreement with the city of Anaheim that essentially granted them many of the concessions that they had been demanding.

Then, Paul Pressler arrived at Team Disney Anaheim in November of 1994, claiming to have come to help push through the WESTCOT project. In reality, he was to be a hatchetman, and the first project to fall at his hands was WESTCOT.

In January of 1995 Disney announced the cancellation of the project citing cost concerns. They stated a continued desire for a second gate, just something "less ambitious" and with more "profit potential" that could be built in phases. Still, they said, the new project might include some aspects of the WESTCOT proposal, and possibly some elements from the Disney's America project as well as a water park. Back into the mix was the shopping district – retail being Pressler's bread and butter. Disney was back to the drawing board.

When Disney unveiled its really-for-real plans for a second gate in 1996, the result was Disney's California Adventure. With an estimated completion date of 2001, and aiming at an older crowd than Disneyland, DCA was a "hip and edgy" solution at the lowest possible price point.

By that time the tourist economy had rebounded and Disneyland was raking in cash on the heels of its very successful fortieth anniversary promotion. Expansion mania was back, and there, amidst the plans, was land earmarked for "future expansion" in a strawberry field that Disney still didn't own.

At long last, this changed. The Fujishige family finally agreed to sell 52.5 of their fifty-six acre farm to Disney in 1998. Combined with the land the company had previously purchased adjacent to the farm, Disney finally had more than eighty acres to build a third park. So what would they build?

Throughout the decade, Disney had considered several options for a third gate. Jack Lindquist, former Disneyland president, told the *Orange County Register* that these included an iteration of the Disney-MGM Studios in Florida (another Eisner pet project, the studio park had also seen attempts at clones in Paris and Tokyo), as well as a design based on the DisneySea concept that had been reconfigured for the smaller urban site in Anaheim.

As many Disney-MGM Studios attractions had already been incorporated into Disneyland and the plans for California Adventure, the DisneySea park appeared the most likely route for a third gate. Other possible projects, such as water parks or more hotels, seemed to be less profitable uses of land that Wall Street expected to see earmarked for a proper theme park. Still, the construction of a third park depended on the success of the second, so groundbreaking was still at least a decade away. Time passed...

As the resort continued to flourish, Disney became convinced that California Adventure was going to be a hit. A *big* hit. Hotel occupancy and turnstile clicks would soar, and soon Disneyland would be a bona fide resort destination just like its little brother in Florida. And this mindset is how, months before California Adventure was to debut, Disney rolled out thirdthemepark.com in the fall of 2000.

> *The proposed project would compliment Disneyland and Disney's California Adventure, possibly including a theme park or a water park, along with integrated retail, dining, and entertainment experiences. The new park would evolve, with a first phase anticipated in 2003, and completion targeted for 2010.*
>
> *- Excerpt from thirdthemepark.com*

It hit the Disney community like wildfire. A new park? And so soon? 2003? And what would be in this park, when California Adventure itself was not yet completed? Reading the website, it was difficult to say.

Dinosaur! Typhoon Lagoon! Winnie the Pooh! Buzz Lightyear! Wait... what? These attractions, along with a mention of Ariel and

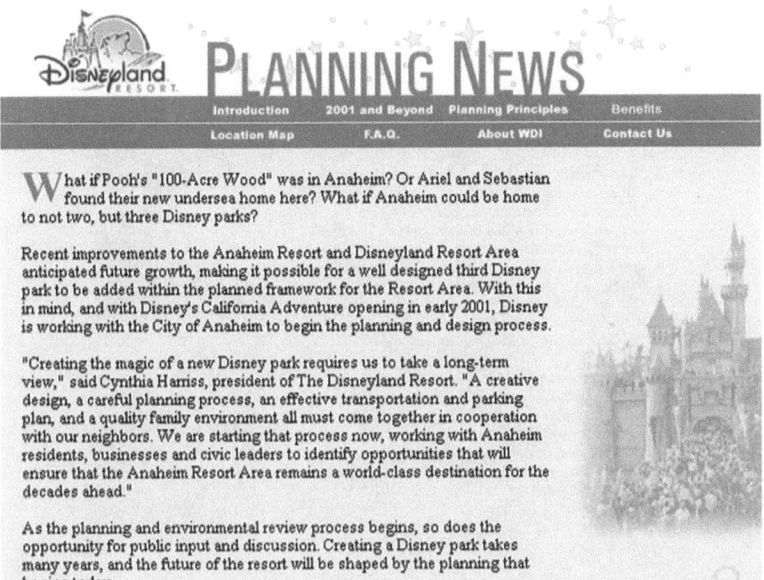

A screenshot of the thirdthemepark.com homepage. © Disney

Sebastian, were thrown into the strange theme park goulash hinted at by the website. While the site was promoting a new park, it seemed difficult to fathom what kind of park it was, or what any of these disparate ideas had to do with the other. It seemed that they were just going to raid the other parks for random ride concepts and throw them all together into… something. And Typhoon Lagoon, too. The idea of "phased" development re-emerged, and there were allusions to shopping, dining, and entertainment areas as well as a bit of hedging on whether it would be a theme park, a water park, or both. Truth be told, it seemed that Disney didn't know themselves.

So why the website? It seemed an odd thing for Disney to do considering their typical secrecy, the obviously protean concept for the park, and their then-reluctant approach to engaging fans on the internet. It was an unprecedented step, and many at the time doubted that Disney was even actually behind the site.

It makes sense, though, that Disney would want to do this. Both Port Disney and WESTCOT had been plagued by clashes with community

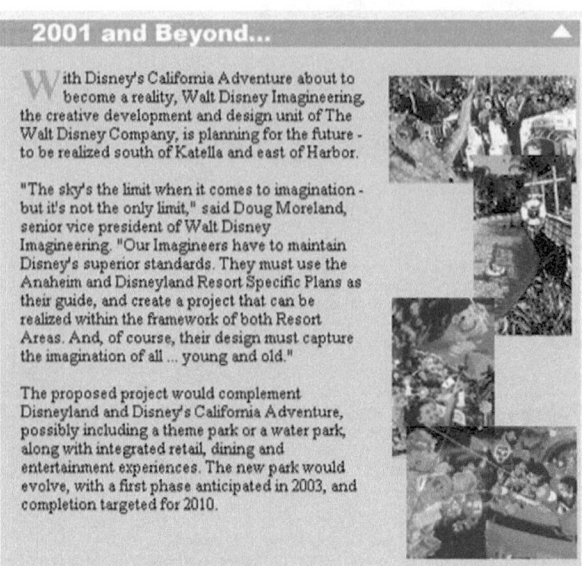

The mysterious melange: the "third theme park" site featured images of *Dinosaur*, Typhoon Lagoon, *The Many Adventures of Winnie the Pooh*, and *Buzz Lightyear's Space Ranger Spin*. © Disney

activists and civic groups. Disney had been roundly castigated for their secrecy and back-room tactics. Putting on a show of openly consulting the public early in the permitting and environmental review process showed that they were taking the community's opinions into consideration, and were behaving like good corporate citizens. It also allowed them to publicly trumpet the benefits of the resort, and the improvements that had already been made to the resort area.

In the fall of 2000, Disney began the process of bringing this new park to life. Draft environmental studies were written, and a series of public meetings were held to reach out to citizens and local businesses. The land for the park had been consolidated and it seemed like this mysterious park was on its way for a 2003 opening. One little thing, though – the fate of the new park depended on the performance of California Adventure.

Amidst all the requisite hype, California Adventure debuted in February of 2001. While the press greeted the new park warmly, guests

Before and After: Much of Disney's efforts to promote resort expansion focused on the aesthetic benefits to the surrounding area. © Disney

were wary. Disney fandom had taken off on the internet, and buzz on the new park was not good. News from previews and soft openings was even worse, and the result was an atmosphere of hostility for DCA's premiere.

Then a funny thing happened – no one showed up. Initial attendance estimates weren't met; they were then lowered, and those weren't met either. Disney first blamed the weather – certainly people would show up for Spring Break. When they didn't, Disney blamed the economy. Summer arrived, but the crowds did not. Disneyland itself continued to pack in guests, bursting at the seams on weekends and holidays, yet DCA sat empty. Disney took the unprecedented step of actually lowering admission prices for the park, and then began to offer free child admissions for passholders. Then they began to distribute thousands of free tickets throughout Anaheim as an attempt to get someone – anyone – through the turnstiles.

Throughout this process, prep work continued on the third park, still without an announced theme but widely reported to be a water park. In May of 2001, Disney began the application process for the park, only to be accused by homeowner groups of attempting to speed up the process and of a return to excessive secrecy. As DCA continued to founder, Disney began to cut staff and costs. While refusing to say that the third gate had been postponed from its announced 2003 opening, Disney spokesman Ray Gomez said that California Adventure's attendance problems would not affect the third gate and that the proposed new park was "at this point completely independent with anything taking place with the existing Disneyland resort".

By June the City Council had rejected a homeowner group's appeal and allowed Disney to start submitting applications for the third park. Many were reticent due to Disney's continuing refusal to disclose what they intended to build, but preparation continued apace. Most of management's attention that summer was drawn towards the critical issues facing California Adventure, but as Disney was trying to figure out what band-aid it could apply to Disneyland's old parking lot, the terrorist attacks of September 11th, 2001, occurred and the entire travel industry went into a nosedive.

The travel drop-off after the attacks gave Eisner cover to slash costs and eliminate staff. Despite the cutbacks, profits continued to drop, and the idea of building a new park seemed to fade. By that November, Eisner told a conference call of financial analysts that, concerning the Fujishige farm, "probably the best strawberries in Southern California will continue to grow there". Disney CFO Thomas Staggs said that while Disney was going to continue the permitting process, they were considering putting a "smaller item" on the site. They would continue with plans, he said, "if time, economy, and the fates line up".

Plans for a third park were mentioned less and less, and while theme park attendance remained soft throughout the Disney empire, it was California Adventure in particular that continued to underperform. As the creative staff responsible for DCA filtered out of the company – Pressler himself left in September of 2002 to run the Gap corporation into the ground – it became apparent that a great deal of money would have to be poured into DCA to make it a desirable destination. When Bob Iger took over as Disney CEO in 2005, California Adventure became Imagineering's main west coast focus, leading to a slate of major additions that remade nearly the entire park.

In the midst of all this corporate wrangling, few probably noticed that thirdthemepark.com was allowed to lapse in the fall of 2002. The third park was on the farthest back of burners, and the site itself was by then outdated. Not only was a 2003 opening date obviously out of reach, but two attractions mentioned on the site – *Buzz Lightyear's Space Ranger Spin* and *The Many Adventures of Winnie the Pooh* – had by then been adapted into attractions inside Disneyland itself. In the years to follow, Ariel and Sebastian would make their Anaheim debut at California Adventure.

Despite the ensuing silence about a third gate, the subject has proven to be continuously relevant. In 2007, it was central to a legal conflict between Disney, the city of Anaheim, and developers that planned a housing development adjacent to the site destined for the third park. Disney argued that the residential development broke with the zoning plans created in the 1990s for the resort district, which kept the area around Disneyland zoned strictly for commercial use. As the development contained a small amount of subsidized housing, the City Council found it difficult to oppose. At the same time, critics said that Disney had abrogated the agreement themselves by failing to live up to the promises they made for developing the old strawberry field. It appeared for a while that Disney might be forced to disclose some plan for a third park to help themselves politically; eventually the announcement of the billion-dollar expansion of California Adventure did that trick.

While the residential development eventually fell through, no light was shed on Disney's plans for a third park, and no rumors have emerged in the years since. So keep thirdthemepark.com bookmarked; you never know what's going to show up.

VII.
Neverworlds

.31

The Disney-MGM Studio Backlot

Long, long ago…
When Michael Eisner and Frank Wells took the reins of The Walt Disney Company, their agenda was clear: Movies. Both executives came from the film business, and they were brought into the studio on that basis. The problems that had faced the previous management team were firmly in the theatrical realm; theme parks were flourishing and a constant, dependable source of income, and the company was successfully branching out into new realms of cable television and consumer products. But the film business was languishing, and the studio had a number of high-profile flops that eventually forced the issue and hastened the behind-the-scenes greenmail and corporate wrangling that led to the executive shift.

And so Mr. Eisner set himself to making movies, churning out a stream of inexpensive comedies featuring somewhat faded (and therefore inexpensive) stars – and it worked. The concept of trying not for home runs, but shooting for singles, doubles, and triples paid off, and the studio's fortunes began to turn. But that wasn't the only reflection of Eisner's Hollywood-centric mindset.

MCA Inc., then owners of Universal Studios, had long planned to bring one of their trademark studio tour theme parks to Orlando – a vacation market that Disney had dominated since 1971. Yet only four months after Eisner arrived at Disney, at his first meeting with the company's shareholders in February 1985, the new CEO announced that Disney would be building their own studio tour in Florida.

This came as a surprise to MCA; its veteran chairman, Lew Wasserman, accused Disney of copying plans for a Universal park in Orlando which, they claimed, Eisner had seen years earlier. In 1981 Universal had approached Paramount as a potential financial partner in the venture and, as Eisner had been president of Paramount at the time, MCA insisted that he had been privy to Universal's ideas for a Florida studio tour. Before Disney's own studio project was announced, Wasserman and MCA president Sid Sheinberg had even approached Eisner and Wells to propose that Universal and Disney embark on a studio attraction together on Disney's Florida property.

Needless to say, the heated accusations that accompanied the announcement of what would become the Disney-MGM Studios Theme Park kicked off the "studio wars" in an atmosphere of open hostility. The situation did not improve in early 1987 when Disney and the city of Burbank announced plans for a new attraction in the heart of the city itself – the Disney-MGM Studio Backlot.

In an attempt to revitalize its city center, Burbank had been working with developers on the $158 million Towncenter mall but, when a fourth anchor tenant failed to emerge, the project fell apart. Brainstorming a way to save the project, Councilman Robert Bowne was said to have asked, "Why don't we let Disney dream a dream for Burbank?" Councilwoman and former mayor Mary Lou Howard ran with the idea and, behind the back of the City Council, approached Eisner with the idea.

Howard and Burbank City Manager Bud Ovrom lunched with Eisner at Disney's executive dining room on January 22nd, 1987, and found the executive to be very enthusiastic about the idea. During a two-hour lunch, Eisner described ideas for the project while sketching on napkins and the tablecloth. As he later recalled, "I was having a fabulous time. That's what the creative process is all about."

On April 24th, Burbank Mayor Michael Hastings traveled to Walt Disney Imagineering for a presentation on the potential project. After the two-hour pitch, Hastings stormed out of the room; "I went out of there like a bull in a china shop," he later said. "I was imagineered into a world none of us had been exposed to. I felt like our staff was being waylaid by Mickey Mouse. I went away thinking, 'Never in my city.'"

Unsurprisingly, Hastings found that few other Burbank residents shared his qualms. After days of discussion with his wife, friends, and city residents, he changed his tune. As he later put it, "The majority of the feedback I got was, 'Tread lightly on it, let's see what it's going to be.' I also started weighing the alternatives, and sorted things out. Then I was slam-dunk in favor of it." He seemed to finally comprehend what a boon a Disney project could be for the city, saying, "Anything else we would put there would be ordinary. It's time that something unusual and unique happens here. We're all used to Burbank being one way. We do a real good job of serving our senior citizens. But, unless we want to expand the Joslyn Senior Citizen Center to cover two-thirds of Burbank, we'll have to do something else for the rest of our demographics." "Something like this," he realized, "would give the whole city a shot in the arm."

To illustrate how "lucky" Burbank was to have such an opportunity, Eisner showed Ovrom and other officials a videotape the company had received from the city of Dallas featuring local businessmen, developers, restaurateurs, and "children in tuxedos" begging Disney to come to their town.

On May 5th, 1987, the Burbank City Council voted unanimously to grant Disney an option to buy forty acres of prime real estate at the corner of 3rd and Magnolia for the bargain-basement price of $1 million. The Council had been wowed by Disney's pitch for "The Disney-MGM Studio Backlot", a new concept for a retail and entertainment district that shared a great deal of DNA with the Disney-MGM Studios Theme Park, then under construction in Florida, as well as other in-development Eisner-era projects such as Typhoon Lagoon and Pleasure Island. The Backlot would showcase "behind-the-scenes Hollywood themes, street performers, live theater, Disney animation tours, and operating radio and TV media centers" at a cost of $150-$300 million.

The deal guaranteed that Burbank would not negotiate with other developers, and that Disney had six months to develop detailed plans, a parking layout, and a proposed construction schedule. After further approval by the City Council, Disney would have six more months to further develop and revise their plans. At the end of twelve months, either side could pull out of the deal if they were dissatisfied with its progress.

Nine drafts of the agreement had been written before the deal was struck; upon signing, Eisner told Councilwoman Howard, "This is your project." Howard herself was pleased, telling the press, "It's time the city had something that Johnny Carson wouldn't make fun of." City Manager Ovrom sounded optimistic, announcing, "I am convinced the Disney development has greater potential to generate more revenue and economic spinoff for the city over the long haul than any traditional center." Yet Eisner himself sounded a word of caution; speaking to the media, he warned, "We're still hoping that this project that we have described is economically feasible. The issue is not what the land cost. It's whether we can deliver the dream, financially."

But what was this dream? For starters, a third of the acreage would be devoted to shopping, with hopes for two major international retailers. Disney's existing studio lot, crammed to the gills with new film and television production, needed satellite office space and expanded backlot facilities; therefore, the Burbank project would also house a relocated feature animation department and Disney Channel offices.

Much like the new Florida park, it would also utilize the MGM film properties licensed by Disney in 1985. A six-story parking deck would be topped by a "Burbank Ocean", and a massive waterfall would conceal the structure from the neighboring I-5 freeway.

We know a good deal about this project thanks to the fact that the 1987 Burbank City Council meeting was aired on local public access television, and featured a fresh-faced young Imagineer named Joe Rohde pitching the project to the crowd.

What's hilarious about this concept is just how many Eisner-era tropes it features: A stranded ship, much like Typhoon Lagoon. Nightclubs, much like the plans for Pleasure Island. Wild visions of backlots and studio tours and buildings with false fronts that you could walk behind and see that they're fake. Something based on *Splash*. And, most importantly, a Ferris wheel. Always a Ferris wheel.

It was very important to the project's success that it serve, primarily, the people of Burbank and integrate well into the local environment. To face the low-lying residential zoning along 3rd Street, the Backlot would present a smaller urban scale before rising up to three or four stories on the side facing the local high school. At the corner of 3rd Street and Magnolia Boulevard would be a two- or three-story anchor department store operated by a major national or international chain. The notion was that the Backlot would present a welcoming and "normal" face to the outside world, melding seamlessly with its environment. But as guests proceeded further and further into its interior, things would get increasingly themed and zany. A regular Burbank shopper would be able to pop in and buy some socks without having to enter the tourist areas, as all the entertainment would be contained at the far end of the complex.

The created mythology of the space was typical Eisner-era mystique of the Meriwether Pleasure variety. Long ago, you see, in days of yore, studios had big backlots where they shot their films. As production techniques improved, however, location shooting became more common and the old studio backlots died off. But at the Disney-MGM Studio Backlot, according to the story, Disney had reclaimed its old, abandoned backlot as a shooting location and it is back in use today! Sure there are shops and restaurants in the old-timey movie sets, but they're still used for shooting! Look! There's Bette Midler shooting her saucy new Touchstone Pictures comedy! Take some pictures, folks – who knows? Tomorrow this set could be a whole other city or Ancient Greece or outer space! Anything can happen in the movies!

These "original" backlot areas would be contained in the Golden State Mall, a shopping district featuring Old West movie sets depicting a town from the Gold Rush era. These sets would be visibly "fake" with half-finished walls and facades separated from interior spaces. One of the first shopping areas guests were to encounter, it would become a performance space at night. One venue, the old train roundhouse containing a country & western and comedy club, sounds particularly atmospheric. Especially interesting would be the old locomotive converted for use as a cappuccino machine, peanut cooker, and "potato roaster" which would also illuminate the stage with its front light. Leftover mining explosives would be used to construct the bar. The idea of having different characters in each area – related, no doubt, to the Disney-MGM Studio Theme Park concept of "streetmosphere" – would result in these different clubs and areas having wacky denizens and proprietors (and also, said Rohde, "girls with long legs doing kicksteps").

Other streets within the Backlot would be themed to New York, European cities, and Tokyo's Ginza district. Ginza was a long-time Imagineering target; it was proposed for the very first version of World Showcase in the 1970s, and was announced as an expansion for Epcot's Japan Pavilion in the 1990s.

Much like old studio lots, the Backlot would also feature streets based on ancient or mythical places, from Pompeii to Angkor Wat to Ancient Egypt. As Rohde promised, we could meet for lunch "under the statue of Ptolemy".

On the upper levels of the Backlot, separated from the shoppers and strollers, would be the nightclubs. Disney envisioned a number of venues ranging from "Club Heaven", located in the Ginza area, to a Caribbean-themed calypso club. Another proposal was for an odd-sounding club where, for entertainment, guests would sit in a chair and operate Audio-Animatronics figures.

In the area themed to lost cities – don't worry, said Rohde, "you don't need to confront the Sphinx" – a club full of mystical artifacts would pull historic figures through time as part of a "cinematic event". In this storage warehouse, guests would be surrounded by props used in great movies which, imbued with magnetic powers, would revive the personalities of the actors who once used them. As guests dined, characters such as Cleopatra, Marc Antony, and Ben Franklin would play out a story around them.

Providing a respite from this madness would be the California Canyon, a quiet and relaxing space where waterfalls and a trout stream would flow in the shadow of two towering structures. Looking down from offices, balconies, or restaurants, all designed in a California bungalow style, people would be able to enter the canyon for an evening stroll among the sycamore groves.

Rising from the canyon, and the "crown of the entire project", was to be the Hollywood Fantasy Hotel. Surrounded by Rohde's trout and squirrels, each floor of this remarkable hotel would be themed to a different film genre. Imagine staying in a room straight out of film noir! At the top, Imagineers planned the Celestial Diner, billed by Rohde as "the most romantic place to have a meal in the entire west". The restaurant does indeed sound spectacular, featuring a chamber orchestra and planetarium ceiling.

From these attractions, guests could enter the more traditional entertainment areas of the Backlot. Straight from plans for the new Florida studio park, the Disney animation department would move to a new campus incorporated into the Backlot complex. Open to tours, and featuring a public museum for the Disney Archives, the campus would also feature a multiplex theater that could house annual animation festivals. In the Star Quality Diner, people could dine surrounded by movie memorabilia while their kids played on catwalks above. The Soundstage Restaurant would cater to family audiences, drawing from the "mythology" of Disney and MGM. This is where the Disney characters could be found, and where character meals would take place.

Also in this area would be a duplicate of Florida's planned *Great Moments at the Movies* ride (soon to become *The Great Movie Ride*), and an attraction teaching about special effects using *Star Tours* simulator technology. A three-camera video production studio would feature an attraction similar to Florida's *Superstar Television* show, and the ubiquitous Videopolis Dance Club (soon to be found at both Disneyland and Florida's Pleasure Island) was there to provide hep teens with food and dancing with a sci-fi spin.

At the farthest extent of the Backlot was to be a waterfront entertainment district surrounding the eighteen-inch deep "Burbank Ocean". Featuring a number of typical pleasure pier attractions, the area was meant to represent the Backlot's old movie studio special effects tank which had been converted for use by guests. The Ocean would stretch to the horizon, blocking out the freeway, and cascading out of sight past the parking garage below. To a guest on the boardwalk, they would merely see the sun setting into the "ocean".

Along the pier could be found a traditional funhouse as well as bumper cars, said Rohde, "with a difference"; the Rockin' Rollerdrome, later to appear at Pleasure Island, was also planned here, offering rollerskating, dancing, and dining while a DJ flew around overhead in a '57 Chevy. Particularly clever was The Deep End, a restaurant with a 1950s beach theme that appeared to be housed at the bottom of a swimming pool. A faux water surface far above would create the illusion, combined with lighting effects and Audio-Animatronics "swimmers" padding overhead.

Yet another Eisner classic was Madison's Dive, a bar once intended for Pleasure Island and themed to the 1984 hit film *Splash*. This crabhouse's windows would look out into aquariums, giving a sense that diners were deep underwater alongside passing sea life.

Emerging from the Burbank Ocean was to be an enormous Ferris wheel, which, lodged halfway into the building like a stuck quarter, would bring guests out of the Ocean six stories above the ground. But this didn't hold a candle to the other attraction sitting on the precipice of the waterfall – the Fish out of Water Restaurant.

Housed in a ship stranded on the edge of the Burbank Ocean, with six stories of waterfall roiling below, this restaurant would be based on the simple premise that – in perhaps the most immortal pitch ever presented by an Imagineer – "Something's wrong, and beef lives in the sea."

Something is wrong. And beef... lives in the sea.

Guests seeking to dine would have to board a rowboat from the pier and make their way out to the stranded ship; inside would be traditional seafood restaurant decor but, instead of fish, diners would find the best steakhouse in L.A. Instead of mounted swordfish, the walls would be lined with stuffed steer. Lobster traps, twelve feet long and modified for cows, would hang from the ceiling. Paintings and pictures would show massive trawlers fishing for cow, schools of cow leaping from the water, Cousteau swimming with the cows, Hemingway showing off a bison he had reeled in…

Tell me that wouldn't be spectacular.

On the deck of the ship, a balcony and bar would provide guests with a tasty beverage and a spectacular view of the Valley. And if that isn't reason enough to mourn the loss of this project, nothing is.

Perhaps unsurprisingly, and immediately upon announcement of the project, MCA Inc. responded to Disney's plans with outrage. The "studio wars" were already two years old at this point, and not only had Universal decided to proceed with a studio facility in Orlando, but it had also determined to expand its entertainment offerings in the hills north of Hollywood. Universal saw Disney's proposed entertainment complex as a direct threat to its plans for a similar district in Universal City (the eventual CityWalk), and lodged a complaint with the Burbank City Council.

Disney, MCA believed, had gotten a sweetheart deal, and other companies should have had a chance to bid on a project for the Burbank land. Burbank admitted that Disney got a good deal, paying $1 million – fifty-seven cents a square foot – for land that other developers might have paid $50 million for. The city had pushed for more money, but Disney stuck to their initial offer. "The break we got in the cost of the land," Eisner insisted, "will be so compensated by what we spend on just bricks and mortar on this property that Burbank will get back its fair amount of investment."

Also contentious was the issue of parking; Disney felt that the city should provide funds for a parking structure, which could have cost as much as $35 million, while the city believed Disney should pay. Eventually the city agreed to give Disney $1-$3 million in property tax breaks to go towards the construction of parking facilities.

In June 1987, MCA filed suit to overturn the deal and force public negotiations with other companies. MCA accused Disney executives of blackmail, claiming they had offered to pull out of Burbank if Universal would abandon their plans for an Orlando park. Disney denied the accusation.

But MCA wasn't Disney's only legal issue. The chairman of MGM-UA, Lee Rich, claimed that Disney had no rights to use licensed MGM properties or names outside of Orlando. "We were very upset about it," Rich said of the Burbank deal. "We're going to do anything we can to get them not to use it." For his part, Eisner felt that it was "crystal clear" that Disney was perfectly within its rights, and pointed out that they already planned to use the MGM name in multiple overseas projects.

As the year passed, more problems emerged. In October 1987 Disney claimed that they'd had problems attracting major retailers to the project and that the Backlot may have to be "scaled back" to become sufficiently profitable. By February 1988, the estimated cost of the complex had risen to $618 million, although Disney had entered talks with British retailer Harrods. Mitsukoshi of Japan, although not yet contacted by Disney, openly expressed interest in the project as well.

But it was not to be. On April 8th, 1988, Disney sent a letter to Burbank officials withdrawing from its agreement to buy the land. Alan Epstein, Vice President of the Disney Design Company, called the decision "extremely difficult" and claimed that Disney had already spent $2.5 million and 22,000 working hours developing the concept.

In the end, the death knell for Burbank's Backlot was a familiar and unwelcome line; in the words of Disney spokesman Tom Deegan, "We gave it the pencil test, and it didn't pass."

Apparently no one told him about *BEEF LIVING IN THE SEA*.

I'm with you on this one, Joe. I'll go to Lowe's and pick up some lumber and meet up at your house. Beef under the sea is an idea whose time has come. Time to start building.

.32

Port Disney

> *Disney's Imagineers have focused their efforts on exploring the myths, romance, challenges, and mysteries of the ocean – the world's last great frontier. Both fun and educational, DisneySea would break down barriers between our guests and the sea.*
>
> *At the rim of the American continent and the Pacific Ocean, DisneySea will be a place of magic and wonder...*
>
> – Port Disney Preliminary Master Plan
> Executive Report, 1990

The early 1990s were a very active time at Walt Disney Imagineering. Disney CEO Michael Eisner had announced the "Disney Decade", which involved an unprecedented wave of expansion in the theme parks division. Imagineering had one park – the then-named Euro Disneyland – under construction, and at least six parks (that we know of) in development. Two of these, the Disney-MGM Studios clones for Europe and Japan, are variations on a theme with which we are familiar. The other four, however, are each exemplars of WDI design and show what a creatively fruitful period this was at Imagineering. It's unfortunate that only one of these projects – California's Port Disney and WESTCOT, Florida's Animal Kingdom, and Disney's America in Virginia – were ever built.

The reasons for the demise of these grand projects vary in the details, but upon examination similar themes emerge. All the projects met with some initial resistance from a vocal minority, which was only compounded when faced by Disney's then-defiant upper-level management. By the time public and private support for the parks rallied and various bureaucratic roadblocks began to fall, fatigue had set in at

Team Disney. The effort expended on these projects, combined with rising costs, the deepening American economic recession, the financial difficulties faced by EuroDisney, the loss of key staff members, and his own health issues, seemed to dispirit Eisner and began the long period of retrenchment that marked the remainder of his tenure.

The Port Disney project began in 1988, when Disney finally achieved its long-time goal of purchasing the Disneyland Hotel. The hotel had been built in 1955 by Jack Wrather as a favor to his friend Walt Disney, who at that time couldn't afford to build the hotel himself. Then-rural Anaheim desperately needed hotel rooms to provide lodging for Disney's guests, so Wrather filled that role. This later proved a problem for Disney, as Wrather refused to sell the property once Disney could afford to purchase it, and an anti-competition clause in their contract prevented Disney from building his own resorts in the area.

After Wrather's death, Disney took control of the Disneyland Hotel by purchasing the Wrather Corporation outright. They divested most of its assets, save for a few key items (Tangentially, one of Wrather's properties was the rights to the Lone Ranger). They also retained Wrather's interests in Long Beach, which included a 66-year lease on the retired ocean liner *Queen Mary*. The lease also included an adjacent 55-acre parcel of land, site of a domed building containing Howard Hughes's fabled *Spruce Goose*, and the right to fill in and develop 250 acres of water.

Disney immediately began to consider development possibilities for the site. Their interest was not with the *Queen Mary*, which had proven to be a costly drain on the city since its arrival in 1967. Instead, Disney was looking to develop the property next to the ship. The planning process continued for several years in secret, with only occasional hints leaking out as to what this "Disney-by-the-Sea" complex would be.

In early 1990, Michael Eisner disclosed that Disney intended to build a second theme park in Southern California. The new attraction would be built in either Anaheim or Long Beach; with typical

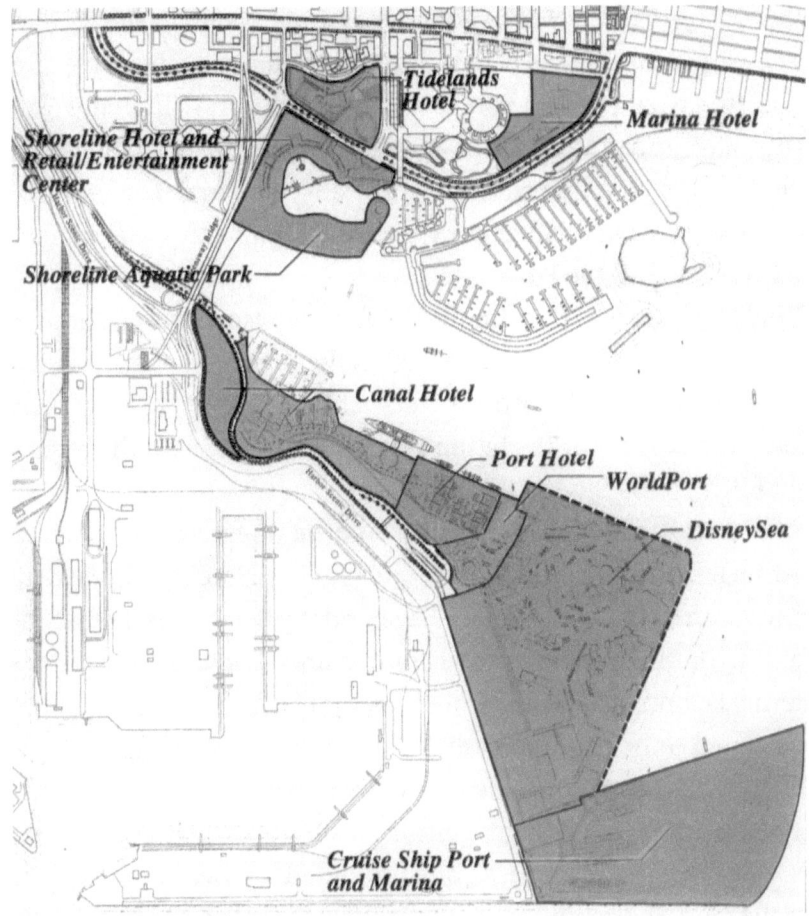

The Port Disney plan as of July, 1990. Expansion of the existing port area would require 250 acres of landfill, and the removal of the *Spruce Goose*, Londontowne development, the Viscount Hotel and Adolph's restaurant, the Reef Restaurant, and Cannon's restaurant. © Disney

Eisner charm it was announced that the decision "depends a lot on which one wants us more." In July of that year, Disney was forced by the terms of their development deal to disclose their plans for Long Beach. They were nothing short of spectacular.

The $3 billion Port Disney resort complex would span roughly 414 acres on both sides of Queensway Bay. The two sides of the resort would be connected by watercraft, monorail, and the Queensway Bridge, crossing the bay on the west side near the mouth of the Los

Angeles River. The resort as announced would contain the 225-acre DisneySea theme park, a cruise ship port, and five – later six – resort hotels that would total 3,900 rooms over 125 acres. The entire area would have integrated design elements typical of a Disney resort, including landscaping, signage, and transportation. The two main areas of the resort, divided as they were by the Bay, were designated the City-Side and the Port-Side.

The City-Side was to contain many of the resort's hotel, shopping, and entertainment areas. Described as the "urban recreational" part of the resort, it would also provide public access to waterways and allow the resort's transportation system to connect with the regional light rail system's Blue Line.

This part of the development would be integrated with several existing facilities, including the Hyatt Regency Hotel, the Long Beach Convention Center, Shoreline Village, and the Downtown Long Beach Marina. The Disney-built hotels in this area would be linked by an internal lagoon system, and hotel-adjacent Shoreline Drive would be redesigned to be more pedestrian friendly. Port Disney's monorail system would run alongside Shoreline Drive, connecting the three City-Side Disney hotels before turning southwards towards DisneySea.

Described as "first-class" and bounded by Seaside Way, Pine Avenue, and Shoreline Drive, the 900-room Tidelands Hotel would connect by pedestrian bridge to the Convention Center and The Pike at Rainbow Harbor, a retail and entertainment development. Set on a 14.8-acre lot, the hotel would be built above a series of parking garages and conference spaces.

Originally designed with a six-acre park and pond, the hotel's layout was altered in early 1991 in response to public pressure. Some residents disliked the design, saying it "faced away" from downtown, and suggested the hotel be moved westward. Disney agreed, and reconfigured the site by moving the hotel to the west and extending its water feature along the entire eastern border of the property. Possibilities under consideration included a freshwater pond or a connection to the existing Shoreline Aquatic Park lagoon to the south.

Disney planned to coordinate with the developers of the then-unbuilt Pike property to the north to ensure that sight-lines to the ocean remained clear.

A separate 25-acre site would contain the 400-unit, all-suite Shoreline Hotel and feature a variety of shops, restaurants, and entertainment along a boardwalk on its ground floor (in fact, it sounds quite similar to the later Boardwalk Resort at Walt Disney World). This hotel would wrap around the northern shore of the Shoreline Aquatic Park lagoon, providing access along the boardwalk to "paddle boats and other non-motor craft". Disney later considered expanding this lagoon as well.

The construction of this hotel would replace the northern section of the Shoreline Aquatic Park, eliminating a seventy-space R.V. campground. In May of 1991 Disney agreed to replace those facilities with a similar campground on the east bank of the Los Angeles River. The rest of the existing Shoreline Aquatic Park would remain, providing continuous public access to the waterfront. A long promenade would extend the length of the development, with landscaped parks and fishing facilities.

The Shoreline Hotel would also house a ferry landing that would connect the City-Side of the resort with the WorldPort and DisneySea across the Bay:

> *The marina esplanade ... is an ideal location for viewing stands for competition and racing activities, such as mini-outboard and hydrofoil races, waterskiing and jetskiing events, and specialized sailcraft, and for other water events, such as fireworks and fireboat displays and water pageants.*

Set on a twenty-acre lot east of the Convention Center, the 700-room Marina Hotel would connect by landscaped walkways to nearby hotels, the Convention Center, and the existing downtown marina.

As guests crossed over the Queensway Bridge or drove along Disney's own access road, they would enter the "fantasy-resort" Port-Side. Access was available by car, ferry, monorail, or pedestrian bridge, and

Guests catch their first glimpse of DisneySea as they turn on to the entry drive under the Queensway Bridge looking southeast. The Canal Hotel is to the right. Said Disney, "The project entry should create a sense of anticipation upon arrival, evoke the waterfront resort feeling, and add a touch of fantasy." © Disney

guests would pass two hotels (one of which was said to evoke Long Beach's historic Hotel Virginia), a guest marina, and the WorldPort before arriving at the jewel of the resort – DisneySea park.

The largest of the Port Disney hotels, the Canal Hotel would house 1,400 guests rooms on a 45-acre site "encircled by a ribbon of water". The hotel would have a 2,300-space parking lot and a 150-slip guest marina. The 20-acre site of the 500-room Port Hotel would be "criss-crossed by 'finger canals'".

These plans changed in May of 1991 when the Canal Hotel was redesigned. This alteration to the plan made way for a new, sixth hotel. Disney designers felt that having three hotels on the Port-Side

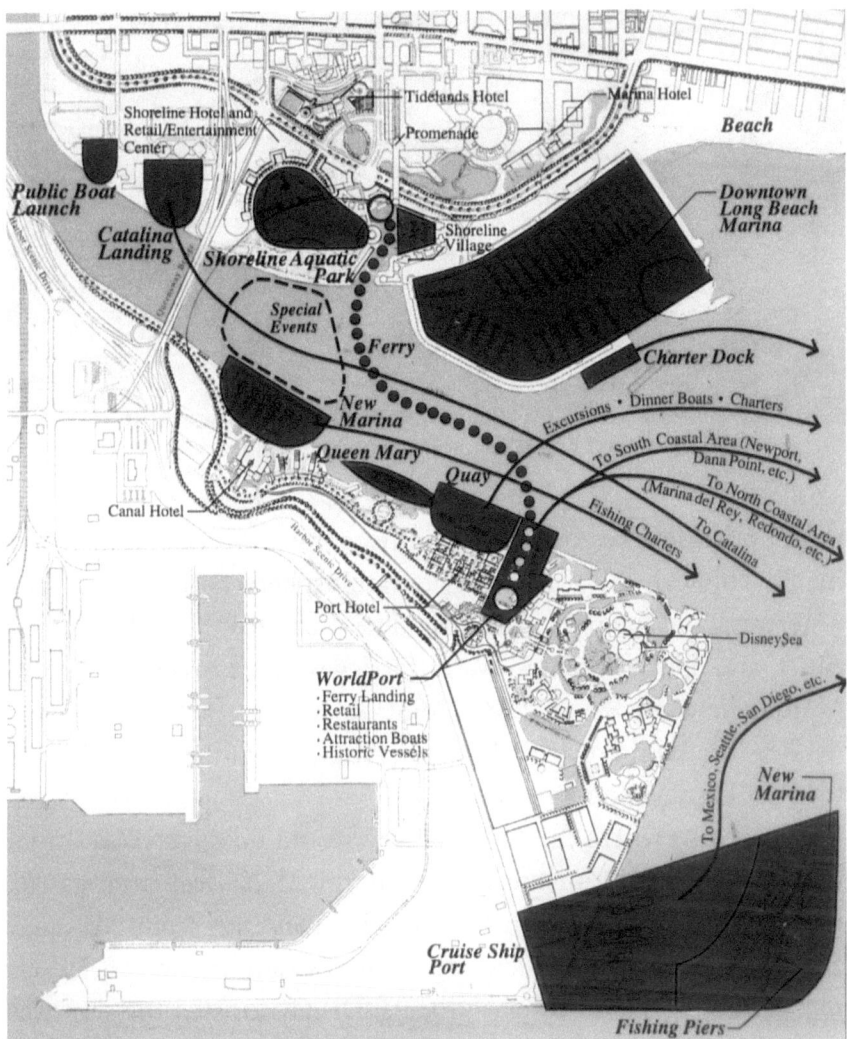

Port Disney would be an active center of aquatic transportation: "Boats of every size, shape, and origin ply the waters of Port Disney offering rentals, excursions, shows, dining, and fun." © Disney

instead of two would allow for smaller, five- to seven-story buildings that would provide a more consistent resort aesthetic. The sixth hotel in Disney's plan, the Regatta, took the place of the Canal Hotel, which was reduced in size and moved closer to the Port Hotel.

The WorldPort, situated on the doorstep of the DisneySea park, would serve as Port Disney's center of activity. Cross-channel and excursion ferries would depart regularly, and a waterfront promenade

Rendering detail of a Mediterranean-styled WorldPort. © Disney

would provide access to shops and restaurants. Dockside entertainment would help create a festive port atmosphere; Disney-controlled waterways and the port plaza would be home to "theme boats, pageants, and special events". Water ferries would provide service to Avalon, Newport Beach, Dana Point, Redondo Beach, and Marina del Rey. The WorldPort would also serve as the southern terminus of the Port Disney monorail line.

This is also where the *Queen Mary* would be docked, as initial Disney plans called for the ship to be moved 700 feet from its current location to sit between the Port Hotel and the WorldPort quay. The actual disposition of the ship in Disney's plan remained nebulous throughout the development process; Disney insisted the ship was an "important visual icon" for the resort, but claimed that they didn't know what they would do with it.

The ship, already converted to a hotel when Disney took over its lease in 1988, was a consistent money loser but had many supporters in the community. The city, having already leased the ship to a number of unsuccessful parties, dumped control of the hotel on the Harbor Department in 1978. Desperate to relieve themselves of the financial drain, they leased the *Queen Mary* to Wrather in 1980. They attached one clause: if Wrather, or later Disney, wished to back out of their long-term lease, they would be forced to purchase the ship from the city for its scrap value and then pay to have it scrapped or scuttled. The city didn't want the *Queen Mary* back – if Disney didn't want it, the ship was dead.

This naturally upset many of the ship's proponents, who argued in favor of preserving its classical beauty and art deco ambience. Disney refused to commit to the ship's role in Port Disney, and after the resort project fell through many feared the worst. Disney divested themselves of the ship in 1992, but after a brief closure it reopened. Despite the city's many attempts to rid themselves of it, the majestic ocean liner still graces the port of Long Beach.

An ironic footnote: although Long Beach officials longed to rid themselves of the *Queen Mary*, when it came time for Disney to construct Tokyo's DisneySea park, they built themselves their own copy – the "S.S. Columbia" sits in that park's American Waterfront area.

At the southernmost tip of Port Disney, a five-berth port would provide cruise ships access to Long Beach for the first time. The terminal, operated by the Port of Long Beach, would have its own parking area and a curving breakwater structure with a 250-slip public marina. As part of later redesigns in May of 1991, the cruise port was reconfigured for easier access. The curved breakwater was altered, and the marina area was moved farther to the north.

The breakwater would also house a landscaped public park, with several fishing piers and an oceanfront promenade that would extend northwards past DisneySea to the City-Side of the resort. Thus, guests could walk or bike from one end of the resort to the other without crossing a road.

These public facilities were crucial to Disney's efforts in obtaining permits for the resort; the Coastal Commission only allows those facilities that require oceanfront access permission to create landfill, and the Commission didn't necessarily see a theme park as fitting those parameters. In order to justify the 250 acres of landfill required to build Port Disney, Imagineers loaded the design as much as possible with coastal-specific uses. These included the marinas, the cruise ship port, the ferry ports, and even the aquarium and research

Model of Port Disney, with the DisneySea theme park. The cruise ship terminal is located in the immediate foreground. © Disney

facilities at the DisneySea park. While this still didn't exactly sway the Commission, and Disney was forced to justify the need for another cruise port in Southern California, necessity proved the mother of invention and helped craft a nicely integrated design for the resort.

The cruise port would offer routes to the north and south along the west coast of the United States and to Mexico, with possible destinations including Mazatlán, Ensenada, San Francisco, Seattle, and Alaska. It would also provide competition for the Port of Los Angeles – in fact, it would make Long Beach the largest cruise terminal on the west coast.

The most important part of the Port Disney project was its centerpiece theme park, DisneySea. The DisneySea park designed for Long

An artistic rendering of the DisneySea theme park. © Disney

Beach incorporated many elements that might appear familiar to fans of Tokyo DisneySea, but it also featured science and research-based aspects reminiscent of Epcot Center's The Living Seas pavilion as well as aquatic attractions similar to Florida's Typhoon Lagoon water park. Guests would encounter live sea creatures and learn about the oceanic environment, but they'd also experience fantastic lands themed to a Grecian village, an Asian water-market, and a Caribbean lagoon. Imagineers would block views of the unsightly cargo port to the west with a massive, 17,000-space parking garage.

Various ports of call themed to places real and imagined would surround the park's centerpiece, Oceana. Inside this futuristic bubble-shaped structure would be housed the world's largest aquarium, "luring guests to a fascinating evolutionary journey through the world's seas".

Oceana's state-of-the-art, two-story aquarium would reach depths of up to thirty feet and contain a volume of 10–12 million gallons. Proposed features would include the Future Research Center, similar to Epcot's Living Seas pavilion. There, scientists from around the

Oceana, the visual centerpiece of Port Disney. © Disney

world would conduct oceanographic studies and other work. At the Hands-On Exploratorium, interactive exhibits would allow "adults and children alike" to learn about the ocean and its diverse marine life. Other ideas included the "Clean Sweep" Exhibit – a hands-on exhibit demonstrating how to clean up an oil spill – and a submarine simulator that would "take visitors on a pretend ride to famous underwater locations".

Sitting in the shadow of a man-made volcano, and said to represent the "scary side" of DisneySea, the Mysterious Island area would bring to life the tales of Captain Nemo and his Nautilus. This area was eventually re-created at Tokyo DisneySea.

One Mysterious Island attraction, *City of Atlantis*, would take guests to that lost underwater city on what was deemed "a modern version of a Disneyland 'E' attraction". Pirate Island, publicized as "Tom Sawyer's Island times ten", would allow children to explore while following clues to buried treasure. Finally, a thrill ride called *Nemo's Lava Cruiser* would suspend guests in the air before sending them careening through underground caverns.

Based on ancient legends, Heroes' Harbor would be themed to an ancient Greek village. It would be where "the myths and legends of the sea come to life". Entrance to Heroes' Harbor would be through the Aqua-Labyrinth, a "challenging maze with walls made only of water". Two attractions would recreate the adventures of ancient mariners, one featuring the Arabian hero Sinbad and the other highlighting the Homeric exploits of Ulysses.

Fleets of Fantasy, a more whimsically-designed area, would sit near the boardwalk, and renderings depict a number of funfair rides with nautical trappings. According to Disney, "a harbor of fabled and fanciful ships, including outsized Chinese junks and Egyptian galleys, would disguise exciting rides and dining and entertainment experiences." It's possible that an outdoor amphitheater was planned for this area.

As a tribute to Long Beach's past, and the former Pike amusement park and historic horseshoe-shaped Rainbow Pier, a nostalgic boardwalk would occupy the side of the park facing downtown. Various renderings depict a Ferris wheel and an old-fashioned wooden roller coaster similar to that later found in California Adventure's Paradise Pier. The Ferris wheel and wooden roller coaster combination was a familiar one in this era of Imagineering, proposed for projects as varied as the Disney's America theme park and Walt Disney World's Boardwalk Resort.

The area of the park called Adventure Reef would be most similar to Florida's Typhoon Lagoon – not surprising, since DisneySea Imagineer Kym Murphy had worked on both that water park and The Living Seas at Epcot. Focused on actual real-life aquatic activity, Adventure Reef would allow guests the opportunity to surf or snorkel through tropical reefs teeming with fish. It was described as a "paradise" setting in which guests could swim and wade. Most surprising in this area was an attraction in which guests would be lowered in a steel cage into a tank full of sharks.

Disney promoted Port Disney as "an 18-hour experience", yet it probably would have been much more:

An evening cruise past Port Disney. © Disney

> *The waterfront at night is also exciting. The shapes of the bridge, boats, and buildings; the reflections in the river, canals, and lagoons; and the City and Port lights illuminate the different character of the nighttime waterfront. In addition, special lighting and special events, such as laser and fireworks shows, boat parades, and evening harbor cruises, provide drama, excitement, and romance to complete the palette of water experiences...*

If only.

What's frustrating is that, ultimately, there was little to actually prevent Disney from going forward on these projects. There were regulatory hurdles, of course, but members of the Coastal Commission in Long Beach, where Port Disney was to be located, ultimately appeared as willing to play ball as officials in Anaheim. Re-living the story through press accounts, one gets the impression of numerous tactical successes by Disney officials on the ground in Long Beach, while the corporate offices in Burbank made one strategic misstep after another. Token resistance was to be expected by those parties that either wanted to protect their own interests or make an example of Disney; executives didn't help their cause with secretive negotiations and a clumsy attempt to purchase legislative support in Sacramento as a shortcut around the jurisdiction of the less-friendly Coastal Commission.

While obviously watchdog groups proved an annoyance to Disney, and grandstanding legislators seemed prone to ridiculous demands for mitigation, in the end the public was in favor of Port Disney. Its obvious benefits for Long Beach would no doubt have led to its approval had Disney not opted to build WESTCOT Center, a west-coast version of Epcot Center, in Anaheim instead.

During the planning process, Disney developed at least two versions of the resort and its centerpiece theme park, DisneySea. The original design, which called for 250 acres of landfill, did not receive legislative support as easily as Disney had hoped, so in the fall of 1991 they unveiled a smaller site plan. While committing to neither version, and always pointing out that both designs were likely to change before construction, Disney at least had a contingency available should the cost of the larger plan prove prohibitive.

This second plan only required fifty acres of landfill, and that area would be mostly used by easily-approved coastal projects such as the aquarium and research facilities. Under this plan, the cruise ship terminal and marina would be built by the neighboring city port, which could more easily obtain the necessary permits and, in turn, reduce Disney's need for landfill. The *Queen Mary* would then be moved from Disney property to the port facility. The existing Harbor Department headquarters would be demolished and relocated to the new terminal site, allowing Disney to occupy its former location.

Ultimately, Disney officials seem to have been displeased with the smaller plan that necessity had forced upon them, and that in part led to the project's abandonment. Delays in the approval process and escalating costs made Port Disney difficult to justify when compared to the cheaper and quicker yet still spectacular WESTCOT option.

One last oddity: in October of 1991 the name of the resort project was changed from "Port Disney" to simply "DisneySea". Previously, only the theme park went by the DisneySea name. Officials from the

Port of Long Beach objected to the Port Disney name, thinking that it somehow was threatening their identity or prominence. Disney made the concession and changed the name, and two months later chose Anaheim for its second gate in California.

In the end, it was money that killed the Port Disney project. Development in Anaheim required only the approval of the city council, which had long ago been wined and dined into submission by Disney. Building on the coast in Long Beach required local, state, and federal approvals; even though Disney had factored the bureaucracy into their scheduling, Anaheim seemed the easier road to take when faced with the option of only building in one site.

Disney would have had to pay for less infrastructure in Anaheim, and would be saved the $50-75 million cost of restoring various wetlands sites to offset the environmental impact of the landfill required to build Port Disney.

A second gate in Anaheim would also benefit from being built adjacent to Disneyland – a situation so sensible that many in Long Beach thought that Disney never really intended to build Port Disney at all. It was, they claimed, merely a ruse to force Anaheim officials to accept a less favorable deal on infrastructure and zoning. If it was all a feint, it was an expensive one. Disney spent several years and many millions of dollars on the Port Disney project, only to give up when many felt success was still possible.

The difficulties involved in getting such massive projects off the ground became an easy scapegoat for executives; in a petulant speech to the World Affairs Council of Orange County in November of 1992, Eisner blamed the state's business environment and environmental obstacles for sinking the park. Eisner used the opportunity to taunt Californians that Disney would build a DisneySea park not in Long Beach but in Tokyo (where, he neglected to mention, the entire bill would be footed by the Oriental Land Company). The story was also an implied threat to Anaheim officials – if they didn't approve $750 million in improvements sought for the resort area, Disney wouldn't build WESTCOT either. Anaheim eventually pushed through the approvals for WESTCOT and the improvements for the resort area – and Disney built California Adventure instead.

But the spirit of Port Disney lived on in plans for Tokyo DisneySea, and while many of the park's details had changed from the Long Beach concept by the time the Tokyo park opened in 2002, it is now considered by many to be the most beautiful theme park in the world.

.33

Disney's America

"Every day, a diverse and unlikely society, made up of every culture and race on earth, is working together to build a great nation. We have a single vision – a new order based on the promise of democracy.

Our resources for building this nation are a rich mixture of land, family, and beliefs – which we apply with our own fiery brand of spirit, humor, and innovation.

As the nation has grown and changed, we are constantly reminded of how impossibly far we've come – and how far we still have to go.

DISNEY'S AMERICA celebrates these qualities which have always been the source of our strength and the beacon of hope to people everywhere."

– Disney Promotional Material, 1994

On November 11th, 1993, Michael Eisner and other Disney officals gathered in Haymarket, Virginia to announce the Disney's America project. The announcement was rushed, as Disney had been forced by press leaks to move the press conference up and thus try and get ahead of the story. Secrecy had allowed Disney to either purchase or option 3,000 acres of property in the area, but it also made them unable to quickly respond to local critics who were both well-connected and very well funded.

Nearly a year later, in September of 1994, Disney would announce that they were no longer seeking to build the park in Prince William County. While the story of Eisner's 'year of hell' and the political and business machinations that helped torpedo the park are fascinating,

"Recall the Past, Live the Present, Dream the Future"
– Disney Promotional Material, 1994
© Disney

what's most important here is the park we missed out on. So let's take a look at the process that brought us the park, and find out what we missed.

The roots of Disney's America were deep indeed. From the time of Disneyland's opening, Walt Disney intended to create an area to educate the youth of 1950s America about their roots and the processes that created the nation. Since then, Americana has continued to be one of Disney's best-executed themes and seemed to be one that Imagineering could most effectively extend to an entire park.

As we've seen in an earlier chapter, Walt himself once intended to create an area directly off of Main Street in Disneyland called "Liberty Street". This cul-de-sac would recreate Colonial America, with various shops and exhibits showcasing crafts and trades in a period setting. These would not be mere merchandise locations, but actual silversmiths, printers, and blacksmiths demonstrating their skills for visitors. The street would end in Liberty Square, a colonial plaza centering on a recreation of Philadelphia's Independence Hall (here called "Liberty Hall").

Liberty Hall would house two major show attractions in the Hall of the Declaration of Independence and the Hall of Presidents of the United States. Both of these shows would rely on the still nascent

Audio-Animatronics technology. Early tests had been done, but the technology was far from ready and these attractions were likely intended to rely on sculpted, life-sized figures with a much more limited range of motion than we have come to expect today.

Eventually, financial and technological concerns led to the scuttling of the Liberty Street concept. Disneyland's expansion budget would go instead to the 1959 Tomorrowland rehabilitation, and the Imagineers would start to focus on the development of a single Lincoln animatronic. With the help of Robert Moses, Walt was eventually able to secure development money for the figure and *Great Moments with Mr. Lincoln* debuted at the 1964 New York World's Fair.

Seven years later, freed from the roadblocks that Disney faced in 1964, the *Hall of Presidents* premiered with Walt Disney World's 1971 opening. The technology and budget were now available to mass-produce animatronic figures (36 presidents at the time), and to present a show similar to Walt's original concept. In fact, some elements of the Florida script and audio recordings dated to the development of the earlier show in the 1960s.

The *Hall of Presidents* was presented in a land unique to Walt Disney World; Liberty Square is a small but highly themed land designed along the lines of Walt's Liberty Street. Intended as an alternative to Disneyland's ornate New Orleans Square (Imagineers thought that Walt Disney World would be too close to the actual New Orleans for that area to be effective), the land reflects the same colonial setting that would much later be used in 1982's *The American Adventure* at Epcot Center and on an even grander scale in Disney's America.

In the late 1980s, Michael Eisner had kicked Imagineering into gear. By 1993, Walt Disney World already had its third gate and a fourth was being secretly designed at Walt Disney Imagineering. Two different second gates had been designed for California, and a second park was in development for Tokyo as well. Euro Disney had just recently opened, and a second gate for the Paris resort had been designed before financial concerns forced its delay.

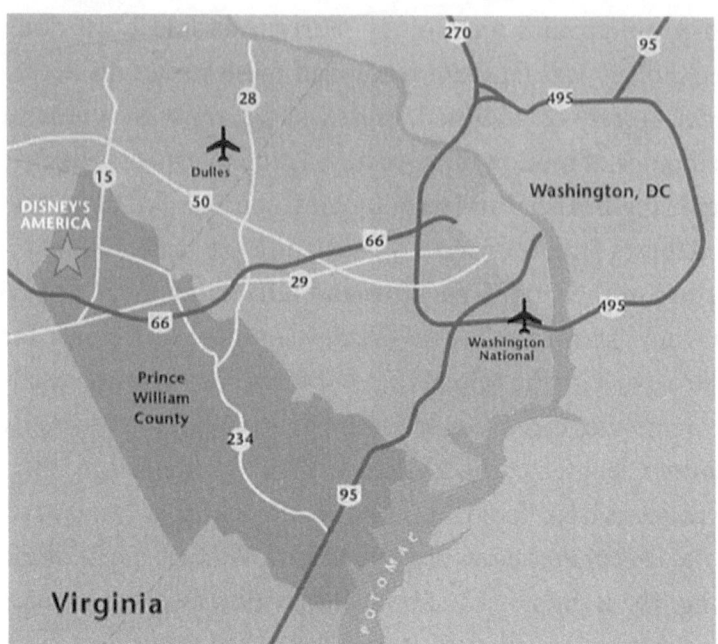

The site: Disney's America would be a close drive to Washington, D.C., as well as a number of historic Civil War sites. © Disney

Following the initial cost overruns of Euro Disneyland, Disney had started looking for ways to build smaller, less expensive parks. In 1991, prior even to Euro Disney's opening, parks head Dick Nunis talked Eisner and Disney President Frank Wells into visiting Colonial Williamsburg in Virginia. Nunis, a Disney veteran, thought that the area would be a ripe opportunity for the company to build a park along historic American themes. Eisner and Wells were interested, but the area turned out to be impractical for development. Eisner tasked Peter Rummell and the Disney Development Company with finding a spot to build, and turned their thoughts to the Imagineering process.

In the fall of 1992, as the DDC looked for an appropriate location for the park, Imagineering assembled the park's design team. Bob Weis, who had led the design of the Disney-MGM Studios, was put in charge of creative development. By the spring of 1993, WDI was at work on the park's design and Rummell had found an appropriate park site near Haymarket, Virginia.

A map of the proposed park. © Disney

Through a stroke of good luck, 2,300 of the 3,000 acres Disney wanted to buy were owned by a single company. Exxon had bought the land in the go-go 1980s for a residential and retail development, only to have the real estate market crash during the elder President Bush's recession. Seeing as it was fairly difficult to find a buyer for such a large parcel, Exxon was excited to unload the property and was glad to give Disney a long-term option on the land. The site was at the intersection of Interstate 66 and Highway 15 in Haymarket, Virginia, and at only twenty miles from downtown Washington, D.C. allowed easy access to a huge tourist population. In fact, at the park's announcement, Weis would trumpet Disney's America as "an ideal complement to visiting Washington's museums, monuments and national treasures".

In initial meetings with the creative team, Eisner asked them to build a park based on complex themes; the fun as well as the serious moments in American history, with all the concurrent highs and lows thrown in. Eisner wanted to use the tools that Disney had invented to take on weighty American stories, seeing this as only reasonable as many so-called 'serious' museums had been trying to do just that at the time.

During the project's first press conference in November 1993, Eisner said that "in Disney's America we will create a totally new concept using the different strengths of our entertainment company – our motion picture and television talent, our park Imagineers, our interactive media and publishing executives as well as our sports enterprise and education executives – to celebrate those unique American qualities that have been our country's strengths and that have made this nation the beacon of hope to people everywhere. We bring seventy years of entertainment experience – many of them creating the world's most original parks – to this project." Peter Rummell claimed that the park would differentiate itself from all others in both subject matter and presentation, and that "Disney's America will allow guests to celebrate the diversity of the nation, the plurality and conflicts that have defined the American character".

These were very preliminary plans. As released, the park pitch was a rough draft to catch the public's imagination, and it was subsequently altered during development. Some ideas were changed, and others added, but this gives a snapshot of what could possibly have happened had the park gone forward.

> "At Disney's America guests may also find themselves piloting a World War II fighter by way of virtual reality or participating in a harrowing Lewis and Clark river expedition inside a Native American Indian Village or in the center of Revolutionary War and Civil War Battle re-enactments. They will even have an opportunity to meet every American president through the magic of Disney's Audio-Animatronics technology."
>
> *– Disney Press Release, 1993*

Guests would approach Disney's America via a newly-widened Interstate 66, entering the park through a dedicated exit that would prevent local communities from being overwhelmed by traffic. The park, resort, and recreation facilities would only occupy 1,200 of the 3,000 total acres the company purchased; Disney continued to be aware of the lessons of Disneyland and would leave a great deal of untouched land as greenbelt, open space, and conservation buffers between guest areas, the adjacent interstate, and neighboring communities. Environmental concerns were also taken into account, as several hundred acres of open space and protected timber would conserve both forest cover and wildlife corridors.

After arriving at the resort and passing through the greenbelt, guests would probably see some of the developments that Disney planned to build on site. The land surrounding the resort, long zoned for a housing development, would give way to hotels, public golf courses, residences, mixed use development, public open areas, and an employment facility. This development was slated to begin after completion of the park in 1998.

If there's one thing Michael Eisner loved (aside from Bette Midler and hockey), it was hotels. So it's no surprise that in the master plan for Disney's America we find a resort hotel. The hotel would have been integrated with the park itself; this was a novelty at the time, as then only the Disneyland Hotel in Paris had been designed at the entrance to a park. While the 'hotel-as-park-entrance' idea would later resurface in Tokyo (twice!) and California, it seemed particularly well suited to Disney's America.

The entrance area of the park, Crossroads U.S.A., was themed to the years between 1800 and 1850, and it seems that the hotel would extend that timeframe a bit by housing guests in a recreation of a Civil War–era lodge. Disney promised guests "lodging amid the hustle and bustle of a themed 19th-century inn". More intriguingly, there is mention of "additional suites spread throughout town" – a seeming elaboration of the WESTCOT concept of guests lodging on upper floors of park ride and show buildings. This would be the Disney's

Crossroads, U.S.A. © Disney

America equivalent of living on the second floor of Main Street U.S.A., and the concept of staying on the upper floors of a highly-themed colonial inn is still appealing in retrospect.

> *"A spirited portrait of mid-19th century commerce, Crossroads USA is the hub of DISNEY'S AMERICA, launching guests on an unforgettable journey through the vivid tapestry of American history."*

Crossroads U.S.A. served as the gateway to the nine "territories" of Disney's America. Guests would enter the park under a covered train trestle from the 1840s, where two antique steam trains would pick up visitors for a grand circle tour of the park. The artwork for this area shows a very busy and lived-in town, and it seems reasonable that there would be some form of river transportation to take guests down the central canal towards the territory of Enterprise.

> *"From the struggle of the colonists and the War of Independence to the formation of the United States and its government, Presidents' Square celebrates the birth of democracy and the patriots who fought to preserve it."*

"Native America" was to feature an authentic Powhatan village as well as a thrilling whitewater attraction. © Disney

Presidents' Square, covering the years 1750–1800, would elaborate on the themes and settings most familiar to guests at previous Disney parks – those of the colonial era. This territory would be designed along similar lines to both Liberty Street and Liberty Square, with another Independence Hall replica housing a second version of the *Hall of Presidents*. Artwork also shows an outdoor amphitheater with a stage built into the doorway of a large barn.

> *"Native America explores the life of America's first inhabitants, their accord with the environment, and the timeless works of art they created long before European colonization."*

Native American culture was definitely in the air at Disney corporate during the development of Disney's America. When Michael Eisner and Frank Wells toured Colonial Williamsburg at the behest of Dick Nunis in 1991, they were fresh off of one of the original story pitches for *Pocahontas*. As the park was developed in 1993 and 1994, *Pocahontas* was working its way to its 1995 release. Disney's America would incorporate these eastern American Indian themes, giving Native Americans a presence in the park that they had not enjoyed since the early days of Disneyland's Frontierland.

The territory of **Native America**, covering the years 1600–1810, would feature a recreation of a Powhatan Indian village. Its highlight attraction was to be the *Lewis and Clark Raft Expedition*, a whitewater raft ride featuring "pounding rapids and churning whirlpools".

Ironclads battle it out on Freedom Bay. © Disney

Imagineers had hoped to create a ride based on Lewis and Clark's journeys going all the way back to the plans for an indoor theme park Disney designed for St. Louis in the 1960s. While it never happened in either Missouri or Virginia, this ride system would later resurface in a slightly different form as California Adventure's *Grizzly River Run*.

> *"Emblematic of our nation's greatest crisis, the Civil War Fort allows guests to experience the reality of a soldier's daily life."*

The **Civil War Fort**, representing the years 1850–1870, would provide a look at the most contentious period of American history (outside of the closure of *Mr. Toad's Wild Ride*). Inside the fort, WDI had planned a Circle-Vision 360 film to surround guests with scenes of a Civil War battlefield. The area around the fort would host period battle reenactments, and the park would stage a "thrilling nighttime spectacular" on Freedom Bay based on the historical battle between the ironclads *Monitor* and *Merrimac*.

Disney's America

A stunning nighttime scene outside *We the People*. © Disney

> *"Framed by a building resembling Ellis Island, We The People recognizes the courage and triumph of our immigrant heritage – from the earliest native settlers to the latest political refugees."*

Another of the park's multimedia attractions, **We The People** was housed in a building that replicated New York City's famous Ellis Island facility. The show would attempt to describe the immigrant experience between 1870 and 1930, depicting how these various cultures helped to shape America. The guest experience would be enhanced by various ethnic foods and music performances found inside.

As an indication of how the park's design would shift after the time of its original announcement, by 1994 Disney Imagineering had started to conceive of this as a more humorous attraction. As an attempt to lighten a rather heavy message and to include the Muppets in the park (Disney was just beginning a decade of contentious negotiations to acquire them), WDI considered telling the American

The fiery furnaces of *Industrial Revolution*. © Disney

immigrant story through the use of Henson's creations. Neither version would ever come to pass.

> "*The factory town of Enterprise plays host to inventions and the innovations spawned by the ingenuity and can-do spirit that catapulted America to the forefront of industry.*"

The territory of **Enterprise**, spanning the years 1870–1930, would pay tribute to the industrial expansion and economic boom that fueled America's rise to world prominence. The key attraction in this area would be a rollercoaster called *Industrial Revolution*. The ride would twist in and around a turn-of-the-century steel mill, climaxing with an escape from a glowing vat of molten metal. Reports indicate that this ride might later have been canceled; Eisner says in his memoir *Work In Progress* that it was thought that the ride could "trivialize and even demean the attempt to portray the steel mill realistically".

As an attempt to smooth over relations with historians, Disney eventually tried to separate the serious themes they were trying to tackle in parts of the park from some of the more "frivolous" theme park attractions they had designed. As Eisner later said, "it was fine to create a Lewis and Clark raft ride, for example, but not to try to explain Manifest Destiny as part of the same experience." *Industrial Revolution* might have been a casualty of these changes.

Victory Field. © Disney

"The flight of the Wright brothers opened a new chapter in American history, bringing with it thrilling exploits and military advancements. With the assistance of modern technology, guests at Victory Field may parachute from a plane or operate tanks and weapons in combat, and experience firsthand what America's soldiers have faced in defense of freedom."

Victory Field represented wartime America during the years 1930–1945, from the vantage point of a military airfield. While this sounds like one of Disney's America's most exciting areas, few details were shared about its actual nature. What exactly is this spectacular sounding E-ticket attraction? What technology would it be based on? What ride system would allow guests to "find themselves piloting a World War II fighter by way of virtual reality"? To parachute from a plane or operate tanks and weapons in combat? None of the park announcements were ever specific. We know about one attraction, though – the park's railroad system would stop here.

Much like the Lewis and Clark attraction, Victory Field's theme might sound familiar to Disney fans. It too was mined for California

A watercolor rendering of State Fair. © Disney

Adventure, this time as the thematic basis for that park's Condor Flats area. While Condor Flats opened as a modern-day Mojave desert airfield instead of a WWII airstrip, many visual elements were retained from the earlier concept.

> "State Fair celebrates small town America at play with a nostalgic recreation of such popular rides as a 60-foot Ferris Wheel and a classic wooden roller coaster, as well as a tribute to the country's favorite pastime, baseball. Amid a backdrop of rolling cornfields, fans may have a hot dog and take a seat in an authentic, old-fashioned ball park and watch America's legendary greats gather for an exhibition all-star competition."

Sound familiar? No, not the part about the baseball – the rest of it. Again we come across one of Eisner's perpetual obsessions – the seaside amusement park with a whitewashed wooden roller coaster and Ferris wheel. He tried to build it here, he tried to build it at Walt Disney World's Boardwalk, he tried to build it at DisneySea, and he was eventually able to shoehorn it in at California Adventure.

DISNEY'S AMERICA 299

The bucolic Family Farm. © Disney

State Fair, set in the years 1930–1945, might seem fairly low key compared to other Disney's America offerings. Still, in the context of the park as a whole and with some highly detailed themeing, even this humble area might have been a cool addition to the Disney park canon. Even a dark ride junkie such as myself would be highly entertained by sitting back with a hot dog and watching some old-fashioned baseball as the cornfields stretched over the rolling Virginia foothills into the horizon.

> *"Offering a cornucopia of pastoral delights and insight into their production, Family Farm pays homage to the working farm – the heart of early American families."*

As we cross to the other side of Freedom Bay, we reach the last of Disney's America's territories. The **Family Farm**, also set between 1930 and 1945, reflects, along with factories and seaside pleasure piers, one of Michael Eisner's fascinations. Family Farm is one of the park's territories least defined in press releases, and probably the one least likely to be found in a traditional theme park. There are no attractions per se, although the park's railroad does stop here. Instead, there are a number of exhibits and demonstrations exploring rural life, including the harvesting of crops, milking of cows, and the making of homemade ice cream. The area seems to focus on interactivity; it is said that guests can "even participate in a nearby country wedding, barn dance, and buffet."

What would have actually emerged from this is unsure. It's no coincidence that this area bears a resemblance to the smaller-scale Bountiful Valley Farm from California Adventure; that farm area lasted hardly a year before before being converted into "a bug's land". One wonders if Family Farm would have had a similar fate.

Little concerning the potential for future expansion of Disney's America was ever released to the public aside from plans for mixed-use developments on the property's borders, and the mention of a possible water park. What would have been inside the park itself on opening day was still up in the air when the park was cancelled; rarely do Disney fans receive such a detailed look into a park more than four years before its opening, and much of what we know about this park would have changed before it opened.

One thing is for sure – there was plenty of room for expansion. The park map shows the railroad attraction's track looping far out into the wilderness; there was lots and lots of room "inside the berm" for whatever WDI could cook up.

> "Beyond the rides and attractions for which Disney is famous, the park will be a venue for people of all ages, especially the young, to debate and discuss the future of our nation and to learn more about its past by living it."
>
> – Bob Weis, November 11, 1993

As with many other projects before the fated year of 1994, Eisner gave the Disney's America creative team a task much greater than the mere design of a theme park. Much like with Epcot Center, Disney heralded the America park as an extension of Walt Disney's desire to educate as well as inspire and entertain. Many of the concepts for incorporating special events into the park's operations hearken back to the ideas of outreach trumpeted for Epcot in 1982. These ideas included various political affairs gatherings, broadcasts, and edutainment events.

The original press release for Disney's America claimed that the park would "have facilities to host and televise political debates, public forums and gatherings of writers, educators, journalists, students, and historians to discuss issues of the past, present, and future." Plans called for the ability to broadcast TV specials and public affairs programming, as well as floating the possibility of establishing a working broadcast newsroom or newspaper bureau on site "so that future generations may learn more about the key roles of media in society and the importance and significance of freedom of the press".

This is the type of heady stuff that always seemed to be announced for projects, only to later go ignored and fall by the wayside. Still, Eisner seemed committed and claimed that the park would additionally broadcast the Disney-created American Teacher Awards. And, lest things get a little too dry and academic, the park would be fully equipped to "stage detailed re-enactments of significant Civil War and Revolutionary War battles".

> *"While only in the conceptual phase, DISNEY'S AMERICA will be different from anything built previously by The Walt Disney Company.*
>
> *"As well as offering rides and attractions for which we are famous, DISNEY'S AMERICA will be a venue for people of all ages – especially American youth – to debate the future of their nation and learn about the past by living its history. This Park will serve as the ideal complement to our nation's leading historical museums, monuments, and landmarks in Washington, D.C. Just as important, the Park will also be a celebration of the diversity of America, the plurality of this Nation, and the conflicts that have defined us as a people."*
>
> *– Disney Promotional Material, 1994*

So after wrapping up our exciting day at Disney's America, one can't help but notice that this park doesn't actually exist. So, why? While Disney's America seemed star-crossed from its inception, Eisner's capitulation in September of 1994 seems unnecessary in retrospect. The battle to put a park in Virginia was one that Disney was winning.

Eisner, in his autobiography, listed a litany of errors in Disney's handling of the park roll-out and public relations campaign. First was the name itself – "Disney's America" appeared, to some, to imply a claimed ownership of American history (this only inflamed the ire of dour academics who, it seemed, desired that ownership for themselves). By August of 1994 the company was considering a name change to "Disney's American Celebration" as a "softer" and "less presumptuous" alternative.

Secondly, the need for secrecy to secure the land for the park prevented the company from reaching out to political allies and starting a lobbying effort in earnest before the story leaked. They never quite managed to get ahead of the story after it slipped away from them, and their enemies already had an in-place network of contacts and influence that always left Disney's lobbying attempts a step behind.

This brings us to the main reason we can't visit Disney's America today – money and power. When you try to build a theme park in Katharine Graham's backyard, near the palatial country estates of American financial royalty such as the Mellons, the DuPonts, and the Harrimans, you can't expect for the smackdown not to come eventually. That's the real story of Disney's America, and perhaps the most American aspect of its development – the ability of the rich and powerful to distort the facts and co-opt the media into convincing the less well-off to act in direct opposition to their best interests.

As soon as Disney announced plans for the park, the horse show crowd developed a severe case of the vapors and mobilized a phalanx of lawyers, P.R. folk, historians, and activists-for-hire to put the brakes to the development. Residents were convinced that their unspoiled countryside would be wiped out and their towns overrun by traffic and burger joints – they would be victims of uncontrolled sprawl.

Rabble rousers rouse rabble. © Associated Press

A cadre of elite historians came out to attack Disney, seemingly offended at the mere idea of history being presented in a way intended to appeal to the masses. Without hearing Disney's plans (and what plans Disney had were very preliminary), they took a stand against the park in any format. It was an insult to actual history, they said, some of which was featured at Manassas Battleground about five miles away. The historians were joined by beltway media and politicians, most of whom were closely tied to the key opponents of the park and who helped form public opinion about the project.

The effect of this campaign cannot be underestimated, even more than two decades later. A cursory internet search reveals a number of discussion threads about the park, most of which are nearly or completely factually inaccurate and many of which involve the same distorted memes that the Washington elite spread to combat the park. According to many, Disney's America would not only have intruded onto several sacrosanct Civil War battlefields, but would wind up "bulldozing" Manassas!

The truth is that the park intruded on no protected lands, no historic battlefields, and after the huge battle to prevent the theme park and its "sprawl", the land intended for the park is currently... an enormous housing development, full of McMansions. There's a Wal-Mart nearby. Shelby Foote would love it.

I-66 never got the widening that Disney would have secured, causing endless traffic delays. Instead of those roads being crowded with cars driving into Haymarket to spend money locally, they're full of commuters passing through to Washington, D.C. to work there and then return to their identical rows of houses on the former site of Disney's America.

Prince William County never got the 3,000 jobs the park would initially create, nor the residual business benefits the park would create in the area. The State of Virginia wound up missing out on $1 billion in projected tax revenues over the first thirty years of park operation, while sleepy Prince William County missed out on $500 million over the same period. Prince William County still has sprawl, it still has traffic – it just doesn't have Disney. For a certain social set, that's how they wanted it; many regular folks, however, who opposed the park at the time now see it as a missed opportunity.

While many historians had mobilized in opposition to the park, others joined forces with Disney and came on to consult and advise the WDI creative team. Though these academics thought that Disney was far from perfect – Eisner reported specific objections to Epcot's *American Adventure* – eventually they were won over to the fact that Disney at least had noble intentions and were willing to listen to criticism.

Eisner explained to them that at the America park they would have a whole day to tell very complex and nuanced stories that just couldn't be done in a single 25-minute attraction like *The American Adventure*. By reaching out in various ways, Disney was able to assemble a team of academics, historians, and intelligentsia that were willing to consult for them and offer advice and criticism. The opposition was not so kind; Eisner would write:

None of this seemed to dampen the resolve of our opponents. Most important, several historians began raising the specter that our park threatened historical sites in the surrounding area, notably Manassas. The leader of these efforts was Richard Moe, president of the National Trust for Historic Preservation. In February, the New York Times *came out editorially in opposition to Disney's America, arguing the same case that Moe was making. "Haymarket is not 42nd Street or Florida's piney woods," the* Times *wrote. "Putting a theme park there degrades a scenic and historic resource for a project that can be built elsewhere. As for parents who want to give their children history, let them – like generations before them – make the trip to Prince William County. Let them sit still at Manassas and listen for the presence of the dead."*

In May, a group calling itself Protect Historic America was launched. Led by Moe, it included a prestigious group of historians, writers, and well-known public figures. On May 11, funded in part by supporters of the Piedmont Environmental Council, they held a press conference that featured several of their most prominent members. David McCullough, the best-selling author of Truman and host for Ken Burns's PBS series on the Civil War, described Disney's America as "a commercial blitzkrieg by the Panzer division of developers." He went on to liken the proposed building of our historical park to the Nazi takeover of Western Europe.

"We have so little that's authentic and real," McCullough said. "It's irrational, illogical, and enormously detrimental to attempt to create synthetic history by destroying real history." Moe warned that if Disney did manage to get the park built, the surrounding countryside would be "overrun, cheapened, and trivialized." The retired Yale historian C. Vann Woodward suggested that "it [is] pretty much taken for granted that Disney [will] misinterpret the past." And Roger Wilkins, a journalist and history professor, described our proposed park as nothing less than "a national calamity."

Perhaps the most telling story about the opposition to Disney's America came at the end of Disney's attempt to build the park. When Eisner decided to pull out of Virginia, he asked Disney Channel president and park consultant John Cooke to use his Washington contacts to reach out to the park's critics and ask them if they would support the park if it were built in a different location, and possibly agree to consult on a future iteration of the park concept. Cooke did so, and according to Eisner received encouraging responses when he asked Dick Moe, David McCullough, and James McPherson if they would consider announcing their support for Disney's right to build the park in another location. Turns out the park wasn't quite the abomination they let on, as long as it was built somewhere else.

Despite this adversity, the park was still within Disney's reach to build. The New York and Washington cocktail party circuit that had started the campaign against Disney's America did not represent the majority of Virginians. Public support was vastly in favor of the park, and the park's management team continued to obtain the necessary permits and government concessions with the ready assistance of Virginia's governor and state government.

Eisner's initiative was instead knocked out by a deadly 1-2-3-4 punch during the dark year of 1994, and by September he was no longer willing to fight. In April 1994, Disney President Frank Wells died in a shocking helicopter accident. Eisner's inability to select a successor for Wells after his death continued to plague the studio for years afterwards; his decision to assume most of Wells's duties himself and skip over studio chief Jeffrey Katzenberg led to Katzenberg's departure in August 1994. To add to his woes, Eisner was forced to have difficult heart bypass surgery that July. By September, Eisner was no longer able or willing to fight for the Virginia park.

Continuing difficulties included the fact that park opponents were challenging every environmental or government approval that the park received from the state of Virginia. The constant litigation was not only pushing back the park's anticipated opening date, but the constant flow of lawyers and lobbyists was draining company funds.

Costs of the park itself had increased by forty percent as the design was refined. In the other column, earning projections had been reduced, as Disney realized that the length of the operating season they had predicted was too ambitious and would have to be scaled back. Due to softening theme park attendance nationwide, the projected admission price points would also probably have to be reduced. Increased costs and decreased earnings predictions pointed to one thing – operating losses, which were a terrifying prospect in the wake of Euro Disney's woes.

While the public remained behind the park and the approvals process continued unabated, Eisner was no longer up to fighting the good fight. On September 15th, 1994, the decision was made to raise the white flag on Disney's America. While Eisner hoped to build the park elsewhere, the plans for Disney's America remain on a shelf at WDI. Americana is one of the things that Imagineering does best, and many a fan dreams of a day when this project could see the light of day.

Appendix

Dining With Disney

Once you've vacationed at a favorite destination a few times, you start to look forward to things besides the obvious attractions and tourist draws. Certain things become part of your travel routine, and they become the special rituals you daydream about when you're sitting in your office or in class visualizing your next vacation.

I'm talking, of course, about food.

Generations of Disney park-goers are no stranger to this phenomenon, and a number of cult foods loom large in theme park legend. From the Silver Banjo BBQ and the Casa de Fritos to the Sunshine Tree Terrace and the Adventureland Veranda, Disney lore is full of unique and bizarre offerings far more fascinating than the standard theme park popcorn-and-churros.

Walt Disney World debuted in the 1970s, and aspired to offer a slate of dining options for urbane adults looking for a night on the town. And so the resort's early years are full of amusingly swanky menus that are definitely "of their era". It was a time when you could get fried ice cream in a hollowed-out frozen peach at the Golf Resort, and when every table had enormous oversized wooden pepper mills.

Over the years Walt Disney World was kind enough to share its recipes with the public so here, for your enjoyment, are a few of our favorites. Try them out as you proceed through the book! A vintage Walt Disney World supper party is always in order.

Island Sunset

If nothing else, while you read the *Progress City Primer* you should make yourself a tasty tropical beverage and put a copy of *Moonlight Time in Old Hawaii* on the hi-fi. This little tummy-warmer is served at the Polynesian Resort's venerable Tambu Lounge.

- ½ oz. Malibu rum
- ½ oz. Captain Morgan's rum
- ½ oz. Melon liquor
- ½ oz. Peach schnapps
- 2 oz. Pineapple Orange Guava concentrate

Blend with ice and serve in a hurricane glass, with an orange slice garnish.

Land Grille Room Cheese Spread

Once upon a time, Epcot's Garden Grill was known as the Land Grille Room (and before that, The Good Turn). This yummy cheese spread was served before meals, and is the perfect appetizer for when you convene the wine and cheese crowd for some retro Epcot fun.

Yield: Five cups

- 3 cups (12 oz.) **Cheddar Cheese**
- ½ cup (4 oz.) **Crumbled blue cheese**
- 1 package (8 oz.) **Cream cheese**
- ⅓ cup **Butter, softened**
- ¼ cup **Heavy cream**
- Dash of Tabasco
- ⅛ tsp. **Worcestershire sauce**
- ⅛ tsp. **Paprika**
- Salt to taste

All ingredients should be room temperature.

Cut Cheddar cheese into one-inch cubes and process half of Cheddar with half of blue cheese in food processor (with a steel blade) until smooth. Transfer to 1½ quart bowl and process remaining Cheddar and blue cheese. Transfer to bowl. Cube cream cheese and add with butter, cream, and seasonings to processor and process with steel blade until blended. Add to Cheddar mixture and mix until blended. Store, covered, in refrigerator and serve at room temperature.

Sopa Azteca

The San Angel Inn at Epcot's Mexico pavilion was an early favorite in my formative Disney years, and this soup was always a mandatory precursor to any satisfactory trip down the River of Time.

Yield: Four servings

- 3 tbsp. Vegetable oil
- ⅓ cup Chopped onion
- 1 ⅓ cups Peeled, seeded, chopped tomatoes
- 1 tsp. Garlic
- 1 qt. Rich chicken broth
- 2 tbsp. Chopped fresh dill weed (or 2 tsp. dried dill weed)
- 2 Chili peppers
- 4 Soft corn tortillas
- ½ Medium ripe avocado, cubed
- 4 tbsp. Sour cream
- ¼ cup Shredded Monterey Jack cheese

Heat two tablespoons oil in a large saucepot. Sauté onion, tomatoes, and garlic until onion is transparent. Add chicken broth and dill weed. Cover and simmer for twenty minutes.

Remove seeds and stems from chili peppers and cut each in two pieces lengthwise. Cut tortillas in ⅓-inch strips. Heat remaining tablespoon of oil in a skillet and fry peppers for five seconds. Remove to a paper towel and fry tortilla strips until golden brown, stirring. Drain on paper towel.

Divide chili peppers, tortilla strips, and avocado cubes between four heavy ceramic or clay soup bowls. Pour the hot chicken broth into the bowls. Garnish each with a spoonful of sour cream and Monterey Jack cheese.

Cheddar Cheese Soup

Another Epcot classic, this soup was a cornerstone offering at the Canada pavilion's Le Cellier "buffeteria".

Yield: Six servings

- ¼ lb. Smoked bacon, finely chopped
- 1 Red onion, cut into ¼ in. pieces
- ½ cup Finely sliced celery
- ½ cup Finely chopped carrots
- 3 tbsp. All-purpose flour
- 3 cups Whole milk
- 2 cups Chicken stock
- 12 oz. Grated white cheddar
- 3 dashes Tabasco
- ½ tsp. Worcestershire sauce
- ½ cup Moosehead Canadian Ale
- 1 tbsp. Thinly sliced chives
- Salt and pepper to taste

Cook bacon in a large heavy-bottomed, non-reactive soup pot over medium heat until wilted but not browned. Add onions, celery, and carrots. Cook until the onion is translucent and bacon has crisped.

Sprinkle in flour and stir constantly for two minutes. Stir in milk and stock, a little at a time, blending well to ensure there are no lumps. Bring to a boil, then cover and simmer for fifteen minutes.

Remove from heat and whisk in cheese, Tabasco, Worcestershire, and ale. Season with salt and pepper to taste. Top with chopped chives.

Fort Wilderness Chili & Beans

Somehow, Fort Wilderness remains off the beaten path for even some veteran Walt Disney World travelers. I can't imagine why. It's the greatest remaining outpost of the "Vacation Kingdom" days, with some excellent recreational and dining opportunities. And *chili*.

Yield: One gallon

- 2 lbs. Coarsely ground beef
- 2¼ cups Coarsely chopped Spanish onions
- ½ tsp. Granulated garlic
- 2 tsps. Chili powder
- ¼ tsp. Ground cumin
- Ground black pepper to taste
- 1¼ tbsp. Salt
- 1 tbsp. Spanish paprika
- 2 cups Tomato catsup
- 3 cups Tomato purée
- 3½ cups Beef stock
- 3¼ cups Kidney beans
- 1 cup Dry bread crumbs

Sauté beef and onions in a 1½ gallon saucepot until meat is slightly browned. Add all spices, catsup, purée, and beef stock. Mix well. Bring to a boil and simmer over low heat, covered, stirring occasionally, for one hour. Add undrained beans and bring again to a boil. Add bread crumbs and remove from heat. Stir for one to two minutes before serving.

Fort Wilderness Cornbread

What's chili without cornbread? This delightful pone is served at the Hoop-Dee-Doo Musical Revue as well as the Trail's End Buffeteria. What are you waiting for? Get to Fort Wilderness!

¾ cup Cornmeal
1¼ cup Sugar
1½ tsp. Salt
1 tbsp. Baking powder
1¾ cup Flour
½ cup Vegetable oil
1 cup Milk
2 Eggs

Blend flour, cornmeal, salt, baking powder, and sugar in a mixing bowl. In a separate bowl, blend milk, eggs, and oil with a mixer.

Using that same mixer, slowly add the blended liquid to the dry ingredients, mixing just enough to incorporate the wet and dry ingredients.

Spray a 9" x 13" baking pan with non-stick food spray and pour the batter into the pan, spreading evenly. Bake in a preheated oven at 375° F for 20–25 minutes or until golden brown.

Allow to cool, slather with butter, and devour ravenously.

Smoky Portobello Mushroom Soup

The greatest soup in the world?
The. Greatest. Soup.
In the world.
Courtesy of Artist Point, at the Wilderness Lodge Resort.

Yield: Eight servings (64 oz.)

9 Medium portobello mushrooms
½ cup Sweet onions
1 cup Chardonnay
2 qts. Heavy cream
24 oz. Chicken broth
1½ tbsp. Garlic, chopped
1¼ cup White roux
Salt and pepper to taste
Croutons
1 cup Light olive oil
1 cup Chives
2 cups Shitake mushrooms
Chives cut for garnish

Cut three portobello mushrooms into thick slices. Cold smoke in a home smoker for one hour. The Wilderness Lodge uses oak chips for smoking.

Thinly slice two cups of shitake mushrooms. Toss with two tablespoons of olive oil and a little salt and pepper. Place on a baking sheet and roast in the oven at 375° F until crispy and golden brown. Cool and set aside.

Prepare chive oil by placing one cup of light olive oil in a blender and adding one cup of chives. Blend for thirty seconds and let rest for one hour. Strain through a fine sieve.

Prepare croutons by pre-heating the oven to 325–350° F. Cut six slices of your favorite bread into ¾-inch squares. Toss in a bowl with ¼ cup melted butter. Place on a baking sheet and season with salt and pepper to taste. Bake at 325–350° F until brown.

Prepare white roux by mixing equal parts butter and flour and cooking slowly over low heat.

Clean the remaining six portobellos by wiping them with a damp towel. Do not wash them! Remove the mushroom gills.

Sauté the onions lightly, to sweat. Add the unsmoked mushrooms to the onions. Add the garlic when the mushrooms are almost cooked. Add the smoked mushrooms. Add the chardonnay and reduce by half. Add the chicken broth and bring to a simmer.

Place in a blender or food processor in batches. Add the heavy cream slowly and continue to blend. Season to taste.

Place the mixture back into the pot. Add the roux and let simmer for twenty minutes. Serve hot and garnish with croutons and roasted shiitake mushrooms, a dollop of sour cream, a drizzle of chive oil, and cut chives.

Lock everyone else out of the house and drink the entire pot in silence, before going to work on the next batch.

KARTOFFELSALAT

The always-innovative Germans, after years of research, hit upon the perfect way to improve salad – make it out of potatoes. This German potato salad has been a staple of Epcot's Biergarten since opening day.

Yield: Three cups

- ⅓ cup Olive oil
- 2 tsp. Mixed herbs (tarragon, parsley, sorrel)
- ½ cup Beef broth
- 1 tbsp. Wine vinegar
- 1 tbsp. Dijon-style mustard
- 2 tsp. Sugar
- 3 tsp. Grated onion
- 4 Large Idaho potatoes
- Salt and freshly ground pepper to taste

Combine olive oil, herbs, beef broth, vinegar, mustard, sugar, and grated onions and set aside.

Steam potatoes until tender. Peel and slice potatoes into sixteenth-inch slices while still warm. Add to oil mixture and mix carefully. Let stand for one-half hour. When half of liquid has been absorbed by potatoes, blend mixture well, without breaking apart potato slices. Add salt and freshly ground pepper to taste.

Nudel Gratin

Another starchy wonder from the Biergarten.

Serves eight to ten

2 cups Heavy cream
2 Eggs
¼ tsp. Salt
1 pinch Ground white pepper
1 pinch Nutmeg
4 oz. Swiss cheese, shredded
4 oz. White cheddar cheese, shredded

1 lb. Cooked elbow macaroni

Preheat oven to 375° F. Spray a 16" x 9" baking dish with nonstick spray.

Combine cream, eggs, salt, pepper, and nutmeg in a large bowl, whisking to combine. Toss cheeses together in a small bowl until combined. Remove one cup cheese and set aside. Stir remaining cheeses into cream mixture.

Cook macaroni until just tender. Drain and add cream mixture, stirring immediately. Pour mixture into prepared baking dish. Cover with foil.

Bake thirty minutes. Remove foil and sprinkle reserved cheese over top of noodles. Bake fifteen minutes longer.

Cool ten minutes before cutting into squares. Serve warm.

Chicken Maori

This lamentably lost delight was once served at the Polynesian Resort's Coral Isle Cafe – now known as Kona Cafe. It was my go-to lunch selection if I slept in too late to get the stuffed French toast.

Yield: Four servings

Sauce:

2 tbsp. Finely chopped onion	1 cup Tomato sauce
1 tbsp. Vegetable oil	½ tsp. Salt
1 cup Chili sauce	2 tbsp. Brown sugar
1 tbsp. Worcestershire sauce	1½ tsp. Chili powder
1½ tsp. Garlic powder	1 tbsp. BBQ spice (¾ tsp. Chili powder, ¼ tsp. Red pepper sauce, ¼ tsp. Oregano)
½ tsp. White pepper	
¼ cup Pineapple juice	1½ tsp. Liquid smoke
1 small Bay leaf	1 tbsp. White vinegar
¾ cup Honey	Cayenne pepper to taste

Sauté onion in vegetable oil until golden brown. Combine with remaining ingredients in a saucepan. Bring to a boil, reduce heat and simmer, covered, for about one hour. Makes three cups.

Chicken:

Four 8 oz. Skinless, boneless chicken breasts	⅛ tsp. White pepper
	Oil or fat for frying
2 Eggs, beaten	4 Kaiser rolls
½ cup Flour	Butter, softened
½ tsp. Salt	Sesame seeds

Pound breasts with wooden mallet until thin. Dip in beaten eggs, then in flour seasoned with salt and pepper. Fry in deep 375° F oil or fat for five minutes. Remove and drain well. Heat Kaiser rolls in oven, split crosswise and buttered slightly. Place fried chicken breasts on each roll. Top with sauce and sesame seeds.

Bobotie

Another fantastic Walt Disney World dining experience I fear many people might overlook is Boma, at the Animal Kingdom Lodge. Off the beaten path and fairly exotic, it might not be on people's radars. But it should. It's amazing.

Yield: Ten servings

1 tbsp. Oil	¼ cup Sugar
1 Onion, chopped	½ cup Pumpkin seeds, sliced
1 tsp. Cinnamon	¼ cup Seedless raisins
2 tsp. Curry powder	¼ cup Golden raisins
2 tbsp. Rice wine vinegar	Salt to taste
2 lbs. Ground lamb (or ground beef if desired)	Topping:
	1 cup Liquid eggs
3 slices White bread	½ cup Heavy cream
1 cup Heavy cream	½ cup Milk

Heat oil and caramelize the onions. Reduce heat and add dry spices. Mix well. Deglaze with rice wine vinegar. Add meat and continue to cook until meat is cooked through.

When the meat is done, drain 90% of the grease off. Then tear the bread into small pieces and add it as well as the cream to the meat mixture.

Add the sugar and mix well. Add a little bit of water if the mix looks too dry. Then add the raisins and pumpkin seeds. Re-season and cool.

In a small container, place the bobotie mixture and top with the egg custard mix. Bake in the oven at 325° F until golden brown and cooked through.

Cottage Pie

An opening-day tradition of Epcot's Rose & Crown pub, this was a particular favorite of mine as a kid.

Yield: Four servings

¼ cup Butter
1 cup Diced onion
1½ lbs. Lean ground beef
Salt and ground pepper to taste
¼ tsp. Ground savory
1 cup Brown gravy
2 cups Mashed potatoes
Additional butter

Heat ¼ cup butter in a nine-inch skillet. Add onion and cook until lightly browned, stirring. Add beef, salt, pepper, and savory and continue cooking five minutes longer. Stir in gravy and heat until bubbling. Spoon into a buttered eight-cup flat casserole dish. Top meat mixture with mashed potatoes. Dot with pieces of butter. Bake at 400° F for fifteen to twenty minutes or until potatoes are lightly browned.

Adventureland Veranda Teriyaki Sauce

Ah, the 1970s. When a hamburger covered in teriyaki sauce was the height of exotic cuisine. When Kikkoman's dearly missed Adventureland Veranda hosted guests in tropical splendor. Here is their fabled teriyaki sauce – put it on anything for an instant island getaway!

Yield: 2½ cups

- 1 cup Soy sauce
- ¼ cup Catsup
- 3 tbsp. Sherry
- 1 tsp. Granulated garlic
- 1 Beef boullion cube, crushed
- 1 Vegetable boullion cube, crushed
- ¼ cup Cider vinegar
- 1 cup Light brown sugar
- 1 tsp. Grated fresh ginger
- 1 cup Water, divided
- 2 tbsp. Cornstarch

Combine all ingredients except cornstarch and ¼ cup water in a saucepan. Cook and stir until bouillon and sugar is dissolved. Dissolve cornstarch in ¼ cup water and stir into sauce. Bring sauce to a boil and cook and stir until mixture is thickened and smooth, about two minutes.

Strawberry Shortcake

One of Walt Disney World's most iconic desserts, strawberry shortcake has been delighting guests at the Hoop-Dee-Doo Musical Revue for decades. Just be sure to serve it to your guests with a high-stepping song and dance routine.

Yield: Four servings

16 oz. Frozen strawberries, thawed
1 tbsp. Sugar
1 tbsp. Cornstarch
2 tbsp. Cold water
1 pint Fresh strawberries
4 slices pound cake
½ cup Heavy cream, whipped

Drain juice from strawberries into a small saucepan. Set strawberries aside. Combine juice with sugar and heat. Dissolve cornstarch in cold water and gradually add to hot juice, stirring constantly. Simmer three minutes. Add defrosted frozen strawberries and chill. Makes 1½ cups frozen strawberry sauce.

Wash, dry, and remove caps from fresh strawberries. Cut in half or slice. Place cake slices on plates. Spoon frozen strawberry sauce over cake. Top with fresh strawberries. Serve with whipped topping or cream.

Ooey Gooey Toffee Cake

This magical confection is served at the Liberty Tree Tavern in the Magic Kingdom. It's enough to make one thoroughly patriotic.

Cake:
1 box Yellow cake mix
1 Egg
1 stick Butter, softened

Mix ingredients and spread into a greased 13" x 9" baking pan.

Topping:

8 oz. Cream cheese, softened	1 lb. Powdered sugar, sifted
2 Eggs	1 cup Semi-sweet chocolate chips
1 tbsp. Vanilla	1 cup Heath Bar pieces
¼ cup Butter	

Preheat oven to 325° F.

Mix cream cheese until smooth. Slowly add eggs and vanilla. Add butter and mix well. Add powdered sugar, slowly. Add chocolate chips and toffee pieces.

Mix until ingredients are barely incorporated evenly. Do not over-mix.

Put on top of cake ingredients already in pan. Bake for 35 minutes. Inside should just be slightly gooey.

Top with vanilla ice cream, crumbled toffee pieces, and chocolate and caramel sauce drizzles.

Berry Cobbler

Another Wilderness Lodge offering, this cobbler has become a family favorite. The perfect end to a day out on the trail. Feel free to alternate servings with giant tureens of mushroom soup. And a few milkshakes from Whispering Canyon. It's the cowboy way.

1½ cups All-purpose flour
½ cup Sugar
2 tsp. Baking powder
½ tsp. Salt
1 stick + 2 tbsp. Cold butter, cut into small pieces
1 Egg
1 cup Heavy cream

12 oz. Fresh blueberries
2 tbsp. Light brown sugar
½ pint each Fresh raspberries and blackberries.
8 Strawberries for garnish

In a medium bowl, whisk together the flour, granulated sugar, baking powder, and salt. With a pastry blender, two knives used scissor style, or your hands, blend in ½ cup butter until crumbly. With a fork, stir in the egg and mix just enough to blend. Add heavy cream and mix just enough to incorporate. Do not overmix!

Preheat the oven to 350° F. Lightly grease a 9" cake pan, line the bottom with wax paper, and grease the paper.

Press the dough evenly into the bottom of the cake pan. Place the blueberries on top of the dough and sprinkle with the brown sugar. Place the remaining two tablespoons of butter pieces over the berries.

Bake for 20–25 minutes, or until golden brown. Cool on a wire rack. Remove the cake from the pan, cut in wedges, and serve with blackberries, raspberries, and strawberries. Serve with vanilla ice cream.

Sunshine Tree Orange Topping

We close out our trip down culinary memory lane with something that truly evokes the early history of Walt Disney World, the orange sauce once used to top cheesecake and other items at the Sunshine Tree Terrace. Put it on everything! Bathe yourself in sunshine!

Yield: 2½ cups

2 cups Orange juice
½ cup Sugar
⅛ tsp. Yellow food coloring
¼ tsp. Orange extract
2 tbsp. Cornstarch
½ cup Water

Combine orange juice, sugar, yellow food coloring, and orange extract and bring to a boil. Dissolve cornstarch in cold water. Stir into hot orange mixture. Cook and stir with whisk until mixture is thickened and smooth.

www.ingramcontent.com/pod-product-compliance
Lightning Source LLC
Chambersburg PA
CBHW020330240426
43665CB00043B/205